WILLIAM AUGUSTUS DUKE OF CUMBERLAND
AND THE SEVEN YEARS' WAR

[*Henry Dixon & Son.*

H.R.H. WILLIAM AUGUSTUS DUKE OF CUMBERLAND.

From the bust by Rysbrack in the possession of the Earl of Ilchester—Holland House.

[Frontispiece

WILLIAM AUGUSTUS DUKE OF CUMBERLAND

AND

THE SEVEN YEARS' WAR

BY

THE HON. EVAN CHARTERIS, K.C.

AUTHOR OF
"WILLIAM AUGUSTUS DUKE OF CUMBERLAND: HIS EARLY LIFE
AND TIMES, 1721–1748" AND "AFFAIRS OF SCOTLAND, 1744–1746"

WITH EIGHT ILLUSTRATIONS AND TWO MAPS

LONDON
HUTCHINSON & CO.
PATERNOSTER ROW

Printed in Great Britain by Hazell, Watson & Viney, Ld.,
London and Aylesbury.

PREFACE

In 1913 I published a volume entitled *William Augustus Duke of Cumberland,* which carried the Life of the Duke down to the Peace of Aix la Chapelle. In that volume I endeavoured to free Cumberland from some of the misrepresentation of which he has been the victim and present a more just and accurate portrait of the man. I have now been able to continue the story so as to include the time which preceded the Seven Years' War and to describe the part played by the Duke during the early part of the struggle between France and England. The present volume closes with the termination of his military services.

Hitherto, Cumberland's share in the war and his responsibility for the Convention of Kloster Zeven have been treated with any fulness by no English historian, and among foreign writers, so far as I am aware, only by M. Charles Waddington, in his well-known *La Guerre de Sept Ans.* Valuable as is that work, M. Waddington did not have access to all the documents bearing on the matter, and these are now for the first time made use of.

While the narrative traverses a well-known period of history, it will be found that a number of the views expressed in the following pages differ from the accepted tradition, more especially as to Newcastle's share in the Diplomatic revolution and his attitude at the time of Byng's condemnation, the relations between Cumberland and Pitt, Cumberland's responsibility for the fall of Pitt in 1757, Pitt's treatment of the Army of Observation, and the respective responsibility of George II and Cumberland for the Convention of Kloster Zeven. I have therefore thought it expedient to burden the notes with very full references to the documents on which those views have been founded. To His Majesty the King I beg leave to record my humble thanks for permission to make use of the Cumberland Papers at Windsor Castle and to reproduce engravings in the Royal Library.

My thanks are also due to the Duke of Leeds and Lord Ilchester, who have allowed me to consult the documents at Hornby Castle and Holland House. Other documents consulted at the British Museum, the Record Office, and in the Archives of Paris will be found referred to in the notes.

The bibliography of the period is so extensive and so well known that I have not thought it necessary to refer to it in detail. But no one writing of the middle period of the eighteenth century should fail to acknowledge his obligation to the more recent publications of Professor Basil Williams, of Lord Ilchester, of Mr. Philip Yorke, and of Mr. Rikker. To M. Rigaud, keeper of the Foreign Office archives in Paris, my thanks are due for his courteous assistance in the search for sources of authority. Like everyone who makes use of the Manuscript Room at the British Museum, I have profited by the help of Mr. D. B. Wood and Mr. R. Coates. Finally I am indebted to Mr. Edward Marsh for his kind assistance in reading through the proofs.

LIST OF ILLUSTRATIONS

MAPS

WILLIAM AUGUSTUS DUKE OF CUMBERLAND AND THE SEVEN YEARS' WAR

CHAPTER I

WHAT brought the War of the Austrian Succession to an end? Why was the Treaty of Aix-la-Chapelle which followed inconclusive? These are questions often dealt with, but to which some answer must here be given if an adequate idea is to be formed of the scene in which Cumberland was called on to play a part.

In 1748 the war had already dragged on for six years. In that year the Newcastle Administration had reached a state of unmeasured despondency: confidence had taken wing from their counsels, and as they surveyed the aspect of affairs on the Continent they were constrained to merge their habitual mistrust of one another in the larger fear of an impending and fatal disaster. At the beginning of the year the failure of the Dutch to supply their quota of troops for the ensuing campaign in the Low Countries, and their demand on the British Government for a loan of one million sterling, had shown clearly enough that it was no use looking to Holland for assistance in carrying on the war. Marshal Saxe with an army of 100,000 men was already in the field, Breda and Maestricht were in jeopardy, and while Cumberland was unable to count on more than 35,000 men for their defence it was feared that the French would shortly be in a position to command the valley of the Meuse and threaten Holland itself with invasion.

Pitt considered peace was "absolutely necessary to our very being"; the Duke of Bedford, to secure the same end, was ready to sacrifice Gibraltar, which he considered "of very little or no utility to this country"; * Chesterfield, who had been

* *Bedford Correspondence*, I, p. 316, Bedford to Sandwich, January 8, 1748.

I

for peace on almost any terms, had resigned as a protest against the continuance of the war; while Pelham, the leader of the Peace Party in the Cabinet, declared, " It must be owned we have fought it to the stumps." Even Newcastle, who had been for prosecuting the war through another year, is found writing to Cumberland in April, "All the world see the necessity of Peace." *

Alike in the military situation, the state of the public finances, and the condition of trade, Ministers discovered what to modern notions must appear disproportionate cause for anxiety and even panic.

The national debt had risen during the war from £48,382,439 to £77,438,940. Trade returns showed that, whereas in 1742 the imports had been of the value of £7,802,353 and the exports £14,625,653, in 1747 the imports had been £8,136,408 and the exports £12,351,433. For 1748 the Estimates were £13,500,000. No longer ago than the reign of Queen Anne, Davenant had predicted that when the annual sum raised amounted to five or six millions England would be on the verge of ruin, while as recently as 1740 an acute critic had regarded the raising of ten millions as " an incredible financial operation." With estimates for £13,500,000 it was, therefore, in accordance with prevalent ideas that a Secretary of State, the Duke of Bedford, should represent to his colleagues that the " country was very little distant from bankruptcy." In every generation it has been the function and the privilege of the alarmist to preach to his contemporaries that ruin was at hand; how seldom has not the succeeding generation derided the fears of its predecessor and envied the burden which to them seemed insupportable? No writer has illuminated this commonplace of experience more clearly than Macaulay. In his essay on *Southey's Colloquies*† he writes:

We cannot absolutely prove that those are in error who tell us that society has reached a turning-point, that we have seen our best days. But so said all who came before us, and with just as much apparent reason. " A million a year will

* Add. MS. 32714, f. 429, Newcastle to Cumberland, April 5, 1748.
† Macaulay, *Essays and Biographies*, Albany Ed., Vol. I, pp. 501–2.

beggar us," said the patriots of 1640. " Two millions a year will grind the country to powder," was the cry in 1660. " Six millions a year and a debt of fifty millions! " exclaimed Swift; " the high allies have been the ruin of us." " A hundred and forty millions of debt," said Junius; " well may we say that we owe Lord Chatham more than we shall ever pay, if we owe him such a load as this." " Two hundred and forty millions of debt! " cried all the statesmen of 1783 in chorus; " what abilities, or what economy on the part of a minister, can save a country so burdened? "

In a debt of seventy-seven millions in 1748, with a population of 6,400,000 in England and Wales and the land tax at 4s. in the pound, there seems to a later generation but slight cause for despairing of the solvency of the country. Yet it was the spectre of bankruptcy which was uniting the Government in their determination to bring the war to an end, and which subsequently gave such unity and zeal to the rejoicings over the signing of the Peace of Aix-la-Chapelle (October 1748).

But if the condition of England was as depicted by its politicians, the plight of France was worse. Reacting more readily to the influence of the hour, and weighed down by a heavier burden of taxation, that nation was giving open and violent expression to the discontent rife in its midst. The *dixième,* or levy of the tenth penny on the income of all estates in the kingdom, the most onerous of all the taxes, which had been suppressed in 1737, was now being revived and extended as a war tax to wages and pensions. Moreover the land tax and capitation tax had been doubled since the beginning of the war, and now fell with intolerable severity on a population among which the large privileged class of noblesse, clergy, princes and princesses of the blood, holders of offices and official positions, and officers of the army and marine were held partially exempt.* Indeed such was the condition of the finances in France that it was said that another year of war would have entirely depleted the country of specie.†

* Bailly, *Histoire Financière de la France* (1830), II, p. 128.
† Add. MS. 35363, f. 233, Joseph Yorke to Charles Yorke, March 5/16, 1749.

Bankruptcies were being declared with ominous frequency.* Trade was at a standstill. Provincial Parliaments were resisting fresh taxation and absolving the people from payment,† while the employment of troops to quell outbreaks of disorder was a sufficient sign of the temper which was abroad. But it was on the sea that the French had suffered most severely. No fewer than 1,700 vessels of their mercantile marine were now captive in English ports, thirty-four of their vessels of the line had been taken by British ships, and their total fighting force was said not to exceed a couple of frigates. For the moment they had ceased to exist as a naval power, and their commerce had been swept from the highways of the ocean. Their conquests on land had in fact been neutralised by their defeats at sea. Fontenoy and Laffelt had found their answer in the victories of Anson and Hawke and the achievements of the British privateers. The systematic and gradual occupation of the fortresses in the Low Countries had proved to be not an end in itself; it had failed to force terms either on Austria or Great Britain; it was evidently a process which could not bring about a political decision, or, so long as naval supremacy was in British hands, give to the French an outlet in the North Sea.

Marshal Saxe, in 1744, in his strategical survey of the projected campaigns in the Low Countries conceived that the political aims of France could be realised by military success. His horizon was bounded by the land, and he failed to allow place in his calculations for the influence which sea power might have on even the most brilliant campaigns. In his own sphere it is true he had succeeded. He had fulfilled every item of his programme. But his victories had not enabled France to impose her will on any one of the belligerents. Indeed it would probably be difficult to find in history a war in which uniform military success had been attended with such inconclusive results. With the exception, as will appear later, of

* Add. MS. 32714, f. 328, Newcastle to Cumberland, March 11, 1748. "Their [the French] trade is absolutely ruined for the present and Bankrupts swarm in all the great French Towns."

† Add. MS. 35363, f. 233, Joseph Yorke to Charles Yorke, March 5/16, 1749.

loosening the bonds between Austria and England, not one of the political aims which France had in view was realised. Furthermore the King, once the idol of his people, had fallen from his high estate. It was said by Napoleon that Fontenoy had prolonged the life of the Monarchy in France by thirty years—with propriety it might be enquired by how many years the influence of Madame de Pompadour had tended to curtail it? Her recent ascendancy was proving one of the most costly ventures hitherto associated with the throne of France. The nation saw with dismay, at a moment of the acutest financial distress, that so far from practising economies or setting limits to the expenditure of the Court, the King at the instance of his mistress was plunging into reckless extravagance. At Crécy, at Celle, at Meudon, costly constructions bore witness to the influence of the favourite; while in Paris the building of the " Hôtel de Pontchartrain " * gave further proof of the King's infatuation.

Immense sums were also being expended on the constant journeys of the Court,† on the plays, the operas, and the fêtes organised by Madame de Pompadour, to distract the King and preserve him from melancholy or the domination of religious ideas.‡ It was said that nothing like it had been seen since the days of Henry III. Whether or not, as the Goncourts would have us believe, the object of this feverish and costly activity was to combat the ennui which they describe as the malady of the age and more particularly of the King, or whether, as seems more probable, it was the mere exploitation and abuse by Madame de Pompadour of novel opportunities for pleasure and amusements and the display of her talents, the material result was the same. Louis XV came to be identified in the mind of his people with the causes of the nation's impoverishment.

Libels and scurrilous verses directed against Louis and his mistress, and freely expressing the prevailing resentment, appeared broadcast in Paris to remind the Court that there was

---

* D'Argenson, *Journal et Mémoires,* Vol. V, pp. 231, 234.

† One journey alone to Havre cost a million livres. Goncourt, *Madame de Pompadour,* p. 57.

‡ D'Argenson, *Journal et Mémoires,* Vol. VI, p. 382.

a mortal side to the divinity of Kings, and that a throne to be secure had also to be respected. Joseph Yorke, then Secretary of the Embassy in Paris, wrote * to Cumberland of his amazement at the disregard in which Louis was held, at the libels of which he was the subject, at the scurrility of the lampoons which were directed against him. He traced it all to Madame de Pompadour and her disastrous influence on the Monarchy of France. Nor was he a little scandalised at seeing the first people of the Court singing and dancing upon a stage, Madame de Pompadour acting with the wife of the King's valet de chambre, and Lieutenant-Generals and Maréchaux de Camp cutting capers before the footlights " in the high stage stile." Such a scene contrasted strangely with a representation of his play, *Mahommed Prophète,* which Voltaire invited Yorke to attend in his house, where a stage had been erected in the garret and " young Bourgeois were rigged up as actors." Here the audience of 160 persons was crowded into a space of 50 feet. Voltaire himself acted as prompter; but, more concerned with the beauty of the lines than the needs of the actors, indulged in frequent outbursts of admiration for passages that had no reference to what was going forward on the stage.† Yorke thought him " as mad as a Bedlamite," and that his head had been affected by the ill success of his *Oreste.* Yorke had been commissioned by Lyttelton to convey to Voltaire a copy of Thomson's poems. Voltaire's reply has never been published and may here be reproduced:

Sr. In spite of agoni franc Voltaire is come to wait upon you, and to receive your orders, were I a man alive I would come to you often, but people belye me when they give out I am alive, as they bely'd Partrige when they gave him for dead. I desire you would let me know whether Mr. Littleton who sends me Thompson's works is not a member of Parliament, and a man of fine genius, I smell the latter, and care little for the former. If per chance I enjoy a moment of good health, I'll come and assure you

* Cumberland MS., Joseph Yorke to H.R.H. Duke of Cumberland, Feb. 18/March 1, 1749.

† Add. MS. 35363, f. 265, Joseph Yorke to Charles Yorke, April 28/May 9, 1750.

that I am with much respect Sr. Your most humble, obedient
servant VOLTAIRE.*

The allusion to "Partrige" was probably suggested by the
fact that *Tom Jones* was at this time having an astonishing
success in Paris and was in every reader's hands, its circulation being much increased by its prohibition on the supposed
ground of its immorality.†

But if the theatre at Versailles was the scene of liberty and
licence it was far otherwise with the theatres of Paris. Here
the suppression of opinion and the limits imposed on art by
a tyrannical censorship were significant of the fears of those
in authority. Joseph Yorke witnessed the arrest of a spectator
at one of the theatres who slightly hissed the line "l'Honneur,
l'ennemi, le Tyran du Bonheur." It may well have been a
case of "tear him for his bad verses," but to the police it was
an attack on an irreproachable sentiment and an offence against
authority. No wonder Voltaire, whose *Mahomet* had been
banned in Paris and whose *Oreste*‡ had been so well received
in England, looked with envy across the Channel. Oppression,
poverty, and discontent were in fact giving an uneasy sense of
insecurity. Apprehension as to the consequences of a prolongation of the war was general.

Another consideration tending indirectly to peace was the
fame of Saxe. The military triumphs of Saxe were viewed
with disfavour and jealousy by a powerful cabal at Versailles.
"Churchmen, Women, Favourites, and Princes of the Blood"
rating peace as more important than patriotism recognised that
the termination of hostilities though it might bring no glory
to France would at least set bounds to the ascendancy of the
Marshal. In Court circles therefore there was no uncertain
demand that the war should end. The King's confessor,§ whose
influence on the shallow and vacillating mind of Louis was con-

* Add. MS. 35363, f. 270, Joseph Yorke to Charles Yorke, May 29/
June 10, 1750.

† *Ibid.* The reason for its suppression was entirely commercial.

‡ Add. MS. 35363, f. 270, Joseph Yorke to Charles Yorke, May 29/
June 10, 1750.

§ Letters to Henry Fox, ed. Earl of Ilchester (Roxburghe Club,
p. 37), Sir Charles Hanbury Williams to Henry Fox, Dec. 8, 1748.

siderable in times of crisis whether moral or political, was enlisted in the cause of peace, and he is said largely to have inspired the policy of the King. These however were but contributory causes. The real justification for the peace was to be found in the internal condition of the country; and if trade was to be restored, if taxation was to be lightened, and if the decline of the King's popularity was to be arrested, the war must be brought to an end.

With such motives at work, the disposition of the French representatives at Aix-la-Chapelle was a factor making consistently for the termination of hostilities.

Under these conditions, the treaty which was finally signed in October by England, Austria, Holland, France, and later by Spain, was everywhere recognised as a suspension of arms rather than a permanent adjustment of differences. Indeed the very terms of the treaty were evidence that the exhaustion of the combatants was a principal cause of its ratification. The status that had existed before the war was in effect renewed by the restitution of conquests—Madras was restored to England, Cape Breton to France, and the Barrier Towns to the Dutch—while Silesia was guaranteed to Prussia, and formal recognition was given to the right of Maria Theresa to the Habsburg succession. At the same time the most vital question of all was left unsolved, nor was any attempt made to settle the boundary disputes between France and England in North America. Such were the main features of the peace signed in October. True, it was the end of the War of the Austrian Succession—but that war had been no more than a preliminary trial of strength, in which the old system had been tested and some of its weaknesses discovered. In the breathing space that followed the Powers of Europe were merely setting the stage and recasting the parts for the inevitable drama that was in due time to follow.

CHAPTER II

Long before the last of the coaches bearing the plenipotentiaries of the Powers of Europe had rolled away from the doors of the Congress at Aix-la-Chapelle, the representative of Maria Theresa had resolved on that trend of policy which was to find its consummation in what is known as the diplomatic revolution of the eighteenth century. Kaunitz had been a witness of the victorious progress of Marshal Saxe in the Low Countries, he had been governor of Brussels when that city had surrendered to the armies of Louis, and both in the theatre of war and in the channels of diplomacy he had been able to gauge the reliance which could be placed on the Dutch. Moreover, if he had not actually fomented, he had at least discerned with his penetrating judgment those causes of dissension which were calculated to trouble the relations of Austria and Great Britain. During the next few years the master hand of Kaunitz was to be largely responsible for the moulding of a new international policy in Europe. But at Aix-la-Chapelle he had formed the conclusion that the " old system " was doomed, and that a regrouping of the Powers was within the range of statesmanship and diplomacy. In March 1749,* on the invitation of his sovereign, he drew up that famous document in which he averred the cardinal aim of Austrian policy must be the recovery of Silesia, and indicated as the sole possible means of executing that policy, an alliance with France. Thenceforward, during the succeeding years of peace, the object of Austrian diplomacy directed by Kaunitz was to secure the goodwill of the Court of Versailles.

British policy, on the other hand, was to be the old policy—on this point Ministerial opinion was emphatic. Austria,

* D'Arneth, IV, p. 362 et seq. See also Broglie, *L'Alliance Autrichienne,* p. 13 et seq.

9

Holland, and Britain were to continue the established alliance. The friendship of Maria Theresa was to be courted by all the artifices of diplomacy. The Dutch Republic was to be persuaded to attend to its finances and improve its military resources, while the system of subsidies on the Continent was to be continued and extended as opportunity occurred.

Newcastle, whose authority in the direction of foreign policy was at this time supreme, laid down what he conceived to be the course for England to pursue. He wrote to Bentinck:

> But there [i.e. the Hague] and everywhere I shall do my best to promote the most perfect union of sentiments and actions imaginable; cultivate our old friends and allies, get new ones if we can; but that, I believe, will be difficult. But above all let us endeavour to re-establish our interior, put our respective Finances on the best Foot we can; endeavour to support our Marine, for by that we have made the Peace; and if that is not neglected and if that can be anyways maintained, France perhaps may not be soon disposed to make war. But all will depend upon our Marine; France stirs Heaven and Earth to revive Theirs: and for God's sake give attention to this in Holland.*

To Newcastle, at any rate, "the only solid system in Europe" was the "old system." He had little faith in Frederick at this time; he believed that the interests of Prussia and France were so unavoidably connected that they were bound to act in concert, and that the only way to preserve the tranquillity of Europe and hinder further hostile action by Prussia was to maintain a superiority at sea.† If, in common with his colleagues in the Cabinet, he failed to foresee the subsequent re-arrangement of the Powers of Europe; if, like them, he made the error of believing that the relations of England and Austria had suffered no irremediable strain, he was at least, together with Hardwicke, superior to them in his perception that the primary hope of England lay in the power of her fleet. "If France," he wrote to Hardwicke, "sees that whenever she breaks with England she runs the same risk for her Commerce and Marine which she has so severely felt this war, neither

* Add. MS. 32815, f. 122, Newcastle to Bentinck, Oct. 31, 1748.
† Add. MS. 35410, f. 86, Newcastle to Hardwicke, Nov. 17, 1748.

France nor Prussia will be encouraged to break the Peace." *
This indeed was the theme on which he continually harped.
" I have always maintained," he wrote in a later letter, " that
our Marine should protect our alliances on the Continent, and
they, by diverting the expense of France, enable us to maintain
our superiority at sea." † A maritime supremacy, in the Duke's
opinion, was not only the means to preserve peace in Europe,
but also the endowment with which to win Austria back to her
former friendship. But Austria was not to be won. She was
possessed by a new order of ideas. Already St. Severin, who
had represented France at the Congress, was boasting that
Austria and England were irretrievably alienated.‡ Already
behind the scenes Kaunitz was working for the reversal of
Austria's traditional allegiance.

In the meanwhile Frederick the Great † was suggesting an
alliance with England to Henry Legge,§ who had been sent to
Berlin as Envoy extraordinary and plenipotentiary. At a remarkable interview in May Frederick disclaimed to Legge

> All connections with France and all desire of future con-
> nections and added strong reasons for his opinion some of
> which I remember were—That he knew France was at too
> great a distance to assist him as critically as he might require :
> that nobody was long the better for an allyance with France
> and that he was too well acquainted with the temper of the
> Court of France not to know the perpetual strong demands
> they made upon those who were called their allies and that
> to be the ally of France was in effect to be their slave. That
> on the contrary he knew the Maritime Powers were so
> situated as to be able to assist him and that the substantial
> Foundation of mutual interest and the strongest natural
> connexions of Religion Policy and Blood would make an
> allyance (with England more especially) solid and to be
> depended upon . . . and that he was ready as soon as a general
> peace was made which would entirely clear him of all obli-
> gations to France to enter into the most strict and zealous

* Ibid.
† Add. MS. 32810, f. 140, Newcastle to Hardwicke, Sept. 2, 1749.
‡ Philip Yorke, *Life of Lord Hardwicke*, II, p. 14.
§ Henry Legge, second son of the Earl of Dartmouth, subsequently
a Lord of the Admiralty and twice Chancellor of the Exchequer.

Union with the Maritime Powers for the future security of
the Liberties of Europe.

These protestations were renewed in July.* It is true that in
his dealings with the Court of Versailles his tone had altered.†
His attitude had become domineering. He had taken to criticising at large and with an overbearing freedom the finances,
the military resources, and the domestic policy of the French;
and although his criticisms were accompanied with protestations of fidelity to the French alliance, they were none the less
galling and calculated to cause uneasiness at Versailles. "What
a man!" exclaimed Maurice de Saxe, after an interview with
Frederick at Berlin. "I am more afraid of him in a tête-à-
tête than of his cousin Cumberland at the head of a hundred
thousand men." Fear was the sentiment which Frederick
most generally inspired on the Continent. Alone among the
Sovereigns of Europe he had benefited by the War of the
Austrian Succession.‡ Silesia, guaranteed to him by the
Treaty of Aix-la-Chapelle, remained as the most irrefutable
evidence of his power, and as a ratified assertion in the eyes
of Europe that in Prussia at any rate force was to claim pre-
cedence over treaty rights or moral obligations. Indifferent to
guarantees, recognising no interest but that of Prussia, possessed of one of the most powerful armies of Europe, himself
the first captain of the age, Frederick came to be thought likely
to prove no less disconcerting as an ally than formidable as
an open foe. In the judgment of Newcastle, at any rate,
the time was not favourable for a definite agreement with
Prussia. He rightly doubted the sincerity of Frederick's
professions. Intercepted letters had made it evident that
the policy of Potsdam was to divide England from her
allies. At the same time Newcastle considered that any

---

* S.P. Foreign, Prussia, Legge to Newcastle, July 1/12, 1748.

† Broglie, *L'Alliance Autrichienne,* p. 43 et seq.

‡ Voltaire, when criticised for making the King of Prussia the
hero of his history, said "he could not avoid speaking advantageously
of the Political Parts of a Prince, the only one who has got anything
by the war, and who knew how to make peace and war opportunely."
Add. MS. 35410, f. 265, Joseph Yorke to Lord Hardwicke, May 29/
June 10, 1750.

separate and exclusive treaty with Prussia at this moment would "overturn the whole system of Europe." * Legge was summoned to Hanover, and reprimanded for the forwardness with which he had met the King of Prussia, George II remarking that "it all came from choosing a man for ambassador merely because he could make a speech in the House of Commons." † Newcastle was careful to point out that in offering a guarded reception to Frederick's advances, he was not attempting to gratify George II's hatred of his nephew, but was reposing his policy on the necessities of the case, and solely in the interests of the "old system," to which he regarded England as irretrievably bound.

Peace, as we have seen, was signed at Aix-la-Chapelle in October 1748. In the course of the negotiations Cumberland had added to his fame. His military failures during the war were attributed with justice to the inefficiency of the allies, and he was now to return to England recognised by statesmen of every party as a man of commanding ability. The Duke of Newcastle, at the beginning of the negotiations, had written to him, "As Your Royal Highness directs the war, you must, without appearing to do it, direct the peace"; ‡ and in every step subsequently taken, up to the signing of the treaty, Cumberland's advice was sought and his judgment deferred to. Bedford and Sandwich wrote of him in a spirit of adulation which promised well for the political alliance later to be formed between Cumberland and those two statesmen. Bedford considered "that the salvation of this country doth greatly depend upon his Preservation," § while Sandwich wrote, "Your Grace judges very well in imagining that H.R.H.'s opinion will have weight with me. I most sincerely reverence his character as a Prince that promises to be the greatest genius of the age he lives in." ‖ And such, stated in

* Newcastle to Pelham, July 14, 1748, Coxe's *Pelham Administration*, I, p. 439.

† Newcastle to Pelham, Aug. 4, 1748, Coxe's *Pelham Administration*, I, p. 444.

‡ Add. MS. 32714, f. 429, Newcastle to Cumberland, April 5, 1748.

§ Add. MS. 32714, f. 401, Bedford to Newcastle, March 28, 1748.

‖ Add. MS. 32814, f. 41, Sandwich to Newcastle, Aug. 29, 1748.

rhetorical terms, was the view widely entertained of the young Duke, now in his twenty-ninth year. So pronounced was the Ministerial confidence in Cumberland's judgment that the despatches directed by Newcastle to Sandwich at Aix were sent first to the Headquarters of the Duke, in order that he might alter or even cancel them, * as he saw fit. Cumberland and Newcastle had been equally desirous of peace. They had been at one as to the means to be pursued, and we find Cumberland alert to censure his friend Sandwich when he deviated from the instructions forwarded to him by Newcastle.†

Even in matters relating to the King, the Ministry now appealed to Cumberland. When it was a question of George II, contrary to the advice of Ministers, proceeding to Hanover in 1748, Cumberland wrote to Newcastle, in answer to a request for his advice, " he [the King] may be told frankly that you and your friends desire an explanation from him in what manner he intends to act." ‡ Later he suggested that it would be better to make a bargain and promise the King two whole years in Hanover if only he would consent to remain for the summer of 1748 in England.§ In the minds of certain Ministers, the doctrine that the King could do no wrong was making way for a belief that George II could do no right. Cumberland, on the other hand, was acquiring a clearer conception of the sovereign's relations with his Cabinet. He saw that every year it was becoming more difficult for the King to act at variance with his Ministers, and he was now determined that there should be no visit to Hanover while the Ministry were opposed to it, or any necessity could be shown for his remaining at St. James's.

From this period dates the friendship between Sandwich and Cumberland, which was to prove such a thorn in the side of Newcastle.

John Montagu, fourth Earl of Sandwich (1718–1792), had succeeded his grandfather in the peerage at the age of eleven. His station in life and his pronounced ability marked

* Add. MS. 32714, f. 360, Newcastle to Cumberland, March 18, 1748.
† Add. MS. 32714, f. 411, Cumberland to Newcastle, April 11, 1748.
‡ Add. MS. 32714, f. 509, Cumberland to Newcastle, May 2, 1748.
§ Add. MS. 32714, f. 385, Cumberland to Newcastle, April 5, 1748.

him out for rapid and easy promotion in the offices of state. In his twenty-first year he had published a dull but scholarly account of an extended grand tour which he had made in the company of his tutor to the Greek islands and the shores of the Mediterranean. From this expedition he had returned to England with a collection of coins and antiquarian relics, to be hailed as a connoisseur and elected as a fellow of the Royal Society. In 1744 he had been chosen as a Lord Commissioner of the Admiralty Board. In the following year, when the Whig magnates were raising regiments to quell the Jacobite rebellion, he became (Sept. 27, 1745) a captain in the Duke of Bedford's regiment. These were times, before Cumberland's influence had permeated the army, when military preferment was adjusted to social rank and political importance, and on October 4 we find Sandwich gazetted Colonel in the army, and on November 22 second Colonel of the Duke of Montagu's ordnance regiment of foot. Thenceforward his promotion proceeded by regular steps to the highest ranks of the army, unaffected by the fact that his military service was never renewed, and that his time was wholly occupied with affairs of state. The success of his work at the Admiralty had induced Newcastle to appoint him in 1746 as plenipotentiary at the Congress of Breda, and to continue him as the British representative throughout the negotiations leading to the Treaty of Aix-la-Chapelle. In February 1748, on the Duke of Bedford's appointment as Secretary of State in succession to Chesterfield, Sandwich became head of the Admiralty. He remained, however, at Aix-la-Chapelle till the conclusion of the treaty, delegating his Admiralty duties to Lord Anson.

Few men during their lifetime have been the subject of such extremes of praise and vilification. On the one hand is the testimony of Churchill as expressed in *The Duellist,** who writes of Sandwich:

> Nature designed him in a rage
> To be the Wharton of his age,
> But having given all the sin,
> Forgot to put the virtues in.

* Works of Charles Churchill: *The Duellist*, III.

> To run a horse, to make a match,
> To revel deep, to roar a catch,
> To knock a tottering watchman down,
> To sweat a woman of the town;
>
> . . . . .
>
> With Wits a Fool, with Fools a Wit,
> Hear him but talk and you could swear
> Obscenity herself was there;
> And that Profaneness had made choice
> By way of Trump, to use his voice.
>
> . . . . .
>
> Too infamous to have a friend,
> Too bad for bad men to commend.

On the other hand, we find the Rev. J. Cooke, his Lordship's chaplain, writing with intimate knowledge of his character:

> Many calumnies equally unjust (as that of holding the clergy in small esteem) were thrown upon the noble Earl; but they have all died away; and his name will descend to posterity in its true colours; never failing to raise, wherever it is received, the warmest sentiments of love, esteem and admiration.*

The truth must be sought between these two views. Sandwich possessed undoubted ability and aptitude for business; he was an industrious and conscientious worker, methodical in his office and famed for his courtesy and benevolence to his subordinates. In the opinion of some, vanity and a tendency to intrigue, combined with a talent for reasoning right on wrong principles, marked him out as a " dangerous minister." † But dangerous or not, he was no match for Newcastle. In debate he could make effective replies, in council he was possessed of a strong and judicious understanding, but his habit of preferring voting power and political influence to efficiency rendered his administration at the Admiralty during his eleven years of office (1771–1782), under Lord North, highly detri-

---

* *Lord Sandwich's Voyage*, p. xxxvii.
† Add. MS. 32815, f. 28, Sir Thomas Robinson to Newcastle, October 17, 1748.

mental to the Navy. He was, however, during that period, responsible for the fitting out of Captain Cook's expedition, and the name given to the Sandwich Islands is witness to the explorer's recognition of the part played by the First Lord of the Admiralty. As a member of the " brotherhood of Medmenham," he acquired a name for profligacy and profaneness of language, and in the very year, 1763, when a newly appointed Secretary of State he attacked Wilkes in the House of Lords as the author of a blasphemous poem,* he was himself expelled for blasphemy by the Beef Steak Club in Covent Garden. †

The attack for party purposes on Wilkes, with whom Sandwich was notoriously associated in the ostentatious proceedings and laboured indecencies of Medmenham, was regarded as an act of the basest treachery. The moral standards of the age were by no means exacting, but a certain honour among confederates was even then expected, and in the reflection of Macheath in *The Beggar's Opera*,‡ " that Jemmy Twitcher should peach me, I own surprised me," the public discovered such appropriateness that ever after, Sandwich was known by the name of Jemmy Twitcher. In social life he was possessed of singular personal charm, and was gifted with a " power of attaching to himself persons of every rank." § He thus had qualities calculated to appeal to Cumberland, and form the basis of that friendship between them which was to play so considerable a part in Ministerial affairs. In appearance he was coarse and uncouth, and the cast of his countenance caused it to be said that he looked as if he had been hung, and cut down before he was dead. In his movements he was a byword for ungainliness, and he used himself to tell that when he asked his dancing master in Paris if he could do him any service, the master replied, " I should take it as a particular favour if your Lordship would never tell anyone of whom you learned to dance." ||

* *Essay on Woman.*
† Walpole, *Letters,* V, p. 396.
‡ Act III, Scene XIV.
§ Charles Butler, *Reminiscences,* I, p. 74.
|| Cradock, *Literary Memoirs and Correspondence,* IV, p. 166; *Dict. of Nat. Biography,* Art. John Montagu.

2

On his return from Aix-la-Chapelle he was much in the company of Cumberland, either at the Ranger's Lodge in Windsor Park, or at Woburn Abbey, where their leisure was spent during the summer months in cricket matches and private theatricals.* In later years his country seat, Hinchinbrook, where he resided with his mistress, Miss Ray, the prima donna, became the scene of famous musical gatherings. Here, with an orchestra of seventy performers, Handel's oratorios were performed, and Sandwich, though he is said by Charles Butler to have had " not the least real ear for music " and to have been " equally insensible of harmony and melody," would play his part with the kettle-drums, while Miss Ray appeared as the principal singer. The same untutored zeal for music made him in London, it was said, " the soul of the Catch Club and one of the Directors of the Concert of Antient Music."

He had shown marked ability in his conduct of the negotiations at Aix-la-Chapelle, but in proposing to ratify without the adhesion of Vienna he had departed from his instructions and incurred the censure of his patron, the Duke of Newcastle. It was no light thing for a youth with ambitions to incur the displeasure of the leader of the Whigs. Newcastle was a faithful foe, and seldom forgave. At this time he stood high in the favour of the King. His supremacy in the Cabinet was hardly contested. His authority in Parliament had been increased by the popularity of the peace. For years his vast patronage had been successfully employed in rendering his position secure. Every branch of the public service was peopled with his nominees. As a territorial magnate he could materially affect the elections in nine of the counties of England. By jobbery, by favour, and by patronage he had turned a preponderating party in the House of Commons into a serviceable and disciplined organisation for supporting himself and his chosen colleagues. Improved relations with Lady Yarmouth, the mistress of George II, had given him auxiliary powers in his dealings with the sovereign. For the moment his horizon was untroubled, save for the breach with Sandwich and a growing jealousy and dislike of the Duke of Bedford, who had succeeded Chesterfield as Secretary of State.

* Walpole, *Memoirs of George II*, I, p. 3.

National Portrait Gallery.

JOHN MONTAGU, FOURTH EARL OF SANDWICH (1718–1792).

From the Portrait in the National Portrait Gallery.

" You can imagine," he wrote at this time evidently with Sandwich in his mind, " I am not a little vain of our success owing as certainly to our measures as any event ever was to a certain cause. Thus vain, I am determined hereafter (Forgive me for saying it *in the greatest confidence to you and to you only*) never to have any Minister in my Department who *tells* me he is wiser than I am; and yet, perhaps I shall be glad to have those whom I may really think so myself." *

By deviating from his instructions, Sandwich had given offence to this powerful Minister, and from the personal antagonism thus established there was to be evolved later a new political faction with the Duke of Cumberland at its head. It was thus in fact that during the long Whig ascendancy changes in Ministerial circles were for the most part brought about. In the case of resignation or promotion it was seldom principles or policy that were at stake. A disagreement, a jealousy, the forwardness of a colleague in soliciting the ear of the King, a disposition towards the Prince of Wales's party, these or personal matters such as these, were mainly responsible for alterations in Ministerial posts.

Sandwich had done his best to repair the consequences of his indiscretion. In October he had written to Newcastle, " I once more make it my earnest request that there may be an entire oblivion with regard to the transactions of some months past, and that you would remain persuaded that I shall prove myself to be upon all occasions with the most perfect attachment your Grace's most faithful and most obedient servant Sandwich." † But Newcastle had been struck in a vulnerable quarter. He conceived that his authority had been defied, his instructions disregarded, and he strongly suspected that Sandwich had been carrying on a secret correspondence with the Duke of Bedford.‡ While preserving an outward decorum of friendly relations, Newcastle made it plain that he was deeply incensed. It was at this moment that Cumberland interposed. Acting on behalf of Sandwich, he endeavoured

* Add. MS. 32815, f. 55, Newcastle to Robinson, Oct. 22, 1748.

† Add. MS. 32815, f. 41, Sandwich to Newcastle, Oct. 19, 1748.

‡ Add. MS. 32815, f. 29, Sir Thomas Robinson to Newcastle, Oct. 18, 1748.

to effect a reconciliation. Newcastle, with less than his usual deference, and even more than his usual resentment, " never honoured the Duke with any answer; left him off; grew cool, impertinent, and inveterate." In the same summer a letter from the Duke of Newcastle to the Princess Amelia had " pert, not to say impertinent expressions in it, which, instead of explaining, he aggravated when he came home." *

Newcastle had thus fallen into the double error of offending both Cumberland and Princess Amelia. In his offence against Princess Amelia had to be reckoned a drop of gall attributable to the remote and shallow passages of love which in former years had passed between them. The Princess was an enemy not to be despised. Her intimacy with Cumberland, her love of intrigue, her influence in society, and her native belligerency rendered her at such a juncture a dangerous adversary. Nor was Cumberland the man to view with any tameness of spirit the rejection of his proffered mediation. Friendship and resentment alike called him to espouse the side of Sandwich. Thus in 1749 events were tending towards the formation of that Cumberland faction which was to comprise in its ranks Bedford, Sandwich, and Fox.

* Fox to Williams, Dec. 15, 1751. Printed Coxe's *Pelham Administration*, II, p. 110.

CHAPTER III

IN September 1748, after an absence of two years, Cumberland left his command in the Low Countries on a flying visit to London, accompanied by his aide-de-camp Lord Bury. He was greatly altered. A severe fever contracted in Holland had injured, if it had not altogether destroyed, the sight of one eye. Always notorious for his bulk, two years of campaigning had but added to his size—so that like "the fat knight" he was in danger of being "beyond all compass," and although as yet only twenty-nine years of age weighed, as we learn from a curious law suit, in which his weight had been the subject of a wager, nearly twenty stone.* In Walpole's letters he now figures as "Nolkejumskoi," a name of which, though the origin is uncertain, the significance may be safely taken as unflattering. No letter writer ever searched so industriously for copy wherewith to amuse his correspondents as Walpole. In the King and Cumberland, in "Messieurs d'Allemagne," as he called them, "who roll their red eyes, stroke up their great beavers, and look fierce," he found one of his richest sources of banter. He relates that the Duke of Modena replied to Princess Emily who enquired if he did not find her brother much fatter, "En vérité, il n'est pas si effroyable qu'on m'avait dit." On another occasion, still exploiting the obesity of the Duke, he describes the scene at a ball given by Lord Sandwich when Cumberland "tumbled down in the middle of a country dance. They imagined he had beat his nose flat, but he lay like a tortoise on the top shell, his face could not reach the ground by some feet." But in spite of the Duke's cumbersome proportions his activity was considerable, and nowhere was he more at home or seen to greater advantage than in the saddle, whether hunting at

* See E. Charteris, *William Augustus Duke of Cumberland*, p. 355.

21

Windsor or campaigning in Flanders. In his long jack-boots, and his blue coat turned back with facings of red, the sleeves wide and rigid at the wrist, and his buff waistcoat with army buttons, a three-cornered hat slightly tilted on his military wig, upright in his carriage and deep in the saddle as he appears in the pictures of Wootton, he is a figure of note invested with much dignity and the spirit of command. After all, it was only in 1735 that Somerville had addressed him in *The Chace*:

> But who is he
> Fresh as a rosebud newly blown, and fair
> As op'ning lilies, on whom every eye
> With joy and admiration dwells? See, see,
> He reins his docile Barb with manly grace.
> Is it Adonis for the Chace array'd?
> Or Britain's second Hope? Hail, blooming youth!
> May all your virtues with your years improve
> Till in consummate worth, you shine the Pride
> Of these our Days, and to succeeding Times
> A bright example;

and though the rosebuds and lilies may have faded under the stress of campaigning, the description may be called in aid to soften the gibes of Walpole. Cumberland was always a great lover and judge of horses, and as will later appear one of the most influential patrons of racing known in the history of the Turf. The pictures of him make it clear that, in his choice of a mount, he had a preference for the Andalusian strain with which the canvases of Velasquez and Vandyke have made the world familiar. But his interest in animals was not limited to horses. He was constantly adding to the collection of fauna at Windsor. His taste in menageries was well known. From the *Gentleman's Magazine* we learn that, on the signing of the Peace of Aix-la-Chapelle, he was presented by the Empress of Austria with a " wild boar, some sheep and goats of an odd make, and a large horned owl as big as an eagle, its two horns several inches long." This was a gift probably more in harmony with his sympathies than that received from Marshal Saxe, who in April 1748 sent a " trumpet " to Cumberland with a copy of Polignac's *Anti-Lucretius,* a volume then making a great stir on the Continent and which was said " by the harmony of numbers to enforce the invincible arguments which prove the existence of a deity and totally overthrow the hypothesis of Epicurus."

In 1749 the Duke acquired three famous horses from Marshal Bathyany in Hungary.* In the same year he is sent a wolf by Colonel Lockhart, an officer whom the Duke had sent abroad at his own expense to recover from his wounds. The wolf is accompanied by a letter to say that " she is as tame as any dog and with a staunch and large hound H.R.H. may have a noble pack of foxhounds." † There is no record that the suggestion was adopted. Colonel Lockhart adds: " I shall as soon as possible send H.R.H. some dozens of partridges and other curiositys for Windsor. I'm informed I can get some very large and curious fowl from Barbary." Lions and tigers also figured in the Duke's collection at Windsor,‡ and to Lord Huntingdon, in doubt what to do with a pair of ostriches sent him by the Governor of Tetuan, Lord Chesterfield wrote advising that they should be offered to Cumberland.§ It was only later that the Duke extended his experiments in the animal world by the breeding of racehorses. But he was active in improving the amenities of Windsor, and in 1750 Fawkener, his secretary, is found writing to the Governor of South Carolina: " H.R.H. the Duke being now a little at leisure in possession of Windsor Great Park turns his thoughts a good deal to the study which has of late prevailed here not a little of the culture of Plants and Forest trees, and is laying out by all the ways he can, to come at a variety of the more useful and beautiful ones," and requests that seeds or cones of American trees and plants may be sent as speedily as possible. The answer was " 3 barrils of seeds " by H.M.S. *Rye.*‖ The same year Cumberland imports " thousands of strawberry plants " from Holland.

* Cumberland MS.

† Ibid.

‡ Walpole, *Letters,* III, p. 251.

§ Francis Stewart, *Lord Chesterfield's Letters to Lord Huntingdon,* p. 80.

‖ Cumberland MS.

A great deal of the planting which to-day makes the beauty of Windsor Forest was done by Cumberland, and much of the verdure in the parishes of Old Windsor, Sunninghill, Winfield, Easthamsted, Oakingham, and Sandhurst * is due to his care and initiative. Planting was extremely in fashion. The subject figures in Walpole's letters with a frequency second only to the Royal Family. A knowledge of trees and planting had become as necessary a part of a polite equipment as the lighter accomplishments of sport and gambling. Henry Fox, Cumberland's friend and ally, occupied the leisure of three years in planting at Holland House, and records in 1753 that during the autumn he had planted sixty-six different varieties of trees and shrubs.†

It was at this period too that Cumberland became interested in the Chelsea factory of china. What the extent of that interest was cannot be exactly determined. Whether he had a financial stake in it or merely gave it his patronage, whether he subsidised it or simply took a purchaser's interest in its products, it is at any rate certain that his name was associated with the early beginnings of the factory, and that he and his secretary, Sir Everard Fawkener, did their best to develop the sales of the porcelain and make it known on the Continent. In a recent book ‡ on Chelsea Porcelain the letter of one Mason, a workman at the factory, is quoted as follows:

> I think the Chelsea China Manufactory began about the year 1748 or 1749. I went to work about the year 1751. It was first carried on by the Duke of Cumberland and Sir Everard Fawkener and the sole management was entrusted to a foreigner of the name of Sprimont, report says at a salary of a guinea per day with certain allowance for apprentices and other emoluments. I think Sir Everard died about 1755 § much reduced in circumstances; when Mr. Sprimont became sole proprietor.

The suggestion in this letter receives some confirmation from

* Cumberland MS.
† Lord Ilchester, *Life of Henry Fox*, I, p. 176.
‡ William King, *Chelsea Porcelain*, p. 31.
§ He died in 1758.

a further letter dated June 9, 1751, and written from Dresden by Sir Charles Hanbury-Williams to Henry Fox: *

> I received a letter about ten days ago from Sir Everard Fawkener who is I believe concerned in the manufacture of China at Chelsea. . . . I find also that the Duke is a great encourager of the Chelsea China and has bespoke a set for his own table.

The Cumberland MSS. yield no further light beyond a letter from one Walters at Rotterdam to Sir Everard Fawkener, dated May 1750, in which the writer says:

> I shall be very glad to have it in my power to make the Chelsea China Manufactory known in this country: the pieces which you are so good as to promise me may be sent off properly packed up, by the Harwich stage to the Captain of the Pacquet Boat.

The evidence either way, it will be seen, is not conclusive; it establishes, however, that both the Duke and Fawkener were concerning themselves with the progress of the factory, and it is not inconsistent with the suggestion that one or both of them were financially interested in the undertaking. In *L'Etat des Arts en Angleterre,* published in 1755, the author, Rouquet, says: " On trouve aux environs de Londres trois ou quatre manufactures de porcelaine; celle de Chelsea est la plus considérable; un riche particulier en soutient la dépense." † Here again is evidence which may well indicate the interested patronage of Cumberland. We know at any rate that the Duke favoured the products of this industry from the fact that in 1766 there was hanging in the principal room at Windsor Lodge " a chandelier of Chelsea China, the first of that manufacture and cost £500." ‡

Cumberland also interested himself in the carpet manufactories at Paddington and Fulham. He paid the debts of the two French workmen who were the foundation of the industry, and made a present of the first carpet they produced to the Princess of Wales in December 1751. Peter Parisot, who sought Cumberland's aid, makes it clear that it was through

* Published by Lord Ilchester, *Burlington Magazine,* XX, p. 361.
† Cited, William King, *Chelsea Porcelain,* p. 32.
‡ *Passages from the Diary of Mrs. Philip Lybbe Powys,* p. 114.

the generosity of the Duke that the industry was able to establish itself and flourish in London.*

But whatever his pursuits, whatever his physical attributes, Cumberland's force of character, his experience, his soundness of judgment and maturity of political capacity had by this time made him an outstanding personality in Great Britain. Since 1744 he had been engaged more or less continuously in campaigning. He had had under his command a larger force than any commander in previous British history. At Dettingen † and Fontenoy he had made himself conspicuous for his physical courage. In the rebellion of '45 he had shown that resolution and the personal prestige of a commander, together with an understanding of the temper of troops, could re-establish confidence and order as well as neutralise the memory of defeat. In the course of the same campaign he had proved his capacity for organisation, and had exactly adjusted the means at his command to the end to be achieved. Under his leadership the fame of British troops had been revived, and they had re-established the reputation which had suffered so grievously at Prestonpans and Falkirk. In the cries of "Now Billy for Flanders" with which he was hailed by his men on the field of Culloden he had recognised a reward beyond all the honours which were subsequently conferred on him.

During six years at the head of allies who failed him at every crisis and were perpetually wrangling amongst themselves he had contested the progress of Maurice de Saxe, one of the first captains of the age, commanding a large and united army with all the resources of a military nation at his call. If the Low Countries were not completely overrun in the first years of the war, if Holland itself was saved from invasion, and if in 1748 it was still possible to make tolerable terms of peace,

---

* *An account of the New Manufactory of Tapestry after the manner of that at Gobelins . . . now undertaken at Fulham,* by Mr. Peter Parisot, pp. 13–15, 17–18. This rare book is to be found at the Bodleian.

† "The Duke of Cumberland behaved charmingly." "The Duke behaved as bravely as a man could do."—Edward Wolfe to his mother. Beckles Willson, *Life of James Wolfe,* p. 35. James Wolfe to his father, *ib.,* p. 37.

the credit was largely due to Cumberland. Indeed the tributes paid to him by the statesmen of the day leave no doubt that this was the view held by his contemporaries. " I must freely own to you," wrote Bedford to Newcastle before the friend-ship between Bedford and Cumberland had been formed, " H.R.H.'s late behaviour and the judgment he has shown in matters of peace as well as war has firmly convinced me that the salvation of this country doth greatly depend upon his preservation." Sandwich, as we have seen, regarded him as a " Prince that promises to be the greatest genius of the age he lives in "; while Newcastle, writing to him on his birthday, April 15, 1748, expressed the hope that he might long continue to be the great " Protector and support of this country and the common cause of Europe." Again, in the Debate on the Address in November 1748, in answer to a motion for an enquiry " as to the causes which rendered the events of the war so little answerable to the bravery of the troops employed," Pelham, replying for the Government, said: " I shall readily acknowledge, Sir, that we owe a great deal to the royal com-mander of our armies; to him we owe our being this day assembled in this House; to him the nation owes the preserva-tion of its liberties, its religion, and everything that can be dear to a people." * But from a military point of view no tribute will compare with that which was paid him by Marshal Saxe at an interview at Dresden with Sir C. Hanbury-Williams. Speaking of the campaign which had just ended, the Marshal praised General Ligonier's cavalry charge at Laffelt and de-clared it to have been " as prudent and as bold an attempt, as at the same time it was well executed." He then went on to speak of Cumberland's conduct of the several campaigns in which he had been opposed to him. Hanbury-Williams, in his letter to Newcastle, wrote: " His [Marshal Saxe's] praise of His Royal Highness was short, but very great: for I heard him declare that he had not found out that His Royal High-ness had committed one fault during his whole command in Flanders." † Cumberland's misfortune in war had been never

* *Parliamentary History*, XIV, p. 350.

† State Papers, Foreign, Poland, No. 70, Sir C. Hanbury-Williams to Duke of Newcastle, Dresden, July 9, 1749.

on any occasion to be on the same side as the strong battalions.

By the end of September he was back in the Low Countries arranging for their evacuation by the British contingent at the conclusion of hostilities. With the war at an end the Ministry at once set to work to cut down the military commitments. The proposed reductions were submitted to Cumberland. He acquiesced with reluctance. The peace time footing of the home establishment, at no time adequate, seemed lamentably deficient to the Captain General in view of the state of Europe. The Royal Marines fell first to be dealt with. This famous regiment, raised to a strength of ten battalions in 1741, incorporated in the line and numbering in the Army from the 44th to the 53rd regiment, were now completely disbanded, not to be revived till 1755, when they were placed for the first time entirely under the control of the Admiralty and reckoned as part of the naval establishment.

During the course of the war they had gained distinction at Portobello, at the taking of Cape Breton, at Quiberon Bay, and in the operations under Admiral Boscawen on the coast of Coromandel. It was in the forces under Boscawen that there was serving one Hannah Snell, a native of Worcester. This woman, following her lover who had been seized by the pressgang, and disguising her sex, had enlisted in the Marines. At the siege of Pondicherry she was wounded in the legs and received a bullet in the groin; the bullet she succeeded in extracting for herself, and treated by the doctor for her other wounds she in due course recovered. Altogether she served seven years. The lover died. She herself returned to England with her regiment. It was only then that her sex was discovered. Cumberland heard the story and at once procured her a pension of thirty pounds a year from the King's Bounty.

To the disbandment of his own regiment of dragoons Cumberland took strong exception, but Pelham considering it " essential to his own credit [as Captain General] and the success of the King's affairs in Parliament," that the reduction should take place, he ultimately consented. Ministers were never on very sure ground when it came to defending a standing army and military establishments in Parliament. It would have appreciably added to the difficulty if a preference had been given to a regiment associated with the Crown through the colonelcy of Cumberland. Political considerations prevailed. The regiment once the Duke of Kingston's and at this time known as the Duke of Cumberland's was duly disbanded. In all 37,885 men were struck off the strength of the Army, leaving for Great Britain a force of 18,995 men,* while 11,850 men were continued on the Irish establishment.†

But while assenting to the proposed reductions Cumberland was insistent that " the forlorn soldier who so nobly fought " and was now to be deprived of his employment should have recognition paid to his services. In the King's Speech for the session beginning November 29, 1748, he caused the following words to be inserted: " You will further consider that those brave men who have served well by sea or land, and cannot now be employed, justly deserve to be the objects of your favour and protection."

Cumberland was more ready to temper his ideas of severity with a measure of consideration than the popular view of him has allowed. Indeed gratitude to those who had fought under him was one of his besetting merits. Together with Lord Halifax, then at the Board of Trade or, as the title went, " first lord of Trade," he now concerted a scheme for despatching disbanded soldiers to Nova Scotia. Fifty acres of

---

* The size of companies in battalions seems to have varied, e.g.:

The 1st Regiment of Footguards consisted of 28 companies at 58 men including officers per company.

The battalions of the line had ten companies of 81 men including officers per battalion.

4,503 Cavalry remained on the Establishment.

Two troops of Horse Guards at 181 per troop including officers.

Two troops of Grenadier Guards at 177 per troop including officers.

1 Regiment of Horse Guards Blue at 37 per troop including officers (9 troops).

1 Regiment of Dragoons at 47 per troop including officers (9 troops).

11 Regiments of Dragoons at 47 per troop including officers (6 troops).

Cumberland to Bedford, W.O. 4, 45 Foreign Expeditions, Oct. 18, 1748.

† The number of men for the Irish establishment could not exceed 12,000 under an Act passed in the reign of William III.

freehold land with an additional ten acres for every child were offered to all ex-soldiers who would emigrate. A free passage was guaranteed, and immunity from taxation for ten years. A company of four thousand, including families, were thus sent overseas under the command of Colonel Cornwallis. And it was hoped that in the founding of the town of Halifax and the stimulus thus given to the colonial system an effective means would be contrived for combating French influence on the other side of the Atlantic. It was, however, fear as much as compassion that directed the Ministerial motives and operated on the Ministerial imagination. The prospect of discharged soldiers roaming the country had in it an element of danger. In the public mind throughout many years of the eighteenth century " soldier " was apt to be synonymous with criminal, and it was the current view that the army was only kept within bounds and restrained from terrorising the civil population by the infliction of those drastic and barbarous punishments, which were then and for many years continued to be part of the military code. However, beyond the Nova Scotian scheme little effort was made by the Government to deal with the problem. Discharged soldiers were abruptly unloaded on the civil population without provision for their support, too often only to fulfil the dark anticipations that they would replenish the gaols and swell the harvests of Tyburn. Indeed, within a year, Horace Walpole was writing: " You will hear little news from England but of robberies; the numbers of disbanded soldiers and sailors have all taken to the road, or rather to the street; people are almost afraid of stirring after it is dark." * In the hope of alleviating the distress thus brought about, Cumberland found work for large numbers of discharged soldiers on the construction of Virginia Water and in the forest and gardens of Windsor.

By Christmas 1748 Cumberland and his whole force had been landed in England. Not a few of the returned battalions † were at once despatched to Scotland to assist in executing the repressive legislation which, passed as a conse-

---

* Walpole, *Letters,* II, p. 423.

† Among them the 20th with James Wolfe, now in his 22nd year, as major.

The Great Bridge over the Virginia River

WILLIAM AUGUSTUS DUKE OF CUMBERLAND SUPERINTENDING THE WORKS AT VIRGINIA WATER.

From an Engraving after Paul Sandby in the Royal Library, Windsor.

30]

quence of the rebellion in 1745, had since its enactment lain largely a dead letter, dusty in the statute book. The laws restricting and regulating the ministrations of the episcopalian clergy, for disarming the Highlands, and restraining the use of the Highland dress,* by which " any one who should wear the clothes commonly called Highland clothes, namely the plaid, philibeg, trews, shoulder belts or any part of the Highland garb, or should use for great coats, or for upper coats, tartans or partly coloured plaid or stuff " should be imprisoned without bail for six months and for a second offence transported to any of His Majesty's plantations for seven years, thus came to be put in operation. These were measures which had excited profound hostility in Scotland. They deeply offended national sentiment, they struck at tradition, and the provision for disarming was wholly at variance with the habits and even the bare necessities of a martial people.

Concealment of arms and evasion of the statute relating to the garb were freely practised. Thus on a journey breeches would be carried hung round the shoulders, or the kilt itself would be worn with the centre sewn up with a few stitches between the thighs, or by reducing the amount of tartan used from twelve yards to four the pleated kilt would be exchanged for a plain straight piece of cloth hanging loose to the knees. To such ingenuous efforts to elude the law the authorities gave no countenance, and to all who were brought up under suspicion an oath was administered which covered every possible artifice and was well framed to awe a primitive and superstitious community.†

True in the end these measures, for which Cumberland was

---

* 20 Geo. II, c. 39.

† Browne, *History of the Highlands,* III, p. 414. The form of the oath was as follows: " I A.B. do swear and as I shall answer to God at the great day of judgment I have not nor shall have in my possession any gun, sword, pistol, or arm whatsoever, and never use tartan plaid or any part of the Highland garb: and if I do so may I be cursed in my undertakings, family, and property—may I never see my wife and children, father, mother, or relations—may I be killed in battle as a coward and lie without Christian burial in a strange land far from the graves of my forefathers and kindred: may all this come across me if I break my oath."

largely responsible, were to prove salutary, in the end they were to show that disaffection could be stamped out and loyalty fostered by legislation. But for the time being they excited an implacable enmity. The old spirit was dying slowly, and in countless hearts fealty to the white cockade, to the King across the water, was still part of an imperishable faith. In 1749 the birthday of the young Chevalier was celebrated at Edinburgh under the very guns of the Castle with all the rejoicing of a national festival. A blue bonnet and white cockade adorned the Lion above the Parliament House. Wherever Cumberland's head figured as a sign, the eyes were picked out. Bonfires were lighted on Arthur's Seat and Salisbury Crags, and at night the town gave itself up to festivity with dances and assemblies to celebrate the occasion.* And so through many of the towns and villages of Scotland and in remote Highland glens the bright but slender flame of Jacobitism still continued to burn, tended by a devout enthusiasm and watched with a fearful hope.

* Cumberland Papers.

CHAPTER IV

HITHERTO Cumberland had held aloof from politics. His gradual entry into that field of intrigue which was coextensive with the statesmanship of the day is not easy to trace. It probably began with his friendship with Sandwich and that statesman's quarrel with Newcastle. Cumberland, as we have seen, intervened, assumed the rôle of a go-between, and was driven ultimately to adopt that of a partisan. Up to that time his conception of the political situation was simple and definite. Briefly stated, he considered Newcastle as personifying Whig ascendancy, and Whig ascendancy he regarded as essential to the support of the Throne and the stability of the Constitution. Now the disagreement between Sandwich and Newcastle had introduced a complication and disturbed the simplicity of his outlook. Newcastle no longer appeared to be so essential— on the contrary his peevish egotism was beginning to interfere with the conduct of affairs. "Lord Sandwich is abominable," Newcastle had written to Lord Hardwicke, " was there ever such a treatment of the King and myself "; and from Henry Pelham he declared that he had " received letters such as no one brother, that has the least affection or regard for the other, ever wrote before." He was in fact in a state of nervous irritation, which made him suspicious of every colleague and querulous in every relation. To Cumberland he had shown an uncommon coolness, and while he considered that the credit for the outward concord at Aix-la-Chapelle was due to his own work at Hanover in the cause of peace, he felt that he was about to return to England without that meed of recognition which his merit deserved and his vanity certainly desired. He was in fact at loggerheads with his principal colleagues. It required all the Lord Chancellor's mellifluous admonitions to keep the peace and prevent an open breach between the brothers.

3

No one understood Newcastle so intimately as Hardwicke, no one could deal so amiably with the Duke's vexations and perplexities or conjure away so successfully his imagined affronts. Moreover he realised the value of Newcastle; he appreciated his boundless industry, his wide knowledge of foreign affairs, his unrivalled capacity for managing the party machine, and the strength of his judgment in political matters: he knew in fact that without Newcastle the Administration would fall to pieces. Thus two camps were forming in the Ministry —on the one side Hardwicke, Newcastle, and Pelham, on the other Sandwich, Henry Fox, and the Duke of Bedford —each with its followers; while William Pitt as Paymaster-General was an uncertain factor, disliked by the King, but for the moment preserving a certain independence, though inclining to the side of Newcastle. Cumberland probably became involved with the Bedford faction owing more to the attitude of Newcastle than to any intentional line of policy on his own part. Newcastle, however, was thoroughly alarmed by "the disposition which I find in the Duke of Cumberland to do nothing which can possibly displease Lord Sandwich."

And as by degrees the alliance between Cumberland and the Duke of Bedford drew closer, Newcastle's alarms increased. He took the gloomiest view of the parties at Woburn. "The sole intent of these parties," he wrote to Hardwicke, "is to declare to the world that the Duke of Cumberland and the Princess Amelia are determined to countenance and support the Duke of Bedford and my Lord Sandwich in opposition to me. Is not every act of their lives a proof of the most inveterate (I am far from saying the most impotent) malice?" *

Events coming within range of Newcastle's hysterical outlook, when they bore upon his prestige or carried a challenge to his social position, acquired an unaccountable significance. The path of the world, and it was the path on which his feet were set, was strewn with thorns. He might well have said, "Il y a peu de choses aussi difficiles et aussi dangereuses que le commerce des hommes." The fabric of his authority rested

* Add. MS. 35410, f. 242, Newcastle to Hardwicke, Aug. 10, 1749.

on a number of precarious and artificial supports. Amongst these not the least to be reckoned was his credit with the Royal Family. It was intolerable to Newcastle that a section of that family should now be showing ingratitude and a scarcely veiled hostility. " I think it a little hard," he wrote to his brother, " that the Duke of Cumberland and the Princess Amelia should use me so cruelly as they have done: excommunicated me from all society, set a kind of brand or mark upon me and all who think with me, and set up a new, unknown factious young party to rival me and nose me everywhere. This goes to my heart. I am sensible if I could have submitted and cringed to such usage, the public appearances could have been better and perhaps some secret stabs avoided: but I was too proud and too inno-cent to do it." * But the fancied evil of social excommuni-cation was largely associated with the machinations of the Duke of Bedford as Secretary of State.

Thenceforward Newcastle's energy and ingenuity were en-listed and concentrated on securing the dismissal of that states-man. He saw in Bedford not only a rallying centre for other elements of disaffection, but a colleague of sufficient ability to prove a dangerous rival, and anyhow likely to be a continual source of vexation of spirit.

John Russell, 4th Duke of Bedford (1710–1771), had succeeded to the title in 1732, the year after his marriage to Lady Dye Spencer, the Duke of Marlborough's sister. In youth he had been educated at home, and later followed the conventional regime of a " grand tour " on the Continent. He was one of the great Whig figures of the eighteenth century, entitled by rank and wealth to participate in the task of governing the country, and qualified by his abilities to play his part with judgment and advantage. When he first entered politics he had been opposed to Sir Robert Walpole; subsequently he had earned the dislike of George II by the infallible method of opposing Carteret and his Hanover measures. In 1744 he had been made First Lord of the Admiralty in the Pelham Ministry, and in 1745 had restored himself to favour at Court by raising, commanding, and even

* Newcastle to Pelham, May 20, 1750. Coxe's *Pelham Adminis-tration*, II, p. 336.

serving with a regiment during the rebellion. In 1748, on
the resignation of Chesterfield, Bedford became Secretary of
State for the Southern Department. He was reckoned by
contemporaries to be violent and headstrong, illiberal and without either "the desire or talent of pleasing." * But he was of
inflexible honesty, and preferred what he believed to be the
interests of the country to his own personal advancement. He
ended his political career as he began, an example of the
limitations, the narrowness, and the unadventurous routine
of Whig principles. In the House of Lords he was an effective debater, and his speech on the Scottish forfeited estates
remains a notable example of Parliamentary oratory. Tainted
less than the majority of his contemporaries with the spirit
of intrigue, he never hesitated to adopt the unpopular cause if
his convictions led him to do so. His attitude on the Militia
Bill (1757) gave rise to a threat of attack on Woburn so
serious that a troop of the blues was sent from London for
its protection. On his return from Paris in 1763, where as
ambassador he had signed the treaty which brought to an end
the Seven Years' War, he was hooted by the mob in London.
In 1765 he figured as a free trader and opposed a duty on
Italian silks; here again he was the object of a popular outburst, and in Bedford House, which he had garrisoned with
his friends, he was attacked by the populace, who were only
driven off by the arrival of a strong body of troops. Later,
in 1769, when visiting his estates in Devonshire, he was set
upon by a Wilkite mob at Honiton, "bull dogs were halloed
at his horse," † he was pelted with stones and escaped with
the utmost difficulty. He had, therefore, in the course of his
career, had more than a common share of public unpopularity.

He exercised on the whole a beneficial influence on political
life, he set a high standard of integrity and independence, and
if his judgments were not infrequently ill-founded, the
course of his political action was often enlightened and
humane at a time when humanity was held in small esteem.
In stature he was small, and he was variously known as the

* *Letters of the Earl of Chesterfield,* ed. Lord Mahon, II, p. 465.
† *Bedford Correspondence,* III, p. lxxix.

" little Duke," " Little Æolus," " John King of Bedford," or the " Cock Dove." Gainsborough's portrait shows features of little distinction but a singularly open countenance, a jaw resolute and thick-set, a high forehead, the eyebrows strongly marked, the eyes far apart and expressing benevolence rather than the violence with which he is credited. If, in the portrait, the benevolence is tempered by a measure of irony, it is at any rate in the story of his life attested by the warm-hearted affection which characterised his intimacies and surrounded him with friends.

He was drawn into politics by his station in life rather than by his inclinations. His real taste lay in sport, in the management of his estate, in the cultivation of the cacti and rare coniferæ of Woburn, and in cricket and private theatricals. It was charged against him that he was a frequent absentee from his office and that he was too often seen riding post to Woburn. Pelham attributed his idleness to " jollity, boyish-ness, and vanity." Newcastle regarded it more seriously and used it as a lever for his dismissal. But he was on the side of gaiety; he did not believe in " filling his house with doleful creatures "; * and Woburn during his tenure became a famous centre of social amusement—here Cumberland and Princess Amelia were constant visitors, here Sandwich beguiled the time with cricket and theatricals, here Rigby delighted a leisured circle with his buoyancy and wit, here Horace Walpole came to exercise his powers of pitiless observation, and here, as Newcastle in jealousy wrote, " all the great men, the fine gentle-men, and the fine ladies " of the fashionable world were wont to assemble. Even Newcastle thought it politic to go the way of the world, smother his jealousies, and accept, if he did not enjoy, the hospitality of the Abbey. It was at any rate the best way to counter the social menace presented by the Cumberland alliance; while in the political world it was clear that the goal for which he must work was the dismissal of Bedford, which, if the King would assent to it, would rid him of a rival and weaken the influence of Cumberland.

The early days of the session of Parliament which opened in January 1749 were taken up with a sharp and vivacious

* Isaiah xiii, 21.

discussion over the clauses of the Mutiny Bill.* Introduced
by the Secretary at War Henry Fox, the Bill admittedly bore
traces of the influence of the Captain General. In effect, it
was said, the Bill continued in time of peace the offences and
penalties which had been prescribed for a time of war. It
contained also innovations to which exception was taken by
the Opposition. It proposed to subject officers on half pay
to military law, and to give power to any commander-in-chief
or commanding officer to require any court-martial to revise
or correct any sentence pronounced by such court-martial.
Both proposals were finally passed. Both were warmly opposed in the Commons and again in the Lords. The usual
arguments against standing armies were reproduced. Covert
attacks in Parliament were directed by Jacobite and Tory
against the person of Cumberland. It was said that the proposal to give power to the Commander-in-Chief to order a
revision of court-martial findings was a dangerous menace to
liberty. This proposal was speciously defended by the Lord
Chancellor.

> Can we suppose [he said] that the judges of a court-
> martial are infallible? Can we suppose them less liable to
> err in their judgment than a jury, or than any of our Courts
> at common law? Do not we know, that when a jury upon
> any trial at common law, brings in a verdict which the
> judge thinks unjust or improper, he may order them out
> again to reconsider their verdict? And do not we know
> that juries have often upon such occasions altered their
> verdict? Why then should we not allow the judges of a
> court-martial to alter their sentence or opinion, especially
> when the crown or the commander-in-chief thinks that they
> have given an unjust or improper sentence? †

In the end the proposal was carried in the Lords without
difficulty. Cumberland attended the debates and voted in the
divisions, a proceeding condemned by Horace Walpole. "Duke
William," he writes, "was there and voted, which was too

---

* First introduced 1689, and with the following exceptions passed
every subsequent year till the Army Act 1892. From Dec. 20, 1691,
to March 10, 1692–3; from April 10, 1698, to Feb. 20, 1701; and from
March 24, 1712–13, till July 25 following, there was no Mutiny Act
on the Statute Book. See *Parliamentary History*, XIV, pp. 434–5.
    † *Ibid.*

indecent in a rigorous bill calculated for his own power ";
on the other hand, for the Commander-in-Chief to have held
aloof and taken no part in a Bill which he considered necessary
for the maintenance of discipline would have placed a forcible
argument in the hands of opponents of the measure. William
Pitt, who was seeking conciliation with Newcastle and anxious
to placate the King, gave his support to the Bill in its entirety,
thereby dissociating himself from the Prince of Wales's party,
which had organised and carried on the opposition and succeeded in getting together a minority of 137 against 203 in
the House of Commons.

The Prince of Wales's Party, or as it was also called the
Leicester House Party, had been showing considerable activity.
In June 1747 a document had been drawn up setting forth the
principles for which the heir to the throne was prepared to
solicit support. " H.R.H.," it began, " has authorised Lord
Talbot and Sir Francis Dashwood to give the most positive
assurances to the gentlemen in the opposition of his upright
intentions : that he is thoroughly convinced of the distress and
calamities that have befallen and are more likely every day
to befall his country from party and faction and a general
depravity of morals diffused throughout this country "—and
at the end of this exordium went on to set forth, as concrete
proposals, the abolition of party, the establishment of a
numerous militia, exclusion from the House of Commons of
all military officers under the rank of colonel and all naval
officers under the rank of rear-admiral, enquiries into the
abuses in offices, and a refusal to accept of more than £800,000
for his civil list.

Few men of his generation had done less to minimise the
calamities attributable to faction or to combat by his personal
example " the general depravity of morals diffused throughout
the country." Nor was the party programme outlined in the
document of a nature to inspire enthusiasm; but it is of
peculiar value as an indication of the barrenness of current
political ideas, directed as they then were to symptoms rather
than causes, and concerned with the Crown and government
rather than with the governed. A moment had, however,
undoubtedly arrived when, if the Prince of Wales was not to

sink into a condition of futile insignificance, some assertion had to be made of his political existence. His reputation had suffered a gradual eclipse, the personality of Cumberland was now filling the stage, the King was advancing in years, the possibility of accession was in sight, and there was no affection between father and son to dispute "the hunger for the empty chair." But it was not till the year now under review (1749) that the Prince's party was able on the Mutiny Bill to gather any noticeable strength in Parliament. On this occasion there was the further incentive that in opposing the measure they were at the same time opposing Cumberland. Indeed the prospects of the Opposition appeared so alluring that such a time-server as Bubb Dodington, whom the Prince himself had once called "that trimming dastard soul," was tempted at the solicitation of the Prince to resign his position as Treasurer of the Navy (March 1749) and take service in the Leicester House Party at a salary of £2,000 per annum as Treasurer of the Chambers, with a reversion on the death of the King to a peerage, leadership in the House of Lords, and "the seals of Secretary of State for the Southern Province." *

Within a few months of the passing of the Mutiny Act an opportunity arose for a further trial of strength at the Westminster election, brought about by the appointment of Lord Trentham the son of Lord Gower as one of the Lords of the Admiralty.

This election, which cost the Duke of Bedford seven thousand pounds, would probably have been unopposed if Lord Trentham's espousal of the French players had not given a convenient opening for a rival candidate. A company of actors from Paris had begun a season at the Haymarket; the war feeling was still active; the populace were determined there should be no enemies within their gates, still less within their theatres, and on the first night indulged in a riot which "the young men of fashion," † of whom Lord Trentham was wrongly reputed to be one, endeavoured to suppress with drawn swords, actually wounding some of the demonstrators. The first advertisement of one of Lord Trentham's meetings

* *Dodington Diary*, p. 5.
† Walpole, *Letters*, II, 416.

produced a counter notice, of which the *Gentleman's Magazine* gives the following account:

" No French stroller will be admitted "—" Peter Wood master of the noted b——y house in the Strand was archly put up in an advertisement ' he having on every occasion distinguished himself for the pleasure of the public ' with this N.B. ' Mr. Wood desires the worthy electors to excuse his not making his personal appearance, a late affair hindering him from it: but hopes they will take notice that he was in no way concerned in the vindication of the French strollers.' "

At the last moment Sir George Vandeput came forward as a candidate with the support of the Leicester House Party. The main topics before the electors were, on the one hand, the suggested Dutch origin of Sir George Vandeput, and, on the other, the French sympathies of Lord Trentham. Westminster was inundated with handbills and squibs in which the " French vagrants " played a principal part. The following is a fair sample of eighteenth-century election wit:

Aux Électeurs Très Dignes de Westminster
Messieurs—
Vos suffrages et intérêts sont désirés pour le Très Honorable mi Lord Trentham,
Un Véritable Anglois.
N.B.—On prie ses Amis de se rendre à l'Hôtel François dans le Marché au Foin.

" To my Lord Trentham
" The King of France (my most glorious Monarch) being touched with a lively sense of the obligations he owes your Lordship, for the powerful protection you have given to his subjects in England, honours you with his thanks, and commands me to assure you that your Lordship shall be the Chief Manager of his Playhouse in England as soon as your Lordship and your friends have brought those insolent rascals, the English, under his dominion, being satisfied the measures your Lordship and Friends now pursue cannot fail of your desired success.
" I have the honour to be
" your Lordship's most obliged and humble servant,
" Mirepoix, French Ambassador, Court of St. James."

The contest was indeed more than usually prolific in verse, caricature, and electioneering humour—the quality of which compares to the advantage of the eighteenth century with modern efforts of a similar character. On the other hand, the pressure brought to bear on voters was in some cases abrupt and drastic, and we find the Duke of Bedford serving on a tenant who had voted against the Court notice to quit or pay double his previous rent.* But pressure such as this was common to both sides, and to George Vaughan, sedan-chair maker to the Royal Family, who had voted for Lord Trentham, came a message from the Prince of Wales that in consequence of Vaughan's vote he was about to order a chair elsewhere. "With all my heart," said Vaughan; "I don't care what they make him so they don't make him a throne." In the course of the election an incident occurred which throws light both on military discipline and Parliamentary practice. A party of soldiers in charge of a sergeant and corporal were marching through the streets to a military duty, when some men in rear of the company infected by the spirit of partisanship joined in shouting "Vandeput for ever!" For not reporting this digression from military reticence, the sergeant and corporal were confined to the Savoy prison and subsequently reduced to the ranks by order of the commanding officer. Later, during the debate on the Mutiny Bill, Colonel George Townshend referred to the incident as illustrative of the dangerous and oppressive powers resident in a commanding officer, and, lest his story should be doubted, brought with him and tendered as witnesses the two victims of the disciplinary measure for examination by the House.

When the poll was declared it was found that Lord Trentham had secured a majority of 200. Nor was the result affected by a scrutiny which was demanded and carried out, backed by the support of Leicester House. It was the first open blow struck by the Prince of Wales, and it had been easily countered. But the kissing of hands, the assignment of offices, the levées and banquets, the fashioning of political schemes, and all the backstairs preparations for a change in the occupancy of the throne continued actively to be carried on at the Prince's residences—Carlton House and Leicester House.

* J. Grego, *A History of Parliamentary Elections*, p. 123.

CHAPTER V

THE Royal House had seldom been more divided against itself than at this time (1749). Ever since that memorable night at Hampton Court when Frederick, Prince of Wales, obeying a reckless impulse, had packed the Princess into her chariot and, together with the midwife and valet, had smuggled her off to St. James's Palace in order that the birth of his eldest child might take place there,* rather than under the roof where his parents were living, the feud had steadily grown. The Queen had followed hard on the wheels of her escaping son and daughter-in-law's conveyance, and arrived at St. James's in the twilight hours of the morning to receive the news that a daughter had already been ushered into the world under circumstances little befitting so august an event. Thenceforward she had shown her determination neither to forgive nor forget the heinousness of her son's offence.

There had followed the expulsion of the Prince and his family from the Palace, and the migration to Leicester House. The frontage of St. James's Palace facing Cleveland Square, built for Prince Frederick on his marriage, and the rooms to which he had brought his Princess Augusta of Saxe-Gotha, and where Miss Vane, the maid of honour, had borne him a son, were abandoned. The Palace was left to the tenancy of George II and Queen Caroline, with place for the King's mistress, Lady Suffolk, the Duke of Cumberland, and the Royal Princesses.

Thereafter, save for ceremonial visits, no communication passed between the two camps. When state occasion brought the heir to the throne into the presence of his parents, "the King would appear neither to see or know that the Prince

* Lord Hervey, *Memoirs of George II*, III, p. 171; Yorke, *Life of Lord Chancellor Hardwicke*, I, p. 169.

43

was in the room," while the Queen "never gave him one single word in public or private." Known in the family by the nick-name of "the Griff," the Prince was equally hated and con-temned by his parents and his sisters.

Not a day passed, if we may believe Lord Hervey, but some member of that volcanic circle at St. James's Palace openly expressed the wish that "the Griff" was dead. But Lord Hervey's account must be accepted with caution. He describes a degree of detestation such as one could hardly look for in a Methodist family one of whose members had developed into a Cæsar Borgia. That Frederick was vain and unstable, that he could be odious to his mother, that in the last years of his life his principal pastime lay in thwarting his father, that his main employment was "intrigue either among men or among women " *—these and failings such as these do not explain the peculiar virulence which Lord Hervey would have us believe poisoned the relations of Frederick with his family. Lady Bristol described him when he first came to England in 1729 as hand-some, lively, and full of duty to the King and Queen. In the course of his career he numbered among his adherents, and among those who regarded him with friendly feelings, Pitt, Lyttelton, Nugent, Lord Egmont, Lord Granville and Lord Bolingbroke, and neither in the voluminous corre-spondence of the Duke of Newcastle, to whom the Prince was consistently opposed, nor in the Chatham, Bedford, or Gren-ville letters, is there to be found any support for the traditional estimate of this despised and much derided Prince of Wales. The extreme hatred of him was in fact confined to the royal palaces; elsewhere—without enjoying the confidence of his contemporaries or engaging more of their esteem than was extorted by right of his rank—he figured as a weak and rather fatuous individual, seldom to be trusted, and perpetually in-triguing, ignorant of the world, a stranger to the significance of events and the graver responsibilities of his position, but in his morals and the unromantic nature of his amours no more deserving of censure than his father or his grandfather before him.

The familiar stories of his resorting to the theatre on the

* *Life of Lord Shelburne,* I, p. 60.

night when the news of Fontenoy reached London, and of his pelting with sugar plums a model of Carlisle citadel with which he had caused his cook to enrich the evening's bill of fare, at the moment the royal troops were endeavouring to wrest that town from the rebels, are typical of the levity which underlay his character. In the same vein may be recalled his comment when Pitt was suggested as Secretary at War, to the effect that "Miss Chudleigh, one of the maids, was fitter for the appointment," and his thereupon dictating a letter to Lord Harrington desiring him to draw a warrant for her and causing the fourteen guests taking part in the supper to sign the letter. But neither the lightness of his mind nor the frivolity of his temperament explains the odium in which he was held by his family; rather has the reason to be sought, if we pass over a mysterious reference by Lord Hardwicke * to some unnamed cause, in his attitude of active opposition and intrigue, and in his constant endeavour to enlist the applause of the people and find favour in the public eye at the expense of his father.

In 1747 he is said to have borrowed £200,000 in order to fight the Court party on the hustings. By promises of future offices and rewards he was tireless in his endeavours to build up his own party in the state. When his father patronised Handel he at once took up the cause of Italian opera at the theatre in Lincoln's Inn Fields. While his father lived in seclusion and remained indifferent to publicity, he lost no opportunity of bringing himself to popular notice. He patronised sport, he took part in the pastimes of the people, he attended bull baitings at Hockley in the Hole, he gave prizes for rowing, he was to be seen at races and fairs. He made a point of supporting home manufactures and giving the go by to the fashions of France. At a fire which broke out in the Temple he was conspicuous in his efforts to extinguish the flames, and rumours of the cries of "Crown him!" "Crown him!" with which his endeavours were said to have been greeted did not fail to penetrate into the sombre home circle of St. James's Palace.

His time was spent at Clifden, or at his residence at Kew,

* Yorke, *Life of Lord Chancellor Hardwicke*, I, p. 179.

or Leicester House, between which places he was perpetually on the move. In 1733 he acquired Carlton House, which had been built by Henry Boyle, Baron Carleton, on land leased to him by Queen Anne, and described as " parcel of the Royal Garden near St. James's Palace and all that the woodwork or wilderness adjoining the said garden." The house, which stood on the site now occupied by the Duke of York's Column, was pompous in design and well adapted to the ceremonial occasions for which the Prince mostly employed it; and here in pointed proximity to the Palace he held his levées and entertained London Society with banquets and balls in vivid contrast to the sedate card parties of St. James's. Bubb Dodington, who gives the diary of a day in 1750, records the essentially informal activities of Their Royal Highnesses. In the morning the Prince and Princess, accompanied by Lady Middlesex, Lord Bathurst, and Mr. Breton, visit Spitalfields to see the silk manufactory; in the afternoon they proceed in private coaches to Norwood Forest to see a settlement of gypsies; then to Bettesworth, the conjuror, in hackney coaches. Bettesworth being away they set out in search of the Dutch dwarf, concluding " the particularities " * of the day by supping with Mrs. Cannon, the Princess's midwife.

In contrast with his father's callousness to art, the Prince showed an appreciation of pictures, he collected miniatures, he purchased drawings, he offered £12,000 for Sir Luke Schaub's works of art,† and in his admiration for Andrea del Sarto he was able to boast a taste to which his father was totally insensible. Nor did he find any difficulty in outdoing the King's charitable donations. In the same way, in writing verses not destitute of a certain elegance, he had no rivalry to fear from George II.‡ Thus in every field and at every step he widened the breach between himself and the occupant of the throne.

To Cumberland this conduct of the Prince was an offence against the guiding principle of his career, loyalty to the Throne; but he remained aloof, and there is no record of his protesting

* *Dodington Diary*, p. 80.
† Walpole, *Letters*, IV, p. 124.
‡ See Walpole, *Memoirs*, I, Appendix.

against or even criticising the measures adopted by his brother.
The stability of his character and his own adherence to that
principle were later to be put to a far higher test; but for
the time being he conformed to what he conceived as his duty
by refraining from interference or expostulation.

Beyond fostering a few intrigues and fanning a number of
ambitions, the opposition of the Prince had a very limited
significance among current political influences. It was a gamble
in futures. And those who had nothing to hope for from
the existing administration could trim their lamps in preparation for the expected change. When the change finally came
it was only to illustrate once more the precarious character of
such gambling. In the meanwhile to Newcastle, who was
alive to every symptom indicating the presence of conditions
in the Constitution adverse to his tenure of power, the only
danger of substance was the Cumberland clique. The efforts
of Frederick could be safely disregarded, they were rather in
the nature of a stimulus to the Court party, and flitted across
the Duke's personal horizon as mildly as summer lightning.

For the King it was another matter, and in the rising popularity of his detested son he saw a hostile factor which he
lacked the power and much of the inclination to combat. He
himself was indifferent to public applause. On one occasion,
when the Quakers' Bill was before Parliament and his departure
for Hanover delayed, he indulged in one of those explosive
outbursts to which he was so liable, and exclaimed: " I am sick
to death of all this foolish stuff, and wish with all my heart
that the devil may take all your Bishops, and the devil take
your Ministers, and the devil take the Parliament, and the
devil take the whole island, provided I can get out of it and
go to Hanover." * That summarised his personal as distinct
from his political attitude to this country. Residence in England was repugnant to him, the English remained a riddle to
his understanding, their Constitution hampered his ideas of
government, their recreations and their politics were alike distasteful to him. Had he not said that the English were king-
killers and republicans, and that, whereas in Hanover he could
reward people for doing their duty and serving him well, here

* Hervey, *Memoirs*, II, p. 274.

he was obliged to enrich people for being rascals and buy them not to cut his throat? Had he not declaimed against the dullness of social diversions in England, against the inability of the men to talk of anything but their dull politics and the women of anything but their ugly clothes? Had he not derided their fox-hunting and their theatres, and shown his indifference to their literature and their art?

Politics, he said, was no trade for a gentleman. He had seen too much of its inner working. Cold, formal, and methodical when his temper was not aroused, he bestowed his favours and administered his censures without magnanimity. His native shrewdness unadorned by grace or culture was devoted to the bare fulfilment of the obligations incurred by his position. But his relation to constitutional government was correct, his intervention in Ministerial affairs was never pressed beyond the strict limits which practice was setting to the prerogative. He recognised that his power was closely bounded. He knew how far insistence could be carried, and when he parted with Walpole and again with Carteret, when he accepted Chesterfield as Lord Lieutenant of Ireland and admitted Pitt to his counsels, he acknowledged that the prejudices of the King could no longer prevail. He was, however, absolute where his authority could legitimately be asserted. In the exercise or refusal of the prerogative of mercy, in the cut of a uniform, in the bestowal of patronage or the determination of a point of etiquette, he brooked no influence or interference. Newcastle unquestionably lived in perpetual fear of him, and was at all seasons tapping the glass to see whether the needle was inclined to fair weather or storm in the royal closet. None the less it was during Newcastle's long administration as a Minister that the relations between Crown and Government came in practice to be almost identical with those which prevailed in the nineteenth century. It was under Newcastle that the Whig oligarchy gradually encroached on the power of the Crown, and by absorbing that power into the hands of the Cabinet increased the authority of Parliament over the policy of the country. Power had passed away from the Council, which was independent of Parliament, to a committee of Ministers and Officers of State responsible to Parliament, whose authority ultimately rested on the support of the House of Commons. There was still to be evolved in its final form the corporate responsibility of the Cabinet as a whole; but here again under George II this element of modern constitutional government rapidly advanced, and by the end of his reign the King's power over his Ministers had in practice been drastically curtailed. It was perhaps well for such a process that Hanover presented a congenial and alternative field for the exercise of the King's German ideas of statecraft. Conflicts were eased and concessions made more palateable for the King in England by the knowledge that elsewhere, in his favourite domain, he could exercise the powers of an absolute monarch.

Horace Walpole says that George II's general disposition was merciful; but there is little evidence of this to be found in those State papers which contain his decisions on capital sentences and the findings of courts-martial, while on the contrary we have two notorious instances in which every opportunity was given to him for the exercise of mercy and where in the one case for political and the other for personal motives he refused to interfere. In the case of Admiral Byng it may be said that the national will was on his side; but in the case of Paul Wells, who was hung for altering the date on a bond for nine pounds in order that his liability might be postponed for some months, the King in refusing mercy acted contrary to the direct advice of the judge, merely it was said because that functionary happened to be the chief judicial supporter of the Prince of Wales.*

Indeed it would be difficult to discover where this reputed gentleness of disposition found expression in his character. Certainly not towards those who had played the part of mistress in his domestic circle. " J'étais extrèmement surpris," he wrote to the Queen, who had informed him of Lady Suffolk's marriage, " de la disposition que vous m'avez mandé que ma vieille maîtresse a fait de son corps en mariage à ce vieux goutteux George Berkeley, et je m'en réjouis fort. Je ne voudrois pas faire de tels présens à mes amis; et quand mes ennemis me volent plût à Dieu que ce soit toujours de cette

* Hervey, *Memoirs*, II, p. 183.

4

façon." *   But at the time of which we are writing the office
of Lady Suffolk had for many years been filled by Madame
Walmoden, then Lady Yarmouth.

Madame Walmoden (1711–1765) in 1735 had been " a
young married woman of the first fashion in Hanover."   But
the first fashion not being without its price, George is said
by Lord Hervey to have secured her complaisance for the sum
of 1,000 ducats.   Thenceforward it is only necessary to turn
to Lord Hervey's quotations from the King's letters to the
Queen to obtain a description of Madame Walmoden's personal appearance and attributes.   It was the custom of the
King to write daily bulletins to the Queen from Hanover,
and inform her " of the growth of his passion and the progress
of his applications," and to give so close a description of the
object of his pursuit that it was said that any painter could
have delineated her from the details supplied in the King's
letters.   In the early stages of his courtship he described her
to the Queen as far from being a regular beauty, but with a
very agreeable countenance and rather genteelly than exactly
made : " Elle n'avait pas un esprit éclatant, mais enjoué et
amusant ; mais à l'égard du cœur elle est sûrement la meilleure
créature du monde."   The Queen welcomed rather than deprecated the advent of this new recipient of the King's favour,
and at her invitation † Madame Walmoden accompanied
George II on his return to England.   Here her influence in
political life was considerable and may easily be understated.
Without the ambition, the mental capacity, or the art of
Madame de Pompadour, and without her inclination to direct
the policy of the King or interfere in the management of
foreign affairs, it may safely be said that Madame Walmoden
exercised a steady and on the whole beneficial pressure on the
course of events in England.

When in 1755 Pitt determined to approach her and submit
to her a plan for his projected Administration and so obtain

* Hervey, *Memoirs,* II, p. 183.

† " If you can," said Lord Hervey to the Queen, " but once get this
favourite to St. James's, she will in three months be everything Lady
Suffolk was but deaf . . . and your only option is whether you will
fear her at a distance or despise her near."   Hervey, *Memoirs,* II,
p. 356.

the ear of the King, George II declared to Lord Hardwicke:
" Mr. Pitt shall not go to that channel any more; she does not
meddle and shall not meddle." * This was a boast that the
King would have found it difficult to verify. She had meddled
pretty consistently for a number of years. It was her mission
to reduce acerbities, to effect compromises, to temporise, and
to secure the King from hasty and impetuous decisions. Her
meddling was in fact more real than apparent. The King
indeed deprecated the appeals to Lady Yarmouth. To Newcastle, who had laid before her the critical circumstances of
the political situation in 1759, he said, "I know you have
been tormenting my Lady Yarmouth about it. Why do you
plague her? What has she to do with these things? The
only comfortable two hours I have in the whole day are those
I pass there, and you are always teasing her with these things." †
In the same mood of irritated despondency he had said, "I
wish I could take a bark now and go to Hanover." ‡

But every Minister in turn saw the necessity of finding
favour in her eyes: every Minister when it came to negotiations with the King recognised her tact and the benefit of her
influence. Newcastle, manoeuvring for position (1749–50)
against the Duke of Bedford, depended wholly on securing her
as his ally. Henry Pelham in 1752, lamenting to Newcastle
that the disposition of Lady Yarmouth for the moment seemed
less favourable, declared what importance he attached to her
goodwill. "There," he wrote in reference to her support,
" was the best ground we had to stand upon: if that shakes I
doubt we have no resource. . . . I cannot but earnestly recom-
mend to you to make up, as soon and as well as you can. . . .
The influence in that quarter grows, and will necessarily and
naturally grow every year." § When Fox desired a peerage
he wrote in almost abject terms to Lady Yarmouth. ‖ In 1754
and again in 1756 the same statesman turns to her as the

* Add. MS. 35357, f. 66, Lord Hardwicke to Col. Yorke; printed
Yorke, *Life of Lord Hardwicke,* II, p. 332.
† Yorke, *Life of Lord Hardwicke,* III, p. 61.
‡ *Ibid.,* III, p. 61.
§ Pelham to Newcastle, Oct. 13, 1732; printed Coxe's *Pelham
Administration,* Appendix II, p. 463.
‖ Lord Rosebery, *Chatham,* p. 296.

surest avenue of approach to the King: it is to her that his resignation is submitted, it is from her that he gets direct advice as to what he should do.* When in 1758 there is a question of obtaining a Garter for Lord Temple, it is Lady Yarmouth who is appealed to.† Or if it is the Princess of Wales who is to be persuaded to influence Pitt in 1758 to send troops to Germany, it is Lady Yarmouth who is selected by the King to act as his emissary.‡ Indeed, whether it was a garter, a bishopric, a pension, an office under the Government or a change in the Administration, the first move in the game was to enlist the support of Lady Yarmouth. The trust not to be put in princes could safely be reposed on the Prince's mistress. None ever had cause to doubt her courage, her integrity, or the sincerity of her motives. She raised no quarrels, she made no enemies, rather was she always on the side of peace, and later will be seen the laudable role she played in assuaging the wrath of the King against Cumberland at the time of the Convention of Kloster Seven. She outlived George II by five years, having retained his affection till the day of his death in 1760.

The member of the Royal Family with whom Cumberland was chiefly concerned next to the King was his sister Princess Amelia. Her devotion to her brother was deep and unbroken, her anxiety for his safety on his campaigns, her sympathy with him in defeat,§ her close co-operation with him in his political activities, all denote the warmth of her affection. In her youth she had been the prettiest of the family, but, with the exception of her brother Frederick, was gifted, according to Lord Hervey, with much the least sense. The Dukes of Newcastle and Grafton had both paid their court to her in former days, ‖

* Lord Rosebery, *Chatham*, p. 461.
† *Chatham Correspondence*, I, p. 361.
‡ *Ibid.*, I, p. 295.
§ e.g. H.R.H. Princess Amelia to the Lord Chancellor: "I must wish you joy from the bottom of my heart that Mr. Yorck hath escaped. You flatter me greatly about my brother's behaviour, but you will allow me to say that I am very miserable from knowing what he feels in having lost so many brave men" (written after the news of Fontenoy).
‖ *William, Duke of Cumberland*, p. 81.

but at the time under review " she had determined to be old
and ugly and out of danger." With the " strength of a
Brunswick lion " she now devoted herself to late hours and
card parties. She was a great talker, and her vivacity and
brusque sayings kept the society in which she moved in a constant flutter of uneasy expectation. Her opinions were expressed with untrammelled freedom, and neither princes nor
foreign diplomatists were immune from the candour of her
views. On the death of Lord Orford, Horace Walpole's elder
brother, she was appointed Ranger of Richmond Park. Here
she was all for privacy and privilege. She refused keys
amongst others to the Lord Chancellor, she put up gates and
denied the inhabitants of the neighbourhood that access to the
Park which they claimed as their established right. Petitions
were presented. An agitation was conducted in the public
press. Meetings were held and protests recorded, all to no
purpose—the Brunswick lion was not to be dismayed. Finally
recourse was had to the law courts, and after protracted
litigation Princess Amelia emerged victorious from the contest.

She had managed to shake off many of the conventions
among which she had been brought up, and had profited by
the freedom she had acquired in her early years hunting in
Windsor Forest, flirting with the Duke of Grafton, or fishing
with Sir Robert Walpole in Richmond Park. At a party at
Bedford House she is seen " supping pell mell with men as it
were in a booth " *—a spectacle which causes Walpole to
speculate as to what would have been the feelings of George II
could he have risen from the grave and been a witness to such
democratic conduct. At Hampton Court she shocks church-
goers by appearing in chapel in her riding clothes with a dog
under her arm.† At the end of a party at Northumberland
House " she thanks my Lady Northumberland like a parson's
wife for all her civilities,"‡ and at one of her own entertainments she showed that her temper could be as explosive as the
King's, and that in the matter of politics she was capable of

* Walpole, *Letters*, V, p. 63.
† *Ibid.*, III, p. 101.
‡ *Ibid.*, V, p. 18.

as fierce partisanship. " None of your wit! " she cried out
in the most outrageous passion, and colouring like scarlet, to
Horace Walpole, who had cynically observed that all politicians
were Whigs when it came to a question of place. " I don't
understand joking on these subjects: what do you think your
father would have said if he had heard you say so? He
would have murdered you, and you would have deserved it." *
But Walpole, though often impatient and nearly always
critical, had an amiable weakness for the Princess; he was a
constant guest at Gunnersbury and Cavendish Square, received
visits from her at Strawberry Hill, and when they met in the
" world " was an habitual player at her table of loo or pharaoh.
One of Walpole's liveliest letters relates to a five days' visit
to Stowe Park—a prospect from which he anticipated no
pleasure.

> A Princess [Emily] at the head of a very small set for
> five days together did not promise well. However she was
> very good-humoured and easy, and dispensed with a large
> quantity of etiquette. . . . We laughed a great deal and
> had not a cloud the whole time.

He goes on to give so complete a picture of the insipidity of
country-house life that the passage may well be quoted:

> We breakfasted at half an hour after nine; but the
> Princess did not appear till it was finished; then we walked
> in the garden, or drove about it in cabriolets, till it was time
> to dress; dined at three which lasted a vast while as the
> Princess eats and talks a great deal; then again into the
> garden till past seven when we came in, drank tea and
> coffee, and played at pharaoh till ten, when the Princess
> retired and we went to supper and before twelve to bed. . . .
> It was a little broken by fishing, and going round the park
> one of the mornings. . . . On Wednesday night a small
> Vauxhall was acted for us at the grotto in the Elysian fields,
> which was illuminated with lamps, as were the thickets and
> two little barks on the lake. . . . It made me laugh as we
> were descending the great flight of steps from the house
> to go and sup in the grotto on the banks of the Helicon;
> we were so cloaked up, for the evening was very cold, and

* Walpole, *Letters*, V, p. 281.

so many of us were limping and hobbling, that Charon would have easily believed we were going to ferry over in earnest.

From the mind of Princess Amelia at any rate nothing could have been further than any thought of Charon and his " hoy "; her vehement personality was still to play a dominant part in London Society for more than a generation, while her exuberant vitality and her indomitable health seemed to defy the frailty of human life. With her judicious understanding of political events, which even Newcastle was fain to acknowledge,* and with the influence she exercised in the narrow social world from which the political life of the day was drawn, she was a factor not to be ignored in the ministerial difficulties that now confronted Newcastle. She was at this time inseparable from Cumberland; together they shared the shelter offered by their father's roof at St. James's, and together they divided the duties of an eclectic hospitality at Windsor Lodge. It was rarely that they paid a country-house visit save in company. When in London it seems to have been an established principle that they should be invited to the same parties, and whether it were at Lord Holdernesse's, or at Norfolk or Northumberland House, or at the Duke of Richmond's, a feature of every entertainment was separate card parties for the Royal pair, one presided over by the Duke, the other held in subjection by the Princess.

* *Life of Lord Hardwicke*, III, p. 401.

CHAPTER VI

CUMBERLAND had watched the passage of the Mutiny Bill (1749) through Parliament with anxiety and impatience. He would have liked to apply the arbitrary methods customary in the field, for he regarded, not without reason, the opposition to the Bill as chiefly factious. It was his first contact with Parliamentary methods. His spirit, never submissive, chafed at the wrangling and delay which were entailed. Six weeks were intermittently occupied with discussions, and it was not till April 10, 1749, that he was able to write to his friend Joseph Yorke at the Hague to announce the end of the struggle.

> I assure you [he wrote] the country was very necessary to me after the bad air and humour I contracted in London, as for want of better employment, the weak and virulent minority had diverted themselves and teared it with dividing upon every clause of the Mutiny Bill for near six weeks together; but which, thank God, we carried through at last without any material alterations.*

The Mutiny Bill was the occasion for attacks from many quarters. Horace Walpole in his letters changes with the times, and joins the clamour which was being continually reinforced by the Jacobites and focussed against the Duke by the Leicester House Party. *The Remembrancer,* a newspaper regarded as the *Craftsman* of the age, was directing all its forces of vituperation against the Captain General. In popular esteem he was losing ground, and stories of his severity were the current gossip of the day.

> His savage temper [Walpole writes] increases every day. George Boscawen is in a scrape with him by a court-martial, of which he was one; it was appointed on a young poor soldier, who to see his friends had counterfeited a furlough

* Cumberland Papers, H.R.H. to Yorke, April 10, 1749.

56

of leave only for a day. They ordered him two hundred lashes; but Nolkejumskoi, who loves blood like a leech, insisted it was not enough—has made them sit three times, though everyone adheres to the first sentence, and swears they shall sit these six months till they increase the punishment." *

With the public, Cumberland's unpopularity had become so marked that Mrs. Pitt, who had succeeded to the beautiful Lady Rochford's place in his affections, was mobbed in the Park " only because this bashaw is in love with her " and rescued with difficulty.† The love affairs of what Walpole calls " the Royals " were always notorious; they became public property with the rapidity of bad news; and the mob from the time of George I regarded themselves as entitled to express their approval or disapproval in the frankest manner.‡

Cumberland had experienced the full fickleness of the crowd. A popular idol in 1745, he had by 1749 passed into being a byword for harshness and arbitrary discipline. The nation which acclaimed him after his campaign in Flanders regarded him now with mistrust and sullen dislike. That the penalty of death appeared in the Mutiny Bill as often as the curses in the Commination on Ash Wednesday was attributed largely to Cumberland's influence. Sedulously did the Jacobites and Leicester House disseminate the view that the King's favourite son was becoming a menace to the State, and gathering into his hands an authority and power that were likely to prove a danger to liberty. The nation, with its habitual jealousy of military ascendancy, was determined to run no risks, and a large section of the public lost no occasion for demonstrating its hostility to the Duke. Cumberland bore this evidence of hatred mildly and said, with more humility than the occasion warranted, that " he would always with gratitude remember the behaviour of the English who received him with transports after the battle of Laffelt instead of impeaching him." George II viewed the decline in his son's popularity with deep distress, and confided to Henry Fox the bewilderment aroused in him

---

* Walpole to Montagu, July 20, 1749, *Letters,* II, 398.
† *Ibid.*
‡ See *William Augustus Duke of Cumberland,* p. 64.

by the alteration. "The English nation is so changeable," he said; "I don't know why they dislike him. It is brought about by the Scotch, the Jacobites, and the English that don't love discipline: and by all this not being enough discouraged by the Ministry." Newcastle might be counted on to see that no such discouragement was forthcoming from the Ministry. The Captain General's unpopularity was a source of solid if secret satisfaction to the Secretary of State. Nothing, however, could shake Cumberland from the course he had set for himself. He was not in advance of the age in which he lived. He had no better inspiration to guide him than that which came from the light of his own times. Slave to the prevailing traditions, and master only of the prevailing methods, he had put his hand to the task of creating a disciplined and efficient army, and from this task pursued along accepted lines no malice or hatred could cause him to deflect for an instant. His massive common sense, his imperative devotion to duty were proof against any temptation to seek a precarious popularity.

Walpole in his letters makes Cumberland the subject of many of his most malicious criticisms—and in doing so portrays a personality devoid of grace or charm, ugly in its weaknesses and ungainly in its virtues. Even when crediting the Duke with "the most heroic bravery" he qualifies it by adding that he had all the severity that levels valour to cowardice, and that while he seemed to love war for itself he was incapable of feeling the passion that it gratifies—phrases which appear more pointed than either just or explicit. He allows that the Duke was gifted with an understanding "strong, judicious, and penetrating," but cannot get over his surprise that Cumberland should have been the author of a *bon mot* on his return from Flanders. It was at the time when Whitefield, newly arrived from his American tour, was at the zenith of his oratorical powers, and leading that astonishing revival which was sweeping over a world notoriously deficient in religious belief. A Colonel Gumley, himself a Methodist, came to report to the Duke that while he was on duty a tree had been set on fire in Hyde Park near the Powder Magazine. The Duke replied, he hoped "it was not by the new light." "This nonsensical new light," adds Walpole, " is extremely in fashion, and I shall not be surprised if we see a revival of all the folly and cant of the last age." With so little discernment could an enlightened observer of the times view one of the greatest religious movements that had appeared in this or any other country. " Methodism," he adds in a later letter, " is more fashionable than anything but brag; the women play devilish deep at both "; and again, " This act increases as fast as almost ever any religious nonsense did. . . . The Methodists love your big sinners as proper subjects to work on, and indeed they have a plentiful harvest. I think what you call flagrancy was never more in fashion."

Cumberland, on the other hand, was quite alive to the significance of the movement, and did much to countenance and facilitate its progress in the ranks of the army. Many years later, in 1771, Wesley, after visiting the triangular tower built by " that active and useful man the Duke of Cumberland " in Windsor Forest, wrote in his journal: " I was agreeably surprised to find many of the books not only religious but admirably well chosen. Perhaps the great man spent many hours here, with only Him that seeth in secret: and who can say how deep that change went, which was so discernible in the latter part of his life "—a reflection, we may be confident, which carried with it a recollection of the encouragement given by the Captain General to the followers of Wesley in the Army.

Methodism appears to have first obtained a foothold among soldiers in 1738. An entry in Wesley's journal for that year shows that he was at that time meeting in Westminster a society which had been formed among the troops quartered in London.* Later in Flanders a small and zealous band of Wesley's followers is to be found taking part in the campaign of Dettingen. Thenceforward not the least ardent and emotional disciples of the new movement were found in the forces of the Crown. Letters preserved by Wesley attest the fervour with which the adherents of Methodism imparted their faith to their brethren in the ranks and with what exaltation they manifested it in the hour of danger. Nor was the movement confined to the

* *The Journal of John Wesley*, Standard Edition (1909), II, p. 93.

"common soldier." Many officers attended the meetings and celebrations of the faith. It had in fact broken through some of the barriers of the fashionable world. A section of " the quality," however, viewed with dismay the encroachments of the new movement. These, secure in the stabilised complacency which was so common in the eighteenth century among those who exercised power or enjoyed the distinction of rank and wealth, were determined to suffer no enemy within their gates. Characteristic of this view, and indeed characteristic of a faith common to a large part of the world of " good breeding," are the words used by the Duchess of Buckingham in a letter to Lady Huntingdon, who had adopted Whitefield as her chaplain and was herself one of the leaders of the Calvinistic section of the Methodists.

Their doctrines [wrote the Duchess after hearing White-field preach] are most repulsive and strongly tinctured with impertinence and disrespect towards their superiors, in perpetually endeavouring to level all ranks and do away with all distinctions. It is monstrous to be told you have a heart as sinful as the common wretches that crawl the earth. This is highly offensive and insulting, and I cannot but wonder that your ladyship should relish any sentiments so much at variance with high rank and good breeding.*

The social and moral conditions were favourable for the infusion of a new faith. The England of 1750 was in fact well prepared for the sudden illumination spread by Wesley, Whitefield, and the host of Methodist preachers who followed in their wake. More than at other times was there an atrophy of spiritual sensibilities. Arid theological controversies were reaching a moment of exhaustion. The rapid growth in physical science had all the appearance of a menace to orthodox beliefs. Deism had failed to effect any transformation in popular faith. At the same time there were noticeable among the well-to-do a callousness to suffering and a cynical indifference to the conditions under which the greater portion of the populace were living. In legislation there was an almost

* Sarah Tytler, *The Countess of Huntingdon and Her Circle* (1907), p. 47.

complete absence of effort in the direction of social reform.* The severity of the criminal code, and the harshness of the penalties by which the governing classes sought to preserve law and order and protect their lives and property, tended to stifle pity and deaden feelings of humanity. The populace were regaled and brutalised by the spectacle of constant executions,† of floggings through the streets, and of the pillory with its accompanying terrors of branding with hot irons, slitting of nostrils, and cutting off of ears.

The state of the prisons was alone sufficient to stamp the age as one aloof from human misery. It is indeed with a sense of deserved retribution that one reads of the infection of fever which, carried by the prisoners from the gaols to the Court House of the Old Bailey in May 1750, proved fatal to Sir Samuel Pennant, the Lord Mayor, Sir Daniel Lambert, alderman, Baron Clark of the Exchequer, Judge Abney of the Court of Common Pleas, Mr. Cox, under sheriff, most of the Middlesex jury, and several of the spectators. Then and then only did the authorities take action. Then and then only were steps taken to ventilate and cleanse these centres of disease, and endeavours made to preserve the health of the prisoners.‡—Horace Walpole, alone perhaps among writers of the day, raises any sort of protest when he exclaims: Could the monthly shambles at Tyburn (that scene that shocks humanity and reproaches our Police!) be exchanged for severe labour, it would reflect honour on a Legislature.§   But if his

---

* Two exceptions should be made to this statement: (*a*) "A Bill for preventing Robberies and Regulating Places of Public Entertainment and punishing people keeping disorderly houses" passed in 1752, in the belief that dancing, gaming, and music were the source of much of the crime of the day, and that by requiring places providing dancing and music or entertainment of a like kind to be licensed by the justices control would be obtained over one of the principal incentives to vice; (*b*) The Gin Act (1751), which by providing for more drastic control over licenses and increasing the penalties for unlicensed dealing sensibly diminished the amount of drunkenness in the country.

† "It is shocking to think what shambles this country is grown! Seventeen were executed this morning." Walpole to Mann, March 23, 1752 (*Letters*, III, p. 88).

‡ John Northouck, *A New History of London* (1773), p. 369.

§ Walpole, *Memoirs of George II*, I, p. 256.

voice is solitary, it is drowned by the abominable cry of George Selwyn, whose *bons mots* are seldom quoted without injury to his reputation as a wit, clamouring for more executions and hurrying from place to place to see men done to death by the law. It may cause wonder that judges should have continued to send men to the scaffold without protest against such barbarous laws. But the conservatism of the Bench is notorious. The business of judges is to administer, not to reform the law, and to that view they have with no little consistency adhered.

The refinements of art, the privileges of education, the luxury of leisure and wealth, were in few hands. The division between classes, always dangerously well defined, was daily becoming more accentuated as industry developed, and as the conditions deteriorated under which the masses, artificially crowded in manufacturing centres, carried on their existence. " Accordez-vous, canaille! " the exclamation of a French officer addressed to the occupants of the pit during the representation of a contentious drama in Paris, very fairly summed up the spirit reigning among the well-to-do in England.

All these things cried out for alleviation. The moral revolt which they engendered, though neither consciously recognised nor outwardly expressed, was giving rise to an inward craving for contrast, for enlightenment, for some guidance which would compensate. And through the exhortations of the Methodists a channel of escape was found from the galling environment which beset the ignorant and humble.

Probably no single influence did so much as the spiritual revival of the eighteenth century to mitigate and assuage those forces in England which, finally running riot in France, culminated in the excesses of the Revolution. By exalting the religious attitude of mind above all others, by embellishing the consolations of piety and faith, and by deflecting the emotions of multitudes of men and women from the inequalities of the social structure, it presented an alternative to worldly evils which otherwise seemed remediable by force alone. That it effected a complete change in the outlook of great masses of the people cannot be contested. It influenced every class of the community. With equal beneficence it penetrated the chosen citadels of the fashionable world, spread through the camp and to the cottage, stood beside the condemned on the scaffold, and brought light into the darkness and misery of the gaols. The field-preacher with his congregations that swarmed in the outskirts of the towns, or gathered at the pit-head, or abandoned at his calling the pastimes of a racecourse, was the substitute for the political agitator and social reformer. And it was probably well for the safety of the existing order in the constitution that the popular oratory of the day was directed to spiritual ends rather than to political change and reform. Moreover it was a time when credulity was easily played on, and the emotions of the mob readily inflamed. Belief in miracles and in supernatural interference, in witchcraft and the magic arts, was widely prevalent. Astrology had many votaries. Certain superstitions of which recent years have seen a revival exercised an unusual sway.

It was the golden age for mountebanks, quacks, necromancers, and wizards. When Mr. Cadwallader played the part of magician in *Peregrine Pickle* he was arrayed, it will be remembered, for his brief exposition of the art, in black gown and fur cap, and was seated before a table scattered with divers books and mathematical instruments, and a long white wand lying across the whole, with "on each shoulder a prodigious black cat which had been tutored for the purpose." In such disguise he was consulted by persons of every age and rank :

In cases of law, physic, and trade over and above the ordinary subjects of marriage and fornication : his advice and assistance were solicited by sharpers who desired to possess an infallible method of cheating, unperceived ; by fortune hunters who wanted to make prize of widows and heiresses ; by debauchees who were disposed to lie with other men's wives ; by coxcombs who longed for the death of their fathers ; by wenches with child who wished themselves rid of their burthens ; by merchants who had insured above value and thirsted after the news of a wreck ; by underwriters who prayed for the gift of prescience that they might venture money upon such ships only as should perform the voyage in safety : by Jews who wanted to foresee the fluctuations of stock ; by usurers who advance money upon undecided causes ; by clients who were dubious

of the honesty of their counsel: in short all matters of uncertain issue were appealed to this tribunal; and in point of
calculation, De Moivre was utterly neglected.*

Cadwallader's clientele was illustrative of the vein of super-
stition that ran through the beliefs of the hour.

Cumberland himself seems to have been no exception to the
prevailing spirit of credulity.   In 1749 he is found responding
with many others to an advertisement which promised that a
man would

> This evening at the Haymarket Theatre play on a common
> walking cane the music of every instrument now used, to
> surprising perfection: that he would on the stage get into a
> tavern quart bottle without equivocation, and while there
> sing several songs and suffer any spectator to handle the
> bottle: and that in a private room he would produce the
> representation of any person dead with which the person
> requesting it should converse some minutes as if alive.

The prospect of such entertainment had drawn a great crowd,
and on the failure of the performer to appear and fulfil his
advertised programme, there was an outbreak of rioting.   Mob
action seldom failed to be drastic.   The inside of the theatre
was demolished, and the contents carried into the street and
there devoted to the purposes of a bonfire.   Many of the
audience emerged from the mêlée poorer for their experience.
Cumberland, amongst others, had his sword stolen—which
gave rise to the following advertisement which subsequently
appeared in the paper called *Old England*:

> Found entangled in the slit of a lady's smock petticoat,
> a gilt handled sword of martial length and temper, not
> much the worse for wearing, with the Spey curiously en-
> graved on one side, and the Scheldt on the other; supposed
> to be taken from the fat sides of a certain great general
> in his retreat from the Battle of Bottle Noddles in the
> Haymarket.   Whoever has lost it may enquire for it at
> the sign of the Bird and Singing Hare in Potter's Row.†

The whole affair known as the Bottle Hoax was said to have
been a jest of the Duke of Montagu.

* Smollett, *Peregrine Pickle*, ed. 1797, II, p. 229.
† Chambers's *Book of Days*, I, pp. 123-4.

But no better illustration of general credulity could be required than the episodes connected with the earthquake in 1750. On February 8 of that year London was alarmed by a shock which, while doing no material damage, was sufficient to drive the populace into the streets and to cause the utmost panic. A month later there was a recurrence of the same phenomenon. "All the women," wrote Walpole, "have taken them up upon the foot of judgments; and the clergy, who have had no windfalls of a long season, have driven horse and foot into this opinion.*

Secker, the Bishop of Oxford, preached to this effect. Sherlock, Bishop of Salisbury, wrote a pastoral letter, a hundred thousand copies of which were bought, declaring it was a visitation for the sinful lives led by the people of London. The possibility of a third earthquake after the lapse of another month was altogether too much for the nerves of the dwellers in the Metropolis. Prophetic warnings from the Bishop of London were supplemented by the ravings of a crazy trooper in Lord Delawarr's regiment,† and resulted in a reign of terror. In three days seven hundred and thirty coaches were counted passing Hyde Park Corner "with whole parties removing to the country." Walpole writing of the affair says:

> Several women have made earthquake gowns; that is, warm gowns to sit out of doors all to-night. . . . But what will you think of Lady Catherine Pelham, Lady Frances Arundel, and Lord and Lady Galway, who go this evening to an inn ten miles out of town, where they are to play at brag till five in the morning, and then come back—I suppose, to look for the bones of their husbands and families under the rubbish.‡

On the fatal night, thousands of the inhabitants careered through the streets, having open spaces for their goal—others sought refuge and spiritual comfort in the churches which were crowded to overflow. Charles Wesley preached for hours during the evening, exhorting his hearers to repentance.

* *Letters*, II, p. 437.
† He was subsequently sent to Bedlam.
‡ Walpole, *Letters*, II, p. 441.

5

Later Whitefield, taking up a position towards the centre of Hyde Park, preached to a vast concourse of terrified listeners. The occasion was exploited to the full by the Church and by the Evangelicals. Penitence leapt into fashion, open profligacy was suspended, and it was only with the appearance of the dawn on April 9 that life in London coursed back into its normal channel.

It was a generation for good or for ill easily wrought on. Its failings were undisguised, its virtues quiescent and only needing to be roused—on the surface a moment of stagnation might have been inferred. Such changes as were in progress were spontaneous and little observed; they were not induced either by legislation or by the self-consciousness which leads to reform and amendment.

Allowances and qualifications have necessarily to be admitted to all statements as general as those which have been made in the text. It would no doubt be possible to point to exceptions, and provide illustrations to the contrary. But the middle eighteenth century is one of the best charted areas of history. Its currents, its channels, its shoals and reefs have been conned and noted by countless searchers and writers. Of no age perhaps is it possible to suggest the broad features with so fair a prospect of approximating to the truth.

CHAPTER VII

DURING the years 1749–51 political life was made up for the most part of personal rivalries. The removal of the Duke of Bedford from his position as Secretary of State engrossed the activities of statesmen, and the vicissitudes which attended that process form the subject of endless correspondence.* For Newcastle it had the quality of a life-and-death struggle. At one moment he was for resigning and becoming President of the Council, at another he was for bringing in Lord Granville —" no longer," he wrote, " the terrible man, non eadem est œtas non mens "—or Lord Chesterfield, or again Lord Holdernesse, who though " Triffling [sic] in his manner and carriage " had " a solid understanding " and was " as prudent a young man as any in the Kingdom."

The essential thing was to manœuvre so that the dismissal of Bedford should appear to result from the action of the King.† That was a difficult thing to bring about. At Hanover, whither Newcastle had accompanied him (1750), the King was showing an indifference and " a sort of reserve "; his behaviour to the Duchess of Newcastle was pointedly lacking in cordiality, and Lady Yarmouth was very obviously avoiding a personal interview. The only solace was the more promising relations with Pitt and his warm approval of Newcastle's foreign policy.

Pitt harboured the hope of succeeding Bedford as Secretary of State. In the debate on the Address at the beginning of the session in 1751, in violation of his former views, he lent his support to the treaty with Bavaria and the policy of granting further subsidies to the electors and princes of the Empire

* Add. MS. 32703, f. 464, Richmond to Newcastle, Dec. 11, 1754: " I fear you will have a great deal of plague with him."

† Add. MS. 35411, f. 94, Newcastle to Pelham, Sept. 2/13, 1750.

in order to secure their votes for the election of the Archduke
Joseph as King of the Romans. That election was the project
issuing from the combined intelligence of George II and his
Minister Newcastle.* Designed to secure to the House of
Austria a further tenure of the Imperial Crown, it was at
the same time intended to cement the friendship between England and the Court of Vienna. And if a charge of incon-
sistency was to be brought against Pitt, he was in a position
to meet it by pointing to the fact that the subsidies and conventions to which he had formerly been opposed were in this
case associated with an object of which he approved, namely
the election of a King of the Romans. It was especially in
his relations with the King that Pitt was anxious for the
mediation of Newcastle: "Nothing," he wrote to that
Minister, "can touch me so sensibly as any good offices in
that place, where I deservedly stand in need of it so much,
and when I have it so much at heart to efface the past by every
action of my life." But the King had neither forgotten nor
forgiven Pitt his opposition to foreign subsidies and his hostility
to the measures proposed for the defence of Hanover in
1743–4. His antagonism was not to be overcome either by
a contrite heart or a change of political principles. More than
that was needed before Pitt could attain the position in which
there would be scope for the exercise of his genius.

Meanwhile he was casting about for the means whereby to
find favour first with Newcastle and next with the King.
Sudden confidences and profuse adulation figure in the correspondence between him and the Duke. In Parliament he
is found supporting measures to which his hostility had
formerly been pronounced. In Ministerial circles his energies
were engaged in softening the acerbities between Newcastle
and Pelham and calming the agitations that ruffled the relations
of that inflammable pair of brothers. His efforts in this regard
were successful, at any rate for the time being.

In August Pitt was able to write to Newcastle, "I should
be foolishly vain with a witness if I ascribed the least part of
the perfect union between you to anything but your own good

* See Add. MS. 35411, f. 86, Pelham to Newcastle, Aug. 31, 1750,
for Pelham's view of the proposal.

hearts and understandings." * " Perfect unions," however,
between the brothers had the impermanence of running waters.
By December Newcastle in disgust and anger was writing that
he would rather be " Mr. P(elham)'s footman than his Secretary of State." † So far as the Ministry was concerned,
" human nature's daily food " was incessant wrangling; that is
the outstanding feature of the politics of the years immediately
succeeding the Treaty of Aix-la-Chapelle. The King himself,
distracted by the kaleidoscopic changes in Ministerial relations,
shared in the violent alternations of feeling. Constant only in
his animosity to Pitt, and his devotion to Cumberland, he
was perpetually veering in his attitude towards Newcastle,
Bedford and Sandwich, nor did even the stable personality
of the Lord Chancellor escape his occasional censures and re-
criminations. Nourishing violent hatreds, and vindictive
towards those who had run counter to his ideas of policy, he
would fiercely reject any overture towards a peaceable understanding. When Newcastle proposed that Lord Harrington,
who had supported the Ministers in the crisis of 1746,‡ should
be given the place of General of Marines on his retirement
from the Lord-Lieutenancy of Ireland, " the King was," wrote
Newcastle in his account of the interview, " more enraged than
ever I had before seen him. He said the General of Marines
was to be the reward for everyone that flew in his face; that
was the case of that old rascal Stair; that my Lord Harrington
should have his ears cut off : he should not have it if he could
hinder it, and at last said he deserves to be *hanged* and I am
ready to tell him so." § Ministers, and above all Newcastle,
had to be very sure of their ground before making direct
proposals. The safer course was to employ some of the
methods of a formal siege, and by parallels and saps to prepare
the position for the final assault. The dislodgement of the
Duke of Bedford was rendered a more critical undertaking

* *Chatham Correspondence,* Pitt to Newcastle, Aug. 24, 1750 (Vol.
I, p. 45).

† Newcastle to Hardwicke, Dec. 15, 1750; cited Yorke, *Life of
Lord Hardwicke,* II, p. 112.

‡ See *Life of William Augustus Duke of Cumberland,* p. 255.

§ Yorke, *Life of Lord Hardwicke,* II, p. 107. Newcastle to Hardwicke, Oct. 10, 1750.

because the Duke had the support of Cumberland; and that
was an asset the exact value of which was uncertain. Newcastle proceeded here with great caution and unusual subtlety.
The final stroke was indirect but effective. The King was
persuaded to remove Lord Sandwich from the Admiralty.
This, it was thought, and the prognosis proved correct, would
lead to the resignation of Bedford.

On June 12th the Duke of Newcastle wrote to Lord Sandwich to acquaint him that the King had no further occasion
for his services. Rumour of the pending decision had reached
Sandwich a few days earlier, and he was determined that
when the blow fell it should find him under the roof of his
friend and patron at Windsor Lodge.

To dismiss him while a guest of Cumberland would show
Newcastle in the light of a hunter who shamelessly pursued
his quarry within the precincts of a sanctuary. It would
make the proceeding more notorious, might even appear to the
King a slight to his son, and would certainly, so Sandwich
declared, have a " good appearance in the world." * It was
accordingly arranged that the message should be handed to
Sandwich at Windsor Lodge. The staging of the episode
failed of its effect. Newcastle's forecast proved perfectly
correct. On June 14 Bedford proceeded to Kensington Palace
to resign the seals of Secretary of State.

Here Bedford was able to settle some old scores, and un-
burden himself to the King on the subject of Newcastle's
conduct. When he left the Royal Presence, George II had
every reason to think less well of his principal Secretary
of State. It had been pointed out to him that Newcastle was
of a temper to live with nobody, that he had forced out three
Secretaries of State, and would do the same by Bedford's
successor, and that everything relating to the King's service
was so concerted as to serve Newcastle's convenience and
increase his power.

It would appear indeed that Bedford had been coached for
this interview by Princess Amelia. From that Princess no
weakness of her father's character was hid. She knew to a
nicety just those allegations which would be the most likely

* *Bedford Correspondence*, II, p. 94. Sandwich to Bedford.

to impress his credulity, and those most likely to prejudice him against his Minister. Malice could desire no more favourable soil on which to work. George II was by temperament, by habit, and in mind antagonistic to Newcastle. He regarded him as an unfortunate necessity: one of the many institutions of the country which he disliked but had no power to alter. There was no getting away from him. Other Ministers came and went, other Ministers he could brow-beat or dispense with, but with Newcastle it was different; there was a sense of permanence about him, proof against every evidence of distaste, and the King also had a feeling of being constantly manœuvred, cajoled, or even forced into doing what Newcastle wanted. Outbursts of temper, coolness, and unfriendly demonstrations had come to be the only means by which the King could express his otherwise rather powerless hostility. He was galled by the periodic consciousness that he was being humoured and outwitted, and the scope of his prerogative gradually curtailed. He was at all times ready to think evil of them that served him, and on this occasion the concert between Bedford and the Princess had been cleverly tuned to the end in view. "Your brother," said the King a little later on the same day to Pelham, "will be jealous of Lord Holdernesse if he continues to be of my parties at Richmond of Saturdays, and if he goes to my son and daughter." * In the sequel the King's coolness and estrangement became more pronounced. Newcastle with his jangled susceptibilities was made to realise that it was he who was to be abased and excluded from any share in the home administration,† while Pelham was to be exalted and taken into the most complete confidence.

But Newcastle was long-suffering. In his encounters with George II he was able to put up with a great deal so long as in the background he had the Lord Chancellor to second him, so long in fact as, like a pugilist in the ring, he could withdraw to his corner and be revived by the ministrations of his henchman. So the Government went on, and New-

---

* Newcastle to Hardwicke, June 15, 1751. Yorke, *Life of Lord Hardwicke*, II, p. 113.

† Newcastle to Hardwicke, Sept. 6, 1751. *Ibid.*, II, p. 117.

castle with it, surviving personal humiliations, and negotiating awkward corners. In this case Newcastle certainly had the best of it and remained master on the field. The Cumberland faction had experienced a distinct set-back. Bedford and Sandwich had both been jockeyed out of high place, while Cumberland, as we have seen, had declined very rapidly in popular favour. The cricket matches and play-acting at Woburn had now lost their significance, the conclaves at Windsor Lodge had no further terrors. Newcastle's exposed flank had been successfully covered, and he could contemplate the ways of Cumberland and his allies with comparative peace of mind.

Cumberland, on the other hand, was absorbed with army matters and his favourite diversions of hunting and gambling, for which his zeal was such that he had succeeded in effecting an unusual combination between the two.

> Lord Sandwich [Walpole writes] goes once or twice a week to hunt with the Duke; and as the latter has taken a turn of gaming, Sandwich, to make his court, carries a box and dice in his pocket, and so they throw a main, whenever the hounds are at fault upon every green hill and under every green tree.*

The gambler is never at a loss for a field in which to exercise his proclivities. And in the eighteenth century he was faced with an unusual variety of opportunity. There were presented for his selection basset and loo, ombre, comet and hazard, picquet and quadrille, quinze and tredrille, trente et quarante, whist, and odd and even, each of which had its patrons and its fashion. Play was high, and could be indulged in at the many coffee houses, at White's, at Littleman's, at Oldham's, Tom's, or Jonathan's, all famous in their day. In private houses gambling was the common pastime, and would be carried on till 2 and 3 in the morning—so much indeed did it become the diversion even of those engaged in the function of maternity that Walpole proposed that " instead of receiving cards for assemblies, one should send in a morning to Dr. Hunter's the man midwife to know where there is loo that evening." †

* Walpole, *Letters,* II, p. 425.
† *Letters,* IV, p. 270.

Cumberland, when not throwing a main out hunting, would now appear to have devoted himself principally to loo, Pharaoh, and hazard. Once when he and his friends were staying at Newmarket for a week they sent for £100,000 to gamble with at hazard.* It was on this occasion that his geniality won as many hearts as he had lost in Scotland; he received everyone at his table with the greatest good humour and permitted the familiarities of the place with ease and sense.† Later we read of him at an evening party losing £450 at loo in less than two hours, the spoil being divided between Horace Walpole and Miss Pelham; or again on Twelfth Night 1752 gambling at St. James's Palace at hazard, when "his most sacred Majesty won three guineas and H.R.H. the Duke three thousand four hundred pounds." ‡ His wagers as an owner of horses and a patron of the fancy will be dealt with later. But no association with the sports and pastimes of the day could stem the tide of his unpopularity with the public.

His enemies were leaving no stone unturned. On February 17, 1751, the day of the meeting of Parliament, great numbers of a document known as the *Constitutional Queries* were circulated by the penny post and dropped broadcast into the areas of houses. The *Queries* made effective propaganda: they gave shape to the doubts about Cumberland which had been so actively stimulated by the Jacobites and Leicester House; they likened the Duke to Richard III, and in the query "Whether, if a younger son of the Crown should ever be invested with absolute power over an army: and at the same time by a factious connexion make himself master of the Fleet, our lives and fortunes might not be dependent on his will and pleasure and the Right of Succession have no other security than his want of ambition?" they gave point to the growing feeling of mistrust. The matter was immediately taken up by Parliament, and a resolution passed by both Houses that the paper should be burnt by the hangman, an operation duly performed on February 22. The queries were framed with no little ingenuity, and betrayed a hand expert

* Walpole, *Letters,* III, p. 152.
† *Ibid.,* p. 155.
‡ *Ibid.,* p. 79.

in hostility to the Duke. Rumour was busy with their origin, and opinion supported the view that they bore the hall mark of Leicester House. Lord Egmont was much suspected.

John Perceval, second Earl of Egmont (1711–1770), was remarkable in his day, but is now a little-known character of that time. In his youth as Lord Perceval he had carried the Westminster election against Sir Robert Walpole's Ministry, and made himself the target of not unmerited ridicule by publishing a history of his family,* which he carried down to his own election, and concluded with the words, "Let us here leave this young nobleman struggling for the dying liberties of his country."

In youth he had been the pioneer of a debating society, and a rostrum erected in his private house had witnessed many contests in eloquence between himself and a set of friends, who met for the purpose of discussion. He was an early contributor to *The Craftsman* and a composer of political pamphlets, one of which, *Faction detected by the Evidence of Facts,* has been described as " one of the best political pamphlets ever written " (1743). In 1747 he became leader of the Prince of Wales's party, and during the succeeding years made a name as a strenuous and ingenious debater, devoting his wide knowledge of history, his powers of application, and his by no means inadequate gifts of oratory to embarrassing the Ministry, and combating the clauses of the Mutiny Bill and the powers of the Commander-in-Chief. He in fact gave coherence and substance to an otherwise flimsy cause. Like Mr. Chain-mail in Crotchet Castle, he had a passion for antiquity, and was for ever attempting to revive feudal tenures—indeed his belief in the past was such that when building a residence at Enmore, near Bridgewater, " he mounted it round and pre-pared it to defend itself with crossbows and arrows against the time in which the fabric and use of gunpowder shall be forgotten." †

Walpole declared he had made as great a figure as perhaps was ever made in so short a time. He undoubtedly showed himself a leader of talent, and in the face of much hostility

---

* *The History of the House of Yvery.*
† Walpole, *Memoirs of the Reign of George II*, I, p. 388.

ended by compelling the attention of the House and the respect of his opponents. His language was described as useful, clear and strong, and his speaking as a combination of fire and method. He was famed for the gravity of his manner. It was said indeed that he had never been known to laugh, and that only once had be been seen to smile and then at a game of chess. But he was no enemy of mirth in others; he would simply adjourn his attention till the laughter was concluded, and he could bring back his company to seriousness and his habitual topic of politics.

In 1756 Newcastle offered him the leadership of the House and the office of Secretary of State. But his ambitions were directed to the House of Lords. In 1762 he was created a Peer,* and in the following year became First Lord of the Admiralty. Of his numerous children, his son Spencer, born 1762, by his second wife Catherine, the daughter of the Hon. Charles Compton, became Prime Minister in 1809.

By the death of the Prince of Wales on March 20, 1751, a sudden end was put to the utility of Egmont as a leader and to the intrigues and aims of the Leicester House Party. The death of the Prince was unexpected. On March 5 he had contracted a chill in his gardens at Kew, but on the day of his death was declared to be out of danger. That evening he was seized with a violent fit of coughing, and murmuring in French " Je sens la mort " passed away in the arms of his favourite German valet de chambre Provanarius. The news reached St. James's Palace while the King was at cards; rising from his place and showing great agitation he leant over Lady Yarmouth and said, " Fritz ist todt." It was the conclusion of a deplorable relationship, but evoked at once the more amiable qualities of the King. Gracious messages passed between the two residences, and the Princess was assured of the friendship and solicitude of the monarch, who in turn received tokens of duty and affection from his daughter-in-law.

On the 31st of the month the King visited Leicester House, and discarding a chair of honour arranged for his reception, subsided on to the sofa, where he sat mingling his tears with those of the widow. On rising to leave he affectionately ad-

* Baron Lovel and Holland of Enmore.

monished the young Princes, saying, "They must be brave boys, obedient to their mother, and deserve the fortune to which they were born." Cumberland, on receiving the news, observed with more bitterness than decorum, "It is a great blow to this country, but I hope it will recover it in time." The event gave opportunity for a fresh outburst against the Duke. In London, as the news was cried through the streets and was received upon Change and in the City, it was freely said, "Oh that it was but his brother"—"Oh that it was but the butcher." * But lamentation was sincere among the Party whose hopes had thus been brought to an untimely end. The gathering of the faction summoned to his house by Lord Egmont within a few hours of the Prince's death, was paralysed by the event and passed the time "in a sort of dumb confusion."

Ill-weaved ambition, how much art thou shrunk!

Probably no member of that group was more afflicted than Bubb Dodington. Only the day before the Prince's death Dodington had put before him a scheme for a union between the Independent Whigs and the Tories and a plan for his first administration. In this plan Dodington himself figured as a Duke and Secretary of State.† Now Dukedom and Secretaryship lay in the dust of mortal things. Writing in his Diary he could only record in a passing mood of unctuous

---

* The occasion gave rise to the well-known elegy:

> Here lies Fred
> Who was alive and is dead.
> Had it been his father
> I had much rather:
> Had it been his brother,
> Still better than another;
> Had it been his sister,
> No one would have missed her:
> Had it been the whole generation,
> Still better for the nation:
> But since 'tis only Fred
> Who was alive and is dead
> There's no more to be said.

† Walpole to Mann, April 22, 1751 (III, p. 45).

piety, " Father of mercy! thy hand, that wounds, alone can save!" * Salvation however required practical steps as well as pious ejaculations, and with cynical promptitude Dodington within a few days was rendering homage at Kensington and seeking that his apology for his defection in favour of the heir to the throne should reach the ears of the King.† This was quickly followed by overtures, favourably received, to the Pelham Ministry. Dodington had in fact crowded into the space of a few days an epitome of his whole graceless career.

Little as the death of the Prince of Wales disturbed the current of events, it was to furnish decisive evidence of the change which had occurred in the contemporary estimate of Cumberland.

The infancy of the Prince of Wales's eldest son made it necessary to provide for a Regency in the event of the death of George II. The King wished that Cumberland should be nominated as Regent. He was too shrewd, however, not to recognise that the feeling in the country and Parliament was strongly opposed to the idea. It would involve a political crisis, and would set him in antagonism with his Ministry. It was lamentable that Leicester House and the Jacobites should have so successfully organised the hostility against his favourite son. But it was impossible to ignore the dread which was apparent on all sides at the prospect of Cumberland being invested with further authority. The Duke had done nothing to conciliate public opinion. He had pursued his own way, he had made personal enemies in high place, he had abated nothing of the severity of his discipline or of his harsh presentment to the world. The devotion and staunchness of his friends, the support of Bedford and Fox and Sandwich, his own commanding personality, and the exalted nature of his calling, these were powerless in the face of the intensity of feeling directed against him. Moreover George II was far too acute an observer to underrate the factors aligned to defeat his project. He knew when to desist and when to compromise. He had a complete understanding of what was constitutional and what was correct. He bowed therefore to the storm, and

* *Diary of George Bubb Dodington*, p. 100.
† *Ibid.*

guided by his Ministers agreed to the nomination of the Princess of Wales as Regent, with a Council consisting of

> The Duke of Cumberland and such persons as for the time being shall be Archbishop of Canterbury, Lord Chancellor, Lord Treasurer, Lord President of the Council, Lord Privy Seal, Lord High Admiral, the principal Secretaries of State, and Lord Chief Justice of the King's Bench, together with any other four whom his present Majesty shall appoint.*

Cumberland himself, much less aware of his own unpopularity than the rest of society, attributed the decision to the machinations of the Pelhams and Lord Hardwicke. This was a view which receives some countenance from Walpole, who writes in his reminiscences: †

> The low ambition of Lord Hardwicke, the childish passion for power of the Duke of Newcastle, and the peevish jealousy of Mr. Pelham combined on the death of the Prince of Wales to exclude the Duke of Cumberland from the Regency.

The distasteful duty of communicating to Cumberland the purport of the Regency Bill which had been agreed on between the King and his Ministers, fell to Lord Hardwicke. Of the answer given by Cumberland the version recorded by the Lord Chancellor himself is more acceptable than that given in the often highly seasoned pages of Walpole's reminiscences.‡

According to Lord Hardwicke Cumberland said:

> I desire you will present my humble duty to the King and return his Majesty my thanks for the honour he has done me by ordering this affair to be communicated to me; that I think it is necessary something should be done in it, and shall $\dfrac{\text{submit}}{\text{be ready}}$ (as it is my duty) to take such part in it as His Majesty shall judge proper for me.§

* *Parliamentary History*, XIV, p. 1000.
† *British Prose Writers*, XXIV, p. 66; cited Yorke, *Life of Lord Hardwicke*, II, p. 45.
‡ Walpole, *Memoirs of the Reign of George II*, I, p. 104.
§ Hardwicke MSS. 243, f. 181; quoted Yorke, *Life of Lord Chancellor Hardwicke*, II, p. 46.

On the other hand, there is every likelihood that Walpole's statement that the Lord Chancellor went to communicate the message " in a great fright " is consistent with the truth. It is highly probable that the Lord Chancellor, during his drive from Kensington Palace to St. James's, was the prey of vivid forebodings.

The debates which followed in Parliament disclosed considerable variety as to the views entertained on the question of the expediency of calling a Council into existence, but none as to the view that the Princess was the proper Regent. Henry Fox alone was found putting forward arguments behind which discreetly lurked a preference for Cumberland. Pitt, on the other hand, who actively opposed Fox in the debates, supported the measure in its entirety—and directed his argument against Cumberland. He contemplated what might happen in the event of the Princess's death if no Council were constituted. He surmised that some person in high station might be induced by his sole possession of the Regency to grasp at the Crown.* He then spoke of the deceased Prince in terms of eulogy, and added his testimony of admiration of the King, who he said " had borne this sorrow with a fortitude surpassing that which Edward III had shown on the death of the Black Prince." How far George II appreciated what was universally regarded as the irony of the reference does not appear. It did little to soften his hostility to the speaker.

It is difficult to find a satisfactory explanation of the line adopted by Pitt. It has been suggested that he desired to placate Newcastle,† in view of the approaching vacancy in the office of Secretary of State, and that by attacking Cumberland he hoped to achieve that object. But in order to secure the office he wished for, it was equally necessary to placate the King. That was Pitt's own view, and he had every reason to think it a correct view. Had he not been kept out of high office for seventeen years, had not his position in Parliament failed of recognition only through the enmity of the King? In a passage which throws much light on his views he wrote that " consideration and weight in the House of Commons

* A. von Ruville, *William Pitt Earl of Chatham*, I, p. 302.
† *Ibid.*

arises generally but from one of two causes, the protection and
countenance of the Crown visibly manifested by marks of
Royal favour at Court, or from weight in the country, sometimes arising from opposition to the public measures." May
not Pitt in his otherwise unaccountable attack have had in
mind the second source of weight and consideration in the
House of Commons? No statesman was more aware of the
influence of the Crown. No man had made greater efforts
to recapture the lost favour of the King.

In 1755 he is found writing: "The weight of irremovable
royal displeasure is a load too great to move under: it must
crush any man: it has sunk and broken me. I succumb and
wish for nothing but a decent and innocent retreat." * It is
not surprising that he regarded his situation in Parliament
as "degraded." † It is surprising that in 1751 he should be
found speaking satirically of the King, and directing his arguments against Cumberland. And of this strange outburst the
mere wish to please Newcastle can hardly be considered explanatory. May it not have been a foreshadowing of an
appeal to an authority greater than the Court, more powerful
than Parliament, to the nation itself, to the tribunal from which
he was ultimately to draw his strength and obtain his sanction?

Cumberland was deeply sensible of the blow which his prestige had suffered. While observing his habitual attitude of
dignity in public, he lamented his situation among his friends,
wishing as he said that "the name of William could be blotted
out of the English annals," and adding that he "now felt his
own insignificance when even Mr. Pelham could dare to use
him thus." A further but lesser mortification awaited him
when he received a visit from his nephew Prince George in
his house in Pall Mall, which appears to have been largely
ornamented with "bruised arms" and the engines of warfare.
To amuse the boy he took a sword from the wall and drew
it, upon which "the young Prince turned pale and trembled
and thought his uncle was about to murder him." The scene
betrayed to Cumberland the ideas which had been inculcated
at Leicester House. He was deeply shocked. The world

* Lord Rosebery, *Chatham: His Early Life and Connections,* p. 337.
† *Ibid.,* p. 331.

WILLIAM AUGUSTUS DUKE OF CUMBERLAND RECEIVING GEORGE III AT VIRGINIA WATER.

From an Engraving after Paul Sandby in the Royal Library, Windsor.

seemed to be turning against him.* But with the settlement of the Regency question, and the cessation of the intrigues at Leicester House, the Duke's name gradually became once more a power in the State. The wounds slowly healed. In public estimation the process of rehabilitation went forward. His former authority by degrees revived.

* Nearly a hundred years later, by an odd coincidence, similar thoughts were entertained of another Duke of Cumberland, and fears were expressed in Radical journals that the future Queen Victoria stood in danger of assassination at his hands (Lytton Strachey, *Queen Victoria*, p. 23).

CHAPTER VIII

THE political annals of 1751 were saved from insignificance if not oblivion by the passage through Parliament of Lord Chesterfield's Bill for reforming the calendar and adopting the Gregorian in place of the Julian reckoning. The old style was still in use only in Russia, Sweden, and England. The inconvenience was constant and unnecessary. The reform was urgently needed. Lord Chesterfield succeeded to admiration in persuading the House of Lords of its expediency. In a subsequent letter to his son, he paused from what Dr. Johnson described as the characteristic of his letters—namely, inculcating "the manners of a dancing master and the morals of a whore"— to betray trade secrets as to the composition and manner of his oratory, secrets more flattering to his own perspicacity than to the intelligence of his audience.

> For my own part [he wrote] I could just as soon have talked Celtic or Sclavonian to them [the House of Lords] as astronomy, and they would have understood me full as well; so I resolved to do better than speak to the purpose and to please instead of informing them. . . . I was particularly attentive to the choice of my words, to the harmony and roundness of my periods, to my elocution, to my action. This succeeded and ever will succeed: they thought I informed because I pleased them; and many of them said, that I had made the whole very clear to them, when God knows I had not even attempted it. Lord Macclesfield, who is one of the greatest mathematicians and astronomers in Europe, spoke afterwards with infinite knowledge and all the clearness that so intricate a matter would admit of; but as his words, his periods, and his utterance were not near so good as mine, the preference was most unanimously, but most unjustly, given to me.*

* *Letters of the Earl of Chesterfield,* ed. Lord Mahon (1845), II, p. 115.

Among the superstitious the change excited a variety of fears and alarms. The death of the Astronomer Royal was attributed to the interference with the Saints' Days,* and Lord Parker, the eldest son of Lord Macclesfield, when contesting a Parliamentary election at Oxford, was assailed by the mob with cries demanding the restitution of the eleven days of which they had been deprived by his father.

The same session had witnessed the last rally of the Prince of Wales's party against Cumberland, when on February 11 Lord Egmont moved to reduce the vote of £16,000 for the payment of the general and staff officers to £11,000. This evoked from Pelham a warm and able defence of the Captain General, in which he set forth the powers of that officer and defined with exactness the limitations to which the exercise of those powers was subject. He pointed out that all commissions in the army and all general orders must be signed by the King and countersigned by the Secretary at War, who was answerable to Parliament for everything which he countersigned; that the Captain General could neither promote nor break an officer in the Army without the King's approval; that even when a vacancy occurred and the Captain General promoted an officer to fill the vacancy, such promotion might be annulled by the King and was only valid if he approved it; in the same way the sentences of courts-martial could not be executed till the sanction of the Monarch had been obtained, the conclusion being that there was little to be feared from the policy of continuing the office of Captain General in time of peace. In the course of his speech Pelham took occasion to eulogise Cumberland as " the great Prince who has so high a claim on our gratitude " and " whose courage and conduct were acknowledged in every part of Europe." † In the end the motion was defeated by 205 votes to 88. The Leicester House Party had been badly beaten. Cumberland, on the other hand, as a result of the debate stood sensibly higher in reputation and the esteem of Parliament.

In August 1751 Cumberland was appointed Lord Warden

* Walter Vernon Anson, *Life of Admiral Lord Anson* (1912), p. 117.

† *Parliamentary History*, XIV, p. 910 et seq.

of Windsor and Lieutenant of the Forest * in succession to the Duke of St. Albans. Forest law had fallen into desuetude. Cumberland at once set about restoring its efficacy and reviving its activities. The Sweinmotes, † or Forest Courts for the prosecution of offenders against Forest law, resumed their sittings, which had been suspended for twenty-five years. Verderers, Regarders, Agisters, and all the company of Forest officials were set in motion, and a new order and discipline penetrated the shades and groves, the "lawns and op'ning glades " ‡ of that sylvan world. Courts of attachment of Vert and of Venison were soon dealing with rights of the chase, with wrongful cutting of wood, with the marking of cattle and the granting of licences to shoot. Offenders found themselves haled before the various authorities, and their accustomed activities curtailed or directed into legitimate channels. Cumberland was determined that, if the Dryads were to be disturbed, the " whirring pheasant " to " feel the fiery wound," and the " circling hare " and " lonely woodcock " " the leaden death," § it should only be at the hands of those who were duly licensed and had paid for the privilege. On the other hand, where the military were concerned he acted with his usual liberality, and gave free licence to officers in the neighbourhood to shoot game without payment of fees. ‖

On November 16, while hunting in the Forest, Cumberland had a severe fall. Three days later he was seized with a violent pain in his side, and was considered by the doctors to be in imminent danger of his life. Not till he had been blooded

---

* Cumberland Papers.

† The following note in the Cumberland Papers shows the constitution and powers of the Court of Sweinmote:

(1) The Court is summoned by the Lord Warden.

(2) The Court consists of the 4 Verderers (who are the Judges), Foresters, Keepers, Regarders and Agisters.

(3) The Steward is the assistant to the Judges and the voice of the Court.

(4) The Freeholders are the Jury and try the indictment.

(5) The Court of Sweinmote convicts but cannot inflict punishment—that is the right of the Lord Justice in Eyre.

‡ Pope, *Windsor Forest*, V, 21.

§ Pope, *Windsor Forest*.

‖ Cumberland Papers.

five times and deprived of one hundred ounces of blood * did his condition improve and hold prospect of a recovery. His illness brought a striking testimony of the affection with which he was regarded by his father and his friend the Secretary at War. Writing to Sir Charles Hanbury-Williams † in December, Fox says:

> The Duke has been so ill by a fall from his horse that he was given over. Never was man so struck as the King was, he told me that if his son had dy'd he must. H.R.H. is now well again. His illness shewed his affection and regard for me to be greater than I ever before presumed to think it. He sent for me and saw me only besides his own family and that for an hour every day. I own I am proud of it, for the reasons that probably occasioned it, because I admire him beyond all men and love him as well as any man whatever.

Pelham, on the other hand, was uttering peevish complaints that Cumberland did not send for him. But if Fox was correct when he wrote, " Mr. Pelham drawn always by the D. of Newcastle and generally dragged has been his agent in whatever has mortified and hurt the Duke most," ‡ the absence of the First Minister is explained.

The Duke, however, was sufficiently anxious to enquire of Fox how the Pelham brothers had acted during his illness. " Both cried," replied Fox; " the Duke of Newcastle overacted it, but Mr. Pelham seemed really in earnest." " Ay," said the Duke, " I know they both cried: for the Duke of Newcastle he cried because he had not been in the morning to know how I did—but for Mr. Pelham he is such a fellow that I can believe he was in earnest." § Fox was for urging Cumberland to exploit the King's emotions, to turn to good account His Majesty's " inexpressible alarms," his tears, and his confidence to those about him that " the nation would be undone, left to nothing but a woman and children." ‖ He repeated that the King had said of Cumberland, " He had a head to guide, to rule,

* *Gentleman's Magazine,* 1751, p. 522.
† Add. MS. 9191, f. 110.
‡ *Ibid.*
§ Walpole, *Memoirs George II,* I, p. 213.
‖ *Ibid.,* p. 212.

and to direct," and that he contemplated him as sole Regent; but when Fox went on to try to persuade Cumberland to remind the King of how much he had done to prevent him occupying that station, Cumberland replied:

> That it was now too late to remedy: that the Regency Bill could not be repealed, and that even if it could, he had rather bear the ignominy that had been laid upon him, than venture giving the King the uneasiness of reflecting, if it were but for two hours in his own room, on the injury he had done him.

Meanwhile the foreign policy of Newcastle and George II was developing on very different lines from those intended.

In a letter to Lord Hardwicke Newcastle had summarised the ends which he had in view when he accompanied the King to Hanover in the spring of 1750.

> The objects of my residence are [he wrote] 1st, the election of a King of the Romans, and the securing for that and other purposes, the Elector and Princes of the Empire; 2ndly, the accession to the Treaty of 1746 with the two Empresses * ; 3rdly, the accommodating the disputes between the Court of Vienna and the Republic of Holland relating to the Barrier, and the putting that in some way of being restor'd; 4thly, the reconciling the King, as Elector, and the other Protestant Princes with the Emperor, upon their present disputes; 5thly, or rather in the first place (if possible) the making up our differences with Spain which now seems further off than ever.

These ends Newcastle steadily pursued.   But his task resembled that of a captain navigating a narrow channel whose soundings were subject to constant alteration, and whose lights or landmarks were perpetually being shifted.   The politics of Europe were in a state of more than usual flux.   Within little

---

* This was a Treaty between Austria and Russia, secret articles of which provided for the restoration of Silesia to Austria and the partition of Prussia.   But as England had guaranteed to Frederick the retention of Silesia by the Convention of Hanover (Aug. 26, 1745) she could be no party to the secret articles, and without these the Treaty, as Lord Hardwicke pointed out, was a mere shell.   See Yorke, *Life of Lord Hardwicke*, II, p. 24.

more than a year Newcastle was forced to recognise that Austria herself was one of the difficulties to be contended with.

I must own [he wrote] I was never more mortified at the Court of Vienna than at present; the evident disregard and reserve that they show to all the King's Ministers in every Court of Europe, especially France and Spain, is so shameful that I must own I have difficulty to persuade the King to suffer me to give you the ample informations contained in my letters. His Majesty sees and thinks himself slighted and ill used.*

It was all very well for the Empress to say that " Mr. Keith knew her too well to suspect her of any penchant for France." † The plain fact remained that she was at variance with the Emperor, holding back from the British scheme for the election of the Archduke Joseph as King of the Romans, and refusing to join in the purchase of the Elector Palatine's vote,‡ which would have been decisive in securing the necessary majority. Her conduct indeed was plainly subject to the influence of Kaunitz, who, as we know, consistently favoured a rapprochement with France as the only means of recovering Silesia. Thus there became apparent a serious flaw in the broad policy of Newcastle, which was designed to bring about a defensive alliance with Spain, Austria, the King of Sardinia, and ultimately the Empress Elizabeth of Russia and the King of Poland.§

Newcastle's general idea was undoubtedly correct. The increasing strain with France was tending to war; it was essential, in order to preserve the peace of Europe or, should war follow, to be in a position to combat the power of France, to have alliances on the Continent. " Some system," he wrote to Hardwicke, " ought to be found, some alliance or party in Europe made, which may prevent our being dependent upon France and enable us to make a stand." ‖ Newcastle deserves

* Add. MS. 9191, f. 39, Newcastle to Keith, Aug. 3, 1751.
† *Ibid.*, f. 73, Keith to Newcastle, Sept. 11, 1751.
‡ *Ibid.*, f. 144, Newcastle to Keith, July 25, 1752.
§ *Ibid.*, f. 40, Newcastle to Keith, Aug. 3, 1751.
‖ Newcastle to Hardwicke, Aug. 25, 1749; cited *Life of Hardwicke*, II, p. 18.

more credit or less abuse than he has received for his policy
in anticipation of the coming war.   In conjunction with
Hardwicke he was continually urging on his colleagues in the
Government the necessity for a " strong marine " :   " I have
always maintained that our marine should protect our alliances
upon the Continent: and they by diverting the expense of
France, enable us to maintain our superiority at sea." *   That
was his creed, that was the bedrock of his policy: it was on this
that he opposed his brother's efforts at economy (backed as they
were in this case by Henry Fox), and supported Pitt when he
resisted the proposal to reduce the number of seamen in 1751;
and it was again in accordance with these notions of preparation
that he was for keeping up the numbers of the Army.   On the
Continent he pursued what we now know to have been a mere
will o' the wisp, namely the Election of the King of the Romans;
this however was but a means to the end he had always in view,
of contriving a party on the Continent which would support
this country in the contest with France—an end in which he
finally succeeded, not by the election but by a treaty with Russia,
which alarmed Frederick the Great into co-operation and
alliance with Britain.

In foreign politics Newcastle had attained an authority almost
dictatorial.   If his views were criticised by his colleagues, they
scarcely ever at this time appear to have been modified.   The
only co-operation which he appears to have regarded as
essential was that of the King.   Foreign policy the King
regarded as his special province, and here he exercised a powerful and certainly not always a beneficial influence.   Love of
Hanover and fear of Prussia were not under all circumstances
consistent with British interests, yet it would be difficult to
instance a case in which one or other of these two considerations
failed to affect His Majesty's views.   Newcastle had an uneasy
task: on the one side was the deep sea of public opinion in
England, on the other the violent opportunisms of the King.
But it cannot be denied that his apprehensions were founded on
wisdom, and his anticipations justified by events.   And under
that cloud of ridicule which hovers about his reputation, ideas
and energies can be discerned at this period which, if they bore

* Cited *Life of Hardwicke*, II, p. 23.

less fruit than could be desired, were far from barren in the realm of statesmanship.

Negotiations for the summoning of the Diet and the election of the Archduke dragged on at great length till they were temporarily laid aside in the winter of 1752. They had offered a broad field for intrigue and the technique of eighteenth-century diplomacy. Frederick of Prussia, "that turbulent yet fearful prince eternally forming groundless fears and jealousies to himself and all Europe, and endeavouring to justify his own conduct by recriminating on that of others," * had steadily worked against the policy of his uncle George II. Nor had he confined his hostility to mere secret negotiations. Recently he had sent as his Ambassador to the Court of France the Earl Marischal, the most distinguished of living Jacobites. He had claimed to review in the Prussian Courts the decisions of the Admiralty Court in London with regard to the capture of Prussian vessels carrying contraband in the War of the Austrian Succession. And on the question of the Silesian loan † he had shown an intention to refuse the payment of further interest. A protest addressed to the French Ministry by the British Chargé d'Affaires on the reception of Earl Marischal at the Court of Versailles had met with an unyielding reply, and been followed by a counter mission to Berlin of the exiled Jacobite Lord Tyrconnel to represent the French King at the Court of Berlin. Thus so far as Prussia and France were concerned the indications were far from friendly. Moreover alarming news was reaching this country from America, showing on the part of France a disposition to hostile action hardly compatible with the maintenance of peace. Austria, whom it was thought to conciliate and attach more firmly to the common cause by the Electoral Scheme, was, as we have seen,

* Add MS. 9191, f. 13, Bedford to Keene, Feb. 11, 1751.

† This was a loan of £250,000 advanced by English merchants to Charles VI during the war between France and Austria 1733-5. The security given for the repayment of the principal was the estates of Silesia. On July 28, 1742, Frederick the Great, having meanwhile taken possession of Silesia, undertook by Article IX of the definitive Treaty signed between England and Prussia to pay capital and interest to the English bondholders: see Sir Ernest Satow, *The Silesian Loan and Frederick the Great* (1915).

showing manifest signs of defection. The members of the Electoral College were treating the election of the Archduke Joseph as a commercial matter, and endeavouring to squeeze what they could out of the interested principals and organisers of the scheme. Notably the Elector Palatine was raising his demands, and causing Newcastle renewed difficulty in the achievement of his aim. Such were the main influences at work on the Continent to frustrate the policy of Newcastle.

At home the difficulties were of a different nature: there was Henry Pelham staunch for economy, offering resistance to any increase in the bribes to the Electoral College; there was the Lord President of the Council * attending Cabinet meetings and "talking like a madman" under the influence of drink,† and making such "lively transitions" ‡ that no man could count on him; there was the Lord Chancellor persuasively critical of the whole scheme; and finally the King himself, like Louis XV, carrying on a private diplomacy of his own, and acting in a double role of Elector of Hanover and King of England. Here was embarrassment enough for a Secretary of State. But notwithstanding these obstacles and vexations Newcastle persisted. By September 1752 he had induced his brother to agree to an increase in the payment to be made to the Elector Palatine for his vote. The Cabinet had recorded their assent. The way seemed open. Nothing was wanting but the King's agreement.

His Majesty, viewing the political situation from Hanover, had said to Newcastle he was sure Pelham would never agree to the fresh demand. The messenger from England arrived. The King's forecast was proved incorrect. The next day Newcastle joined the King and his Court as they were hunting in the Forest. The King showed "all the joy and satisfaction in his face and manner that ever I saw. He began, ' You knew your brother better than I did, you have great reason to be pleased with him, you see the support you will have.' " All was for

---

* Lord Granville.

† Pelham to Newcastle, Aug. 28, 1752; printed Yorke, *Life of Lord Hardwicke,* II, p. 34.

‡ Pelham to Newcastle, June 19, 1752; Coxe, *Pelham Administration,* II, p. 433.

the best. The King mounted on a Hanover horse—hunting a Hanover stag—Lady Yarmouth by his side, with the hounds running well and the sport prolonged into the summer evening, " kept his good humour and remained in the highest spirits " till late at night. The next day, to the consternation of Newcastle, the King had swung round. There was no haste necessary, the election was less important than Newcastle thought. The negotiations need not be forced—perhaps the Emperor would pay the whole and the Elector Palatine accept less. " In short so altered a man was never seen." The truth being that the King had drunk deep of the pleasures of Hanover, and did not mean to be hurried back to England by Newcastle or by any political crisis. The mere mention of the yachts and the return journey had produced an instantaneous intention not to budge. That was Newcastle's interpretation of events. In that view he was confirmed by Lady Yarmouth. Further, the King had been negotiating with the Austrian Court as Elector of Hanover. In return for the election of the Archduke he had asked for the Bishopric of Osnaburg for Cumberland. He had advised the Empress not to contribute more than a certain sum for the election. Moreover he had a secret destination for the money if it was to be withheld from the Elector Palatine. He intended that it should be used for subsidising Russia.* He was playing his own hand. He was " countermining " " the most faithful ministers engaged in executing his avowed orders." † It was one thing to be Constitutional in England, but to combine that with double dealing when the affairs of Hanover were concerned was to justify all the rhetoric and abuse that had been levelled against that Principality and its harmful influence on the course of English politics. That for the time being was the end of the Election Scheme: but the negotiations had illuminated the state of feeling in Europe. They had shown the temper of Prussia and France, the untrustworthiness of Austria, and the precarious character of the prevailing peace.

* Newcastle to Pelham, Oct. 3, 1752; printed Coxe, *Pelham Administration*, II, p. 455.

† Lord Chancellor to the Duke of Newcastle, Oct. 6, 1752; Yorke, *Life of Lord Hardwicke*, II, p. 36.

Cumberland was personally opposed to the subsidising system of the Government. He regarded it as an extravagant gamble. You might secure peace-time promises by purchase, but when it came to war there was no guarantee that the promises would be fulfilled. Some more solid foundation of common interest was requisite. In the absence of such it was erecting an edifice that might collapse at any moment. Events indeed were to prove the policy wrong and to show that these treaties were "all paper and pack thread." The treaty with Bavaria (1750) which in exchange for £20,000 a year was to secure a force of 6,000 infantry, and the treaty with Saxony (1751) to secure the same number of men for £32,000 a year, both expired in 1756 on the outbreak of war.* The improvidence of the policy stood exposed. But it was a policy dear to the King. He was mesmerised by the constant menace of Prussia. His settled pursuit on the Continent was a policy which, while as far as circumstances would admit it was acceptable to Britain, would have the effect of making Hanover more secure. He was for ever seeking to construct outworks for his Electorate, to erect small Principalities and Powers into buffer states between himself and his dreaded nephew. Cumberland, as we know, was entirely governed by his notions of loyalty and he refrained from open opposition, but his party in Parliament laboured against the Pelhams and indirectly against all their works. They were playing for the reversion of the leadership, to which the title of Henry Fox, the Secretary at War, was becoming more incontestable as each session went by.

In those days, and indeed till a much later date, it was possible to remain a Minister and yet oppose a Government measure, just as it was possible to be a member of the Cabinet and yet have no responsibility for Ministerial policy, the determination of which was left to the inner council of the Cabinet, to those who were singled out for "the circulation of papers." But the privileges of free criticism and opposition were probably never so fully taken advantage of as by Fox, the Secretary at War, and Pitt, the Paymaster. The Pelham Administration existed, if not in a constant, at any rate in a frequently recurring state of anxiety as to the course likely

* Yorke, *Life of Lord Hardwicke*, II, p. 3.

to be taken by these two statesmen, the one acting for himself and an exiguous band of followers, the other for a faction rendered formidable by its inclusion of Cumberland. It is no doubt due to this that Dodington was justified in writing in 1754 that the Ministry, of late years, had been like children round a fire, telling stories of spirits, till they frightened one another and did not dare to look behind them.*

Thus Fox had exposed the Regency Bill to destructive criticism, and now (1753) on the Clandestine Marriage Bill, but acting probably for himself alone, he made a sensational attack on the Lord Chancellor in denouncing the provisions of the measure. This he followed with a belated panegyric, in deference to the view that the attack had been excessive and uncalled for. The Lord Chancellor was not slow to reply:

> Men of riper years and graver had opposed . . . another dark, gloomy, and insidious genius [Fox] who was an engine of personality and faction, had been making connexions and trying to form a party, but his designs had been seen through and defeated. That in this country you must govern by force or by law; it was easy to know that person's principles, which were to govern by arbitrary force . . . but [he concluded] I despise the invective and I despise the recantation: I despise the scurrility (for scurrility I must call it) and I reject the adulation.

A display of temper and vehemence rarely seen, at any rate, in the public utterances of a Minister in reference to a colleague.

Discussing the episode later on, Cumberland said to Fox, "The Chancellor meaned me by arbitrary force," and though Fox demurred to the suggestion, Cumberland was probably right. The question which followed indeed admitted of but one answer. "Why, do you think that he imagines you would govern by an army without me?" Cumberland recognised only too clearly the fears of him entertained by the present Whig Ministry, and the scantily veiled hostility with which they viewed his influence and authority. Continuing his conversation Fox said, "Sir, how will the King act on what has happened?"

* Dodington, p. 267.

" The King," replied the Duke, " would part with you or even with me to satisfy them : but if you can maintain yourself for six months, he will like you the better for what has passed, for he thinks you a man, and he knows none of the rest have the spirit of a mouse." *

The activities of the Cumberland party in Parliament seem to have been limited to those occasions most calculated to embarrass the Pelhams, or advance the claims of Fox. Dodington † brings accusations against Fox of perfidy to Pelham, and would have his readers in one case regard Cumberland as a fellow-conspirator. He relates that on the occasion of the motion to. repeal the oath in the Bribery Act Fox gave his word to Pelham at two o'clock " that he would *not* speak for the repeal and then went to the House and *did* speak for it," and draws the conclusion that in the interval Fox had seen Cumberland and received sailing orders from his chief. Fox was quite capable of pursuing such a course on his own initiative; and beyond the fact that Sandwich was in the gallery of the House and left when Fox had spoken, there is nothing to connect Cumberland with what was done. Displaying perfidy himself or stimulating that vice in others is certainly not one of the offences which even the harshest critic of Cumberland could allege against him. For the rest there was little in current legislation to engage the attention of Parliamentary critics. The annual Mutiny Bill evoked the time-worn arguments against standing armies. The conversion of the debt into 3 per cent. Stock, and the foundation of the British Museum (1753), the main practical achievements of Pelham's Administration, were accepted with general approval. On the other hand, the Bill for the Naturalisation of the Jews provoked serious opposition. Passed in 1752-3 after animated debates in the House of Commons, when evils were predicted threatening the very existence of the Christian faith, it roused throughout the country so fierce a storm of protest that in the following session it was thought politic in view of an approaching election to introduce a Bill for the repeal of the Act.

Whether the allegation so frequently made in reference to the

* Walpole, *Memoirs*, I, p. 351.
† Dodington, p. 265.

eighteenth century that it was devoid of enthusiasms be true or not, certain it is that it was conspicuous for its gusty outbursts of popular clamour. Not outbursts engineered and inflamed by the Press, or initiated and fostered by political zealots, but springing from the spontaneous and untutored opinion of the mob; starting abruptly—quickly reaching a climax of violent expression and then as rapidly subsiding—leaving vague traces of resentment and slumbering hostility. Such was notoriously the case in the affair of the Naturalisation of the Jews. Seized upon by the populace and the " very lowest of the Clergy," * within a few months of the passing of the Act it had set the nation aflame and was being denounced in every quarter of the country. " The little curates preached against the Bishops for deserting the interests of the Gospel: and Aldermen grew drunk at county clubs in the cause of Jesus Christ, as they had used to do for the sake of King James." † The country was inundated with pamphlets, the rage of the people was described as " ungovernable." ‡ It was said in the most popular of the pamphlets " that the Jews have no God, no king, no country, and never act on any higher principle than self-interest; that the present set of Bishops is the only one since the time of Christ, that would have countenanced so anti-Christian a measure." § Typical of the feeling rife throughout the country was the experience of the Bishop of Norwich. That prelate, one of the most respected in the Church, and tutor to the young Prince of Wales, was openly insulted in his diocese for having voted for the Bill; youths at Ipswich called out to him for circumcision, and a notice affixed to the church door declared that the next day being Saturday his lordship would confirm the Jews, and the day following the Christians. Ministers with a mind to the coming election quickly yielded to the outcry, and on the very first day of the 1754 session Newcastle moved to repeal the Bill, excusing its

* Walpole, *Memoirs,* I, p. 357.

† *Ibid.,* p. 358.

‡ Dr. Birch to Hon. Philip Yorke; *Parliamentary History,* XIV, p. 1431 n.

§ *An Answer to the Considerations on the Jews Bill.*

original introduction on the ground that it had only been a point of "political policy." *

Pitt in the Commons supported the repeal, and compared the relation of Parliament to the people to that of a father dealing with the insistence of a peevish and perverse son, claiming something which was not quite right, but if granted could not be attended with any very bad consequence, and went no further than to add: "Thus, sir, though we repeal this law out of complaisance to the people, yet we ought to let them know, that we do not altogether approve of what they ask." † The repeal was duly carried. Nor was this striking avowal of the fallibility of Parliament without its reward. At the general election in March 1754 the Government position was so unassailable that not more than forty-two seats were contested. The easy compliance of the Ministry had in fact foiled the Opposition.

* It appears from Spence's *Anecdotes,* ed. 1820, p. 77, that in the reign of Queen Anne the Jews offered Lord Godolphin £500,000 if the Government would allow them to purchase the town of Brentford, with leave of settling there entirely.

† *Parliamentary History,* XV, p. 154.

CHAPTER IX

HENRY PELHAM, whose health had been failing for some time, died unexpectedly on March 6. It was a day rendered odious to the orthodox by the publication of Lord Bolingbroke's works, an event which provoked Dr. Johnson to one of his most surcharged outbursts, and elicited from Garrick verses with the following stanza:

> The same sad morn to Church and State
> (So for our sins 'twas fixed by fate)
> A double stroke was given;
> Black as the whirlwinds of the North,
> St. John's fell genius issued forth,
> And Pelham fled to Heaven.*

What followed was no ordinary scramble for office. The situation was limited to a contest between personalities. Neither of the parties to the contest could claim any divergence of political principles. On the one side were the Lord Chancellor and Newcastle, determined not only that power should not pass from their hands but that none should share it; on the other were Fox and Pitt, by far the ablest Parliamentarians, both subordinate members of the Administration, but bent on participating in that power on something approaching equal terms. Under such circumstances it is not to be expected that human weaknesses, intrigue, and even self-abasement should be absent from the scene.

Pelham died at 6 a.m. The news must have been conveyed to Fox without loss of time. Before 8 o'clock he had called on Lord Hartington and also at Pitt's house, and within a few hours had approached the Duke of Newcastle and written to the Lord Chancellor " no less than three very humiliating and

---

* Boswell's *Life of Johnson*, ed. 1887, I, p. 269.

apologizing messages." * Pitt, chained to the seclusion of Bath by gout, on hearing the news wrote to Newcastle: " You have a great occasion for all your strength of mind to exert itself. Exercise it for the sake of your master and your country and may all good men support you." † Even for so towering a figure as Pitt there comes a moment when

> 'tis better
> To praise the sun than reason why it shines.

To his followers, Lord Temple, Sir George Lyttelton, and the Grenville brothers, Pitt wrote directions as to the course to be steered. Conscious of his powers and justly mortified by his long exclusion from high office, he desired promotion. Knowing Newcastle and Hardwicke, and measuring the hostility of the King, he realised the caution that was necessary. This was the procedure which he counselled:

> Give me leave to recommend to your Lordship a little gathering of friends about you at dinner, without ostentation. Stanley who will be in Parliament: some attention to Sir Richard Lyttelton I should think proper; a dinner to the Yorkes very seasonable: and before things are settled, any of the Princess of Wales's Court. John Pitt not to be forgot: I know the Duke of B—— nibbles at him: in short liez commerce with as many members of Parliament, who may be open to our purposes as your Lordship can. Pardon, my dear Lord, all this freedom, but the conjuncture is made to awaken men, and there is room for action. I have no doubt George Grenville's turn must come. Fox is odious and will have difficulty to stand in a future time. I mend a little. I cannot express my impatience to be with you. ‡

Fox was the natural successor to the position which Pelham had occupied in the House of Commons. But Newcastle being prostrate with grief, discussions with the King were conducted by Hardwicke, and Hardwicke had not forgotten Fox's attack in the debate on the Marriage Bill. He would even have preferred Pitt, but to this idea, if the Lord Chancellor's ver-

* *Grenville Papers*, Pitt to Earl Temple, March 11, 1754, I, p. 112.
† Add. MS. 32734, Pitt to Newcastle, March 7, 1754.
‡ *Grenville Papers*, Pitt to Earl Temple, March 11, 1754, I, p. 112.

sion of what occurred is accepted in its entirety, the King opposed a direct negative. * Here, as so frequently happened, there cropped out the fear of Cumberland. Fox and Cumberland were of one party, and to hand over control of the Commons to Fox, "a proper Minister to overturn the constitution and introduce a military government," † for so he was regarded in some quarters, would mean "The Treasury, the House of Commons, and the Sword joined together." ‡ This was a bogey which appears to have exercised a real or simulated sway over the minds of both Hardwicke and Newcastle. It was difficult to put it as an argument before the King, who was in favour of Fox. Indeed to attack Fox was indirectly to attack Cumberland. The subject had to be broached warily.

I have thrown out several considerations to His Majesty from day to day and so have others [wrote Hardwicke]. These have made an impression upon him, and he has been more *deliberative*. He begins to find that all the world is not for Mr. Fox, as he had been told: for in truth it is a very narrow clique and many of them of the worst sort. If he should succeed to the plenitude of power which Mr. Pelham had, there is an end of this administration, and of all that you and I wish well to in that respect. He would also by his connection in a certain place [Duke of Cumberland] have another power added to it, which Mr. Pelham had not for several years, the army.

It is straining credulity to believe in the sincerity of this fear of Cumberland and Fox. Hardwicke writes of them as might Osman II of his corps of janissaries before his dethronement and murder. Yet there was no more devout and loyal supporter of the Throne than Cumberland, no more approved

*Add. MS. 32736, f. 413, Hardwicke to Newcastle, Sept. 3, 1754: "There are some who will say that I threw out to the King a person to whom I knew he had an inclination, on purpose to defeat Mr. Fox: though your Grace knows *that* was not the case and that no hint was given of Sir Thos. Robinson till after Mr. Fox had refused and the King had put a negative on Mr. Pitt."

† Earl Waldegrave, *Memoirs*, p. 22.

‡ Lord Chancellor to the Archbishop of Canterbury, March 11, 1754.

§ *Ibid.*

and convinced adherent of the Constitution than Fox. However, the motives at work are of but secondary interest. What is clear is that the two Ministers so long and faithfully conjoined in the political arena were determined to distribute as little as possible of the power they enjoyed, and that in all they did they acted in harmony. Fortunately for the course of British history, it was their last success in the frustration of talent. Never again were they to bar the door. A power was growing which they could not curtail. In due course retribution was to attend their singular and fatal blindness to the claims of Fox and the genius of Pitt.

The situation, and it is one that has been the subject of an amount of investigation out of proportion to its importance, was described with far more accuracy than is generally found in contemporary explanations by Horace Walpole.* On the day after Pelham's death, when Fox after his first uneasy search for favour had subsided into a more decent quiescence, and when Pitt taking his survey of the situation and swathed in bandages at Bath was issuing his first suggestions to his followers, Walpole wrote:

> The three apparent candidates are Fox, Pitt, and Murray; †
> all three with such incumbrances on their hopes as make
> them very desperate. The Chancellor hates Fox; the Duke
> of Newcastle does not (I don't say, love him, but to speak
> in the proper phrase, does not) pretend to love him: the
> Scotch abominate him, and they and the Jacobites make use
> of his connexion with the Duke [Cumberland] to represent
> him as formidable: the Princess [Wales] cannot approve
> him for the same reason: the Law, as in duty bound to the
> Chancellor and to Murray, and to themselves, whom he
> always attacks, must dislike him. He has his parts and
> the Whigs, and the seeming right of succession. Pitt has
> no health, no party, and has, what in *this* case is allowed
> to operate, the King's negative. Murray is a Scotchman,
> and it has been suspected, of the worst dye: add a little of
> the Chancellor's jealousy: all three are obnoxious to the
> probability of the other two being disobliged by a preference.
> There is no doubt but the Chancellor and the Duke of New-

* *Letters*, III, p. 216, Walpole to Mann, March 7, 1754.
† The claim of Murray at this time was scarcely considered.

castle will endeavour to secure their own power, by giving an exclusion to Fox: each of them has even been talked of for Lord Treasurer; I say talked of, though Mr. Pelham died but yesterday; but you can't imagine how much a million of people can talk in a day on such a subject! It was even much imagined yesterday, that Sir George Lee would be the Hulla,* to wed the post, till things are ripe for divorcing him again.

Hardwicke having the ear of the King inspired him with the view that a separation should be made of the offices held by Pelham. It was agreed between them that the matter should be referred to the Lords of the Cabinet Council. Hardwicke explained this in a letter to the Archbishop of Canterbury, for whose benefit he drafted the terms of his Grace's reply concurring in the suggestion that the office of First Commissioner of the Treasury should be filled by the Duke of Newcastle, and the office of Chancellor of the Exchequer by someone to be nominated from the House of Commons—as barefaced a case of packing the jury as could be imagined. The meeting was held on March 12. The Archbishop wrote as directed. The Minute was unanimously passed.† The King acquiesced with the terms of the Minute. The Duke of Newcastle became Prime Minister and Mr. Legge Chancellor of the Exchequer.

Thus the first move was very visibly in favour of the existing combination. The next step was the least straightforward of the whole transaction. Obviously recognition had to be given to the claims of Fox. How could this be effected without any substantive increase of power? The problem was solved by the offer to Fox of the office of Secretary of State for the Southern Department with the leadership of the House of Commons. The offer was accepted. The next day Fox learnt from Newcastle himself that, although leader

* "Nom que l'on donne en Turquie à celui qui devient pour un seul jour l'époux d'une femme répudiée, afin que le premier mari puisse légalement la reprendre" (Littré).

† Those present were: Lord President, Lord Chancellor, Lord Steward, Lord Chamberlain, Duke of Devonshire, Duke of Argyll, Marquis of Hartington, Earl of Holdernesse, Lord Anson.

of the House, he was to have no hand in the disposal of the secret service money, and that both in Ministerial nominations and the management of the coming general election, arrangements were only to be communicated to him after they had been made. This was a complete departure from what had been understood when the offer was made and accepted. It meant place without power, promotion without aggrandisement. Fox had been shamelessly outmanœuvred. He might well feel, as Walpole writes, "that he was bubbled." * Newcastle had shown himself an astute tactician, and was resolute to hold the results of his work. His procedure even had the effect of increasing the King's respect for him. The King was no more indifferent to success than the humblest of his subjects, and within a few weeks Newcastle, in high spirits, had the satisfaction of being told by George II that he regarded him as the "best Secretary of State he had ever had," † a circumstance he "could hardly write without blushing," even to Hardwicke. Hardwicke replied with many congratulations, and to cheer still further the Duke, who was expected at Wimpole, ended his letter: "Your Grace may be assured that your Bed is thoroughly air'd: for it has been lain in this fortnight." ‡ Airing of beds was a hobby of Newcastle; even on the Royal yacht he was never satisfied until he had learnt that some of the ship's crew had been detailed to air his own and the Duchess's bed by sleeping therein. But in spite of the King's short-sighted commendation Newcastle, together with Hardwicke, had been playing against Fox with loaded dice. Moreover it was quite useless to argue with the Prime Minister. He had won, and meant to enjoy the fruits of his victory. Fox consulted Cumberland § as to what he should do. Cumberland very strongly counselled resignation. He considered that the terms of the offer had been infringed before even they were ratified. ‖ Cumberland by this time was thoroughly convinced that no more good was to be derived from the con-

---

* Walpole, *Memoirs*, I, p. 383.
† Add. MS. 32734, f. 392, Newcastle to Hardwicke, Sept. 1, 1754.
‡ Add. MS. 32734, f. 436, Hardwicke to Newcastle, Sept. 7, 1754.
§ Walpole, *Memoirs*, I, p. 384.
‖ *Ibid.*

tinuance of Newcastle in power. On the other hand, he wanted Fox as Secretary at War. Storm centres were forming in Europe, the scene in America was threatening and charged with menace, there was needed in authority at home a statesman capable of vigorous and decisive action. It was no moment for a hesitating and tentative policy, the time for going up and down Europe driving bargains with minor Princes was past, the economy and caution of Pelham had to give way to more effective methods. The country was drifting, and neither accomplishing its aims on the Continent nor preparing for war with sufficient insistence at home. Such was the view of Cumberland. And to remedy this state of things the sooner Fox was in power the better. Pending that contingency Cumberland considered Fox more likely to be useful as Secretary at War. On March 14 Fox resigned the office of Secretary of State.

Meanwhile by March 15 Newcastle, " this august remnant of the Pelhams," had so far surmounted his grief as to appear at Court. There sinking down and bursting into tears he had to be assisted into the royal presence by two Yeomen of the Guard, and when deprived of this support flung himself at the King's feet, crying " God bless your Majesty! God preserve your Majesty!" and if Walpole is to be credited, " lay there howling and embracing His Majesty's knees." * The outcome of the interview was the appointment of Sir Thomas Robinson as leader of the House. " The Duke might as well have sent us his jack boot to lead us," was the comment of Pitt.† To some, however, it was preferable to be governed by the King's Boot rather than by Mr. Pitt's Legge.‡

Sir Thomas Robinson, now after a long and honourable career in diplomacy emerging on a stormy sea of political strife, was unfortunate in the moment of his new publicity. Born in 1695, after a career of some distinction at Trinity College, Cambridge, he entered the diplomatic service, and in

* *Letters*, III, p. 220, Walpole to Richard Bentley, March 17, 1754.

† Leadam, *The Political History of England*, 1702–1760, p. 430.

‡ Holland House MS., Hanbury-Williams to Fox, Feb. 15, 1757. " I would rather be governed by the King's Boot than Mr. Pitt's Legge."

1730 was appointed ambassador at the Court of Vienna. There for eighteen years his efforts were directed to stabilising relations with that elusive ally of Britain, and during the precarious period of the War of the Austrian Succession to reconciling the Empress Maria Theresa to the loss of Silesia and to the repugnant necessity of negotiating with Frederick. The Empress's hesitation to join in the general pacification in 1748 led to his recall from Vienna and his appointment as joint plenipotentiary with Lord Sandwich in the peace negotiations at Aix-la-Chapelle. Here his relations with Newcastle became of a more confidential character, and to his diplomatic functions was added the business of scrutinising the correspondence of Sandwich and reporting to Newcastle any symptoms of independence which might be shown by that wilful and mutinous young peer.*

In 1748 he was returned to the House of Commons for Christchurch. No record exists of his having spoken in Parliament before his appointment as Secretary of State, but it seems that as a diplomatist he would address the Court to which he was accredited, and Frederick, with whom he negotiated, in a " wordy high droning way as if he were speaking in Parliament," and on occasions could move Maria Theresa to tears by his eloquence. He stood high in favour with the King, whom he had represented abroad with discernment and credit, and to whom he was endeared by his knowledge of foreign affairs and his sympathy with the King's German interests. In 1750 he enjoyed with numerous others, including Horace Walpole, the fame of being robbed by the fashionable highwayman, McLean, who by his sallies from his lodgings in St. James's Street had added to the perils which even then made of Hyde Park a scene of adventure and an area not lightly to be traversed in the hours of darkness. On the fall of Bedford, Robinson was already spoken of as a possible Secretary of State; but it was not till the death of Pelham that he received a definite offer of the post. While worthily transacting the administrative side of his office, he was so alien to the manner and temper of the House of Commons in his form of oratory, effective though it had been with Maria Theresa,

* See page 19 ante

that even those who loved and esteemed him were on occasions unable "to preserve a friendly composure of countenance." * To George II this was a consideration of little importance, and after six months' experience he was able to tell Newcastle that, with the exception of Newcastle himself, he regarded Robinson as the best Secretary of State he had ever had.† Robinson as leader in the Commons might have remained for better or for worse inconspicuous, had he not been rendered notorious by the attitude of Fox and Pitt.

When Newcastle apologised to Pitt for the necessity of placing Robinson in his then position, he described him as "An honourable and able man, extremely well qualified in every respect for the execution of that office—and who without departing from that rank and figure which belonged to his office, had not those parliamentary talents which could give jealousy, or in that light set him above the rest of the King's servants there." ‡ That indicated with some exactness the unfortunate position Robinson was called on to occupy. But it was not only in the House of Commons that he was to give no jealousy—the claim was to be of more general application, and had he not been the creature of Newcastle he might have continued in office. Be that as it may, if Newcastle had any hopes that Robinson would be able to tire the bowling, he was speedily disillusioned. No sooner had the new Parliament assembled than Pitt and Fox, his colleagues in the Government, set to work to undermine Robinson's authority and expose his unfitness for the position—a task highly congenial to such masters of Parliamentary dialectic, and carried out with obvious relish till a change in political circumstances brought their alliance to an end. In November 1755 Robinson resigned the seals which had proved so burdensome, and became Master of the Wardrobe with a pension on the Irish establishment. In April 1761 he was raised to the peerage as Baron Grantham, and died in 1770.

* Waldegrave, *Memoirs*, p. 32.
† Add. MS. 32734, f. 392, Newcastle to Hardwicke, Sept. 1, 1754.
‡ *Chatham Correspondence*, p. 97, Newcastle to Pitt, April 2, 1754.

CHAPTER X

CUMBERLAND was now a well-defined figure in the political life of the country, nor is it difficult to discern the object he had in view. He saw the power in the State tending to become a monopoly in the hand of Newcastle; he saw the House of Commons, in the words of Pitt, " only sitting to register the arbitrary edicts of one too powerful subject."

It became therefore his purpose to infringe and break down that monopoly, and so secure that abler men should be free to step in and assist in the administration of the country's affairs. His friend Fox he regarded as the head of the assaulting column, and Fox was quite willing to have his movements directed by the Captain General. Cumberland therefore welcomed and encouraged the alliance between Fox and Pitt which Newcastle had indirectly brought about, and, as will be presently shown, deprecated the severance of the alliance when political changes rendered its dissolution imminent.

Apart from politics, little is known of his movements during the early fifties. In 1750 his former tutor, Stephen Poyntz, died, and Cumberland at once made an allowance out of his own purse of eight hundred pounds a year to the two sons and sent them to the Continent, at the same time securing places for his other children.* Those who would enforce the accepted view that Cumberland was a bye-word for harshness and brutality, may well soften their opinion by the record of this and kindred acts of humanity. He resided at this time either at Windsor Great Lodge or St. James's Palace. He was, as is well known, a regular attendant at Newmarket and other race meetings.†

* Walpole, *Letters*, III, p. 25, Walpole to Mann, Dec. 19, 1750.
† See post, p. 212.

In connection with pugilism, which at one time claimed his most intimate support, he is heard of no more. The blow which defeated his famous protégé Jack Broughton, in his contest with Jack Slack, while incidentally it cost the Duke £10,000 in bets,* appears at the same time to have put an end to his interest in boxing.

Occasionally he is heard of at Woburn, or staying with his sister at Gunnersbury, and Walpole records a visit to Strawberry Hill in terms which leave no doubt that the Duke's bulk did not decrease, little as he allowed it to interfere with his recreations and activities.

> Nolkejumskoi [wrote Walpole] has been to see it [Strawberry Hill].† I can't conceive how he entered it. I should have figured him like Gulliver cutting down some of the largest oaks in Windsor Forest to make joint stools in order to straddle over the battlements and peep in at the windows of Lilliput."

He was a familiar figure at masquerades, against which the Puritan spirit was constantly murmuring its protests, and he was a great frequenter of Ranelagh and Vauxhall, then at the zenith of their fame. Less than most things do the recreations of succeeding generations vary one from another. Under different forms and under varying banners the same objective of social communion, of meeting in the market-place, of eating and drinking, of dancing or of listening to music, and of staring and being stared at, is catered for and achieved. And though to more sophisticated seekers after pleasure the forms in use at Ranelagh and Vauxhall wear an air of tameness, in essentials they differ not from those of to-day. The famous Rotunda at Ranelagh not only offered facilities for promenading with the throng on the circumferences of imaginary circles at varying distances from the great fireplace in the centre of the building, but here the visitor could listen to an admirable orchestra or enjoy the skill of Dr. Burney on the organ, or if not feasting himself could stare at the parties supping in the tiers of boxes that adorned the sides of the amphitheatre. Here it was that Dr. Johnson experienced " an expansion and

---

* See *William Augustus Duke of Cumberland*, p. 291.
† Walpole, *Letters*, III, p. 210.

gay sensation of the mind, such as he never experienced any-
where else." And here society moved and displayed its lighter
side for the purpose of recreation through many years.
Canaletto thought its proportions worthy of record on canvas,
and every memoir of the time pays a tribute to its artistic
pretensions and the liveliness of its atmosphere.

Vauxhall, situated opposite the present Tate Gallery, was more
extensive and ambitious in its resources; there for the payment
of one shilling the visitor could wander through gardens,
through avenues and bosquets, could admire flowing waters
and cascades and artificial grottos, and dazzle himself with
the illumination provided by a thousand lamps. On special
occasions he could witness a firework display, and at all times
there were to be had good eating and drinking, chicken and
slices of ham renowned for the wafer-like thinness with which
they were cut, with a regale of coffee and tea. If the pleasure
was to be enhanced, the excitement to be made more sensational,
a party would embark in a barge at Whitehall stairs or the
Temple, and so, either floating on the tide or propelled by
watermen and accompanied by an orchestra or a "music of
French horns" conveyed in a corresponding craft, the revellers
would come to the witchery of Vauxhall with "the fragrancy
of its walks and bowers, and the choirs of Birds that sing
upon the trees." The very process of landing could be one not
devoid of incident, and to not a few must have occurred the
experience of Cumberland, who on one occasion fell gigantically
between the vessel and the stairs into the waters of the Thames.
If across the years the pleasures of Vauxhall and Ranelagh
appear to us a little remote or insipid, and their significance
falls rather faint on ears which would catch something of
the music they played to their generation, we have to recognise
that they formed a generous part of the life of the day, of
its laughter, its gaiety and intrigue.

In London Cumberland was a familiar figure in the Mall as
he passed from St. James's Palace to the Horse Guards at
Whitehall (the offices newly erected—1752—from designs by
William Kent), where the chiefs of the Army were already
installed. At other times he was to be seen walking with his
father, a circumstance which the *Gentleman's Magazine* would

have us believe was a source of delight to those fortunate
enough to be witnesses of the spectacle.   Indeed in a family so
subject to violent strains it was a scene not destitute either of
domestic or political significance.*   Or again he was to be
heard of sauntering in Hyde Park with Lady Coventry,† to
whom he was at that time (1754) devoting his attention.
How far his suit was favoured there is nothing to indicate.
Lady Coventry was well known at any rate to have other
commitments.   Like her sister the Duchess of Hamilton, Lady
Coventry was famed not only for her beauty, which excited
something approaching a national interest, but also for the
lack of felicity in her sayings.   To George II she said that
she was tired of masquerades and surfeited with most sights,
and that what she most wanted to see was a coronation—a
story repeated afterwards by the old King with great good
humour.‡

Meanwhile during these years Cumberland had been regaining his popularity.   Once more he had become a great
figure in the State, acclaimed by the populace when he appeared
at reviews and inspections; § esteemed by those in authority
for his judgment, and looked up to by a considerable party
in Parliament.   He was no longer pursued by the misrepre-
sentations of Leicester House; he had ceased to be good copy
for the Jacobites.   The abuse which had followed Culloden
had died down; and as Jacobitism each year became a fainter
political cry, so did the gratitude to Cumberland for his victory
in Scotland reassert itself in the nation.   Here and there were
still to be heard reverberations of the Stuart cause; information was constantly trickling through to the Ministry; Pickle
the Spy, Young Glengarry, was busy transmitting intelligence
from the Continent; rumours of plots, of a rising in London,
of a projected expedition to Scotland, of utterly wild and
impossible schemes, would hold attention for a moment and
then flicker away into nothingness.   And Charles himself,

* Walpole, *Letters*, III, p. 419.
† Formerly Miss Gunning.   Her sister married first the Duke of
Hamilton, secondly the Duke of Argyll.
‡ Walpole, *Letters*, III, p. 407.
§ See *Gentleman's Magazine*, XXV, p. 327.

still the symbol of a generous cause, still the idol of a romantic loyalty, was now drifting an ineffectual figure across the face of Europe, unespoused by the Courts to which he turned for help. He is heard of in Sweden, or in Berlin, or in Paris, or in Basel. Few disguises were strange to him. Few hiding-places were unknown to him. At different times he appears as an Abbé or a lacquey, or with blackened eyebrows, or a painted face, or as a friar, and so slinks through dark streets to dingy inns and secret meetings with his followers or with foreign emissaries; always spied on, but at times baffling pursuit, his movements shrouded under a veil of mystification, his identity lost to the most vigilant of his observers; at one time promised help from Prussia, at another encouraged by the Court of France, exalted for a moment to serve a purpose and create embarrassments for England, then as cynically cast aside and disavowed.

In 1750 he was undoubtedly in hiding for some days in London, rubbing shoulders with the populace he still sought to rule, viewing that capital which, on January 7, 1744, he had left Rome disguised as a Spanish courier to conquer, and catching sight, it well may be, of the soldier who had crushed his aspiration for a crown on the field of Culloden. It was on this occasion also that, in a belated bid for Protestant support, he was received into the Anglican Communion. Later there are grounds for the belief that he was again in England in 1752, in furtherance of one of those vain and restless projects which periodically disturbed the equanimity of Whitehall and stirred sleeping hopes among the faithful. Then once more he becomes the wanderer on the Continent, resumes his disguises, intrigues with foreign Ministers, hopes against hope for some turn of destiny, and so continues till the death of James his father in 1766, when he retreats a discredited exile to a Court of meaningless ceremonial and shadowy tradition in Rome. "My heart is broke enough, without that you should finish it," he had written in 1754 to Earl Marischal. It needed no Earl Marischal to accomplish that end. Charles was fallen from his high estate, and in the sorry figure that presided at Rome was seen the final solution of all fears of a Jacobite restoration.

The management of the House of Commons in the new Parliament elected in April 1754, when Newcastle's wire-pulling had been so successful that only forty-two seats were contested, had become increasingly difficult. Throughout the session Pitt and Fox were carrying on a veiled but studied opposition to the leadership of Sir Thomas Robinson. Holdernesse, Newcastle, and Hardwicke were not very successfully trying to dig themselves in and hold the position without any change in the tactical disposition of their forces. Moreover the King seemed well disposed towards Fox. Fox was making frequent visits to Lady Yarmouth. He had actually bragged in public that Lady Yarmouth had lent him her post-chaise.* He had been invited by Lord Hartington to a formal meeting with young Mr. Walmoden, the son of Lady Yarmouth.† He was being received at the King's Levées ‡ with decided cordiality, and in the closet had gone so far as to attack Holdernesse. "Mon ami Monsieur Fox," wrote Holdernesse to Newcastle, "m'a donné un plat de son métier et a tâché de m'appliquer un coup de grife dans le cabinet." § To Newcastle these trifling occurrences were more than mere straws in the wind, they were indications of an altogether alarming drift in Royal favour, and always in the background was Cumberland, a menace not easy to deal with. It was difficult also to appreciate how far Cumberland's authority extended, and to what degree he was calling the tune. By September 1754 it was clear to the governing Junta that something must be done, and that Fox or Pitt or both of them must be called in to garrison the citadel of power.

It all tends to one point [wrote Hardwicke] to prove the necessity of a single leader in the House of Commons, and they know that as the King is prejudiced against others, that must centre in Mr. Fox. When that is attained in the degree they mean it, there will, in my apprehension, be an end of your Grace's chief power as the Minister of this country.||

* Add. MS. 32736, f. 388, Newcastle to Hardwicke, Sept. 1, 1754.
† *Ibid.*
‡ *Ibid.*, f. 392, Newcastle to Hardwicke, Sept. 3, 1754.
§ *Ibid.*, f. 330, Holdernesse to Newcastle, Aug. 24, 1754.
|| *Ibid.*, f. 584, Hardwicke to Newcastle, Sept. 27, 1754.

Curiously enough Newcastle had come to the same conclusion, and almost at the same time was writing to Hardwicke:

> Thus the grand secret is out the Three Great men Fox,
> Pitt and Legge have agreed upon this Principle that there
> must be a Minister in the House of Commons and the two
> first or perhaps all three think they have a chance for it.*

This letter had been preceded by an uncommonly disagreeable interview with Legge, who had told Newcastle that the
cards must be new shuffled, that Fox must be promoted, means
be adopted to satisfy Cumberland, and Lord Sandwich be
given a pension, adding that " the House of Commons would
not go on without a Minister in it, a Cabinet Councillor if you
will, who shall go to the King *himself* and speak from *himself*."† So long as the House of Commons could be kept
from representing public opinion, so long as it could be filled
with placemen and nominees and the creatures of the ruling
Minister, it was possible to depress the power of that House.
But this state of things was coming to an end, and in the letters
quoted above is to be found a recognition, dimly entertained,
that a new phase was opening in Parliamentary history. Fox
and Pitt, and with them Cumberland, had each been assisting
in his own way to bring it about. It meant that the House of
Commons was to be given its due voice in the government of
the country, and public opinion a freer say in the conduct of
affairs. It meant that a force more powerful than corruption
was coming into existence, and that the day of mere management was drawing to a close.

By December Newcastle's plan of operations was complete.
Fox was to be detached from Pitt. Cumberland foresaw what
was intended, and recognised the danger that would attend a
separation of the two statesmen. He warned Fox. He coun-
selled him not to abandon Pitt. " I don't know him," he said to
Fox, " but by what you tell me, Pitt is what is scarce, a man.
If they should give you this Cabinet-Counsellor's place and
Pitt should hereafter attack the Duke of Newcastle, and you

---

* Add. MS. 32736, f. 591, Newcastle to Hardwicke, Sept. 28, 1754.
† *Ibid.*

should not defend him, they will say you have broke your word." In a letter written on November 27, 1754, after stating that he regarded Fox's decision as " more critical than when Mr. Pelham died," he advised Fox in these terms:

> If you should have improper offers from the Duke of Newcastle, I hope you'll desire to give your answer to the King yourself, and without mentioning what is pass'd, repeat your promises of not opposing and declining the offers, as they would not enable you to remedy the disorders now risen in the House of Commons.*

But the idea of promotion had been too insistent in Fox's mind to be put aside. In a humble letter he submitted the terms on which he could accept. On December 12 † it was intimated to him by Newcastle that he was to be admitted to the Cabinet. The intimation emphasised the limitation to which it was subject. " It was not," wrote Newcastle, " intended by the King in the least to interfere with or derogate from the Priority belonging to His Majesty's Secretary of State in the House of Commons." Thus it was really no more than an attempt to underpin the precarious authority of Robinson, and mitigate some of the hazards which threatened that Minister's troubled tenure of office.

* Lord Ilchester, *Henry Fox, first Lord Holland*, I, p. 233.
† Much confusion has arisen owing to the erroneous dating of letters in the *Chatham Correspondence*. Lord Ilchester has finally cleared the matter up. See his *Life of Henry Fox*.

8

CHAPTER XI

THE Speech from the Throne at the beginning of the session in November 1754 was, except for a guarded reference to "protecting those possessions which make one great source of our commerce and wealth," remarkable for its reticence on the prospects of peace and war. No such reticence, however, was observed in the Debate on the Address. The speeches of Members of the House of Commons were concerned with pressing on the Government the desirability of immediate action, and discussing the strategy to be adopted in the almost inevitable event of war with France. In those years relations with foreign Powers were referred to on the floor of the House with a degree of freedom and provocation that seems astonishing to later and more circumspect generations. Seldom was any effort made to mask or palliate the asperities of an international situation. In debates on the Army or Navy, it was considered superfluous to veil the truth in the form of a hypothetical case, or to prefer suggestion and innuendo to the cruder method of direct designation. France was the enemy. That was the accepted postulate of every discussion. The dictum of Lord Grantham, "I hate the French, and I hope as how we shall beat the French," was the traditional view * and expressed the current sense of the nation. And, however delicate the negotiations being carried on by secret diplomacy might be, so far as public discussion on foreign affairs was concerned the susceptibilities not only of France but of other nations as well were allowed little recognition in debate. Thus, though a declaration of war was to be delayed for nearly two years, and the course of negotiations between Versailles and London gave hope at that time for a peaceful issue, we find a Minister of the Crown (Henry Fox), in discussing the extension of the

* Lord Hervey *Memoirs*, I, p. 42.

Mutiny Bill to North America in December 1754, speaking of "our success in the war now like to happen," while every speech in the debate treated of the measure in relation to its effect on the troops to be engaged against France.

Though such references would ill accord with modern practice, they do not appear to have affected the course of events or to have done anything to retard or accelerate the hour of the conflict. But it is necessary briefly to recall the well-known events which were leading up to the outbreak of the Seven Years' War, and direct attention to the considerable part which Cumberland played in the shaping of them.

The failure of the Treaty of Aix-la-Chapelle to settle the question of boundaries between France and England on the American continent had left open a field of dispute, bristling with difficulties and opportunities for hostile action. On the one hand were the English Colonies on the seaboard of the Atlantic divided from the interior by the formidable and desolate ranges of the Alleghanies; on the other were the French, who, having seized the St. Lawrence and planted the Fleur de Lys in Louisiana, were indomitably penetrating south from Canada and north along the waters of the Mississippi, thus tending to effect a junction between their northern and southern possessions and hem the British settlers into the area between the sea and the mountains. Here then were all the elements of conflict.

Traders from the British settlements were continually pressing westwards across the mountains down into the fertile valleys towards which the French were extending their posts from the north; support from France and England to the claims and activities of their respective settlers was given with reluctance or with freedom according as the negotiations between the two countries faltered or progressed. France, however, was the more adroit in catering for the needs of her colonists. By those on the spot no stone was left unturned, no agency was neglected to secure the goodwill of the Indians. Not wholly realising the challenge offered to their supremacy, the Five Nations which comprised the Indians inhabiting the central region from the great lakes southward were divided amongst themselves, siding now with the French and now with the English. Trade, religion, bribery, menace, and cajolery were each in turn made to serve the supreme end of securing a friendly footing with the tribes. French missionaries, with intrepid activity, were untiring in their efforts to convert them to the Faith. The zeal with which the missionaries proclaimed the Kingdom of Christ was accompanied by unremitting vigilance in extending the empire of the Most Christian King, and inspiring their converts with fear and hatred of the English race while inciting them to attacks on English settlers. The French, indeed, with more fervour for the country of their origin, enjoying the advantages of unity of administration and command, their fidelity not shaken like that of the English, by a series of insensate restrictive enactments, and receiving from Europe a greater degree of encouragement than the English settlers, were pressing forward on strategic lines and slowly diminishing the unclaimed area to the west of the Alleghanies. They were showing promptitude and foresight. They were forestalling and checking at many points the activities of the English traders. They were conducting to an inevitable collision the claims of the two great Powers of Europe.

The establishment and demolition of forts and stations, the advance and withdrawal of outposts of empire, the fluctuation of dealings with the Indians, the ebb and flow of the claims of possession, the alternations of success and failure in trading enterprise—these were the occurrences in progress since the Treaty of Aix-la-Chapelle which, centring for the most part about the headwaters of the Ohio, were to light a conflagration in Europe and usher in the Seven Years' War.

In Nova Scotia, or Acadia as it was then called, the rivalry of the two nations was even more active and acute. Louisbourg, wrested by the enterprise of the Colonies during the War of the Austrian Succession from the French, had been restored to France by the treaty of 1749. In that year, as has already been shown, at the instance of Cumberland and Lord Halifax, a party of emigrants, mostly disbanded soldiers and their families, embarked for Acadia, and landing in June at Chibucto, on the south coast of the peninsula, began that settlement which was to form the town of Halifax. Each succeeding year saw a fresh influx of emigrants from the mother country. By the year 1752, the population of the town numbered over four thousand. In the growth of Halifax the French recognised a possible menace to Louisbourg and their position in Canada. Their policy, under La Jonquière, governor of Louisbourg, encouraged at intervals from Versailles, was steadily directed to spreading disaffection among the Acadians who had been declared by the Treaty of Utrecht to be British subjects, to stirring up the Indians to harass the settlers of Halifax, and to defeating the measures of security taken by Cornwallis, the governor of the Colony. Here again French Missionaries were tireless in their endeavours to seduce the Acadians from their rightful allegiance and withdraw from the British jurisdiction. By prompting the Indians to acts of savagery against the inhabitants, by withholding the sacrament and suspending their religious ministrations, by the offer of land and monetary support, the missionaries, directed by the famous Monsieur l'Abbé Le Loutre, were successful in drawing off numbers of the Acadians and establishing them in French territory.* Aggression by one side was followed by aggression on the other, thrust by counter-thrust, claim by counter-claim. Yet in Europe the nations remained at peace, and in Paris, year after year, the Commission appointed to settle the question of boundaries between France and England in America dragged out its ineffectual existence, examining archives and precedents, piling document upon document and drafting interminable reports, while across the Atlantic the destiny of empire was being disputed, if not in terms of war, at least by acts which bore the character of covert hostility. The struggle in Acadia indeed was a struggle between national temperaments and methods. On one side the French, bold, impetuous, and at the same time subtle, neglecting no means of policy to attain the end in view, inspired by an emotional patriotism, and suffering considerations of legality to be swept aside in the zeal of their enterprise; on the other the English, deploying their spirit of political tolerance, patiently pursuing a policy open to the world, methodically encroaching on their opponents, carrying forbearance almost to a point of weakness, and seeking by conciliation to counteract the more violent and less conscientious methods of the French.

* Parkman, *Montcalm and Wolfe*, I, p. 105 et seq.

Newcastle, writing to Albemarle, then Ambassador in Paris, in October 1754,* summarised the proceedings of the French as follows:

> Every year since the peace, troops have been sent from Europe to the Mississippi and Canada, Indians have been collected, with which Force they have actually hostilely invaded our possessions, drove us from our Forts and are making a chain from Canada to the ocean by the Mississippi to cut off all our colonies from commerce with the Indians, and building forts on the back of our possessions on ground actually belonging to the Crown of Great Britain, all this done in full peace without saying one word of it to us and in breach of the agreement that nothing of the kind should be done till the Commission had reported on the boundaries.

The description was fully justified. In 1753 the Marquis Duquesne, the new governor of Canada, in pursuance of the French policy of aggression, launched an expedition with the object of taking definite and final possession of the headwaters of the Ohio. Before the summer of that year had passed, the French had established themselves at Presqu'isle and Fort-le-Bœuf, thereby gaining access to the Alleghany River and the main stream of the Ohio. Here they prepared to winter, ready in the following spring to continue their southward march. But news of the movement had reached Robert Dinwiddie, the governor of Virginia. To leave the French action unchallenged was tantamount to an admission of the legality of their possession. He had communicated with the Government at home. In reply he had received instructions, dated August 23, 1753. He had been told to build forts on the Ohio at the cost of the Colony, and that if any number of persons should presume to erect any fort within the limits of the province of Virginia, he was to require them peaceably to depart, and in the event of their failing to do so, he was authorised to expel them by force.

> I must desire you to acquaint me [accordingly wrote Dinwiddie to Legardeur de Saint-Pierre, commander of Fort-le-Bœuf] by whose authority and instructions you have

* Add. MS. 32851, f. 51, Newcastle to Albemarle, Oct. 16, 1754.

lately marched from Canada with an armed force, and invaded the King of Britain's territories. It becomes my duty to require your peaceable departure, and that you would forbear prosecuting a purpose so interruptive of the harmony and good understanding which His Majesty is desirous to continue and cultivate with the Most Christian King.

Thus it was that while this advance guard of the French was abiding the passage of the winter, remote from civilisation, but secure in their desolate and now strongly stockaded post, a youth in his twenty-second year, with a guide and a handful of followers, was threading his way across wilderness and forest, often deep in snow, and through territory ranged by Indians, bearing the momentous despatch from Dinwiddie. On the evening of December 11, a few moments after sunset, French officers in Fort-le-Bœuf were roused from the monotony of their winter routine by a figure on horseback issuing from the forest and approaching the cleared space by which their fort was surrounded. It was the bearer of the challenge from Virginia. Reading the document after the explanatory formalities of greeting had been exchanged, they learnt that the name of the youth before them, who bore all the marks of the hardships to which for weeks he had been exposed, was George Washington. History might be ransacked in vain for an equally dramatic conjuncture or for a moment holding so great a measure of hidden destiny. Washington was at the time Adjutant-General of the Virginia militia. As a British subject he was carrying the formal challenge of the Crown of Britain to the right of the Crown of France to invade lands which were ultimately to be owned by neither Britain nor France, but by a nation not yet in being, of which he was to be the first and one of the greatest rulers. But for the moment he was concerned with defeating the aims of France. Saint-Pierre in reply stated that he would forward Dinwiddie's despatch to the Marquis Duquesne, meanwhile remaining in possession of the territory he had invaded.

By the middle of January 1754 Washington was back in Williamsburg, and had reported to Governor Dinwiddie the result of his mission. There now became apparent the need of a directing force in colonial policy. It was in vain that

Dinwiddie appealed to the neighbouring states and exhorted them to vote money and men for an offensive against the French. Knit by no common bond, unless a certain critical aloofness from the mother country could be so described, each with its own constitution, its own special characteristics of religion, of politics, of trade, and even in some cases of race, the states composing the North American colonies viewed with very different eyes the advance of the French. Virginia, it was said, was the colony primarily concerned. Virginia must therefore deal with the situation. The absence of co-operation was complete, united action was not to be hoped for. Indeed a union between the colonies was no part of the policy of the mother country. As late as September 1754, when the necessity for such a union had become doubly urgent and obvious, and after Cumberland had again and again pressed on the Government the necessity for a measure of this kind, Newcastle was still afraid that there was an " independency upon this country [England] being to be apprehended from such an Union." * With such views entertained at home, co-operation on the other side of the Atlantic in the cause of the mother country was a counsel of perfection. North Carolina alone responded to Dinwiddie's appeal. Finally, with the assistance of two independent companies in New York and one in South Carolina, a force was got together, under orders from the Home Government, and in the spring of the year launched on the fatal expedition which had for its object the construction of a fort on the falls of the Ohio. In August news reached the Ministry in London that Washington with his whole force had capitulated at Fort Necessity after a fight against a superior body of French and Indians, and withdrawn with the honours of war.

* Add. MS. 32736, f. 554, Newcastle to Hardwicke, Sept. 20, 1754.

CHAPTER XII

THE situation in America at this time has been described as a state of hostile intercourse short of war.* In so far as such a state could ever have obtained recognition in the comity of nations, it has now been rendered impossible by rapidity of communication. If we can conceive the news which reached Newcastle weeks after the event, arriving almost concurrently with its happening, we can then reconstitute the crisis that would have arisen. Representations would at once have been addressed to the French Government, satisfaction would have been required, and assurances of good faith demanded. In other words, the intention of the French Government would immediately have been tested. But arriving so long after the event, the news brought about no such crisis. It was impossible to say what had happened in the meanwhile; the matter was in the hands of the commanders on the spot. The French might have withdrawn or terms might have been negotiated. In any case it was not necessary to interpret what had occurred as evidence of intention. That was a matter which required further probing and discussion. Of course the cumulative effect of these proceedings might to some minds carry the conviction that war was intended. But that was a question of inference and opinion. That indeed was the difficulty and at the same time the weakness in the English Ministry's position. They still believed in the possibility of peace: they did not desire war themselves; but they had no means of knowing what France wanted—they could only surmise. The occurrences in America which to-day would either mean war, or an ultimatum followed by the giving of satisfaction,

* Julian Corbett, *England in the Seven Years' War*, I, p. 26. A number of caricatures at this time were published under the title of *Half Peace*.

in the eighteenth century denoted a middle state, one neither of peace nor of war. They left room for hopeful negotiation. To Cumberland, however, and those who thought with him, the matter presented no such difficulties. His mind was clear on the subject. From the first * he was convinced that France meant war; and he found confirmation for his conviction in every fresh manifestation of the state of "hostile intercourse." He did not believe in waiting till a formal declaration of war should set at rest all doubts as to intention. He was for forcing the pace. He was for a definite assertion of British rights in America by military means, not because he wanted war, but because he was convinced that France intended war and was in the meanwhile only amusing, to use a word of the period, the British Government with negotiations and proposals.

But not till September 1754 had the Captain General been consulted with regard to the action to be taken. After that date he plays an influential part in all discussions; his view runs clear and decided through the hesitations and pauses of Ministerial opinion. Convinced that war was inevitable, convinced, moreover, that England was in no condition to wage that war on the continent of Europe, he was for striking while there was time and striking hard both on the high seas and in North America. On September 15, 1754, Robinson informs Newcastle † that the King had given leave for Cumberland to be consulted as to the nomination of a general officer and half-pay officers for North America, and that Cumberland on being appealed to had said that he could not advise unless he knew "the extent of country to be defended, the particular places properest for operations, what were the number of forces to be employed, and what was to be the particular service of the half-pay officers, whether to discipline only the American troops or to be regimented." ‡

* Holland House MS., Cumberland to Fox, April 2, 1755: "The return of Mirepoix's courier does not alter my opinion in the least, for I always thought that France was resolved for War. Will the King still go abroad?"

† Add. MS. 32736, f. 529, Robinson to Newcastle, Sept. 15, 1754.

‡ Cumberland as early as April 2, 1755, was urging Fox to send off the recruits for Gibraltar and Minorca "without loss of time whilst the sea is still free" (Holland House MS.).

These were questions deeply embarrassing to the Ministry, who so long as there was a hope of peace appear to have seen no necessity for clear ideas on the steps to be taken in the event of war. Indeed, it was undoubtedly in a large degree due to Cumberland, as the unofficial head of the War Party, that the speeding up of definite preparations was forced on the Ministry and that they were driven into adopting immediate measures for the safety of the country. Newcastle was still endeavouring to keep alive that drooping relic of the past " the old system." Keith in Vienna and Joseph Yorke at the Hague were busy easing the constant friction over the Barrier Treaty. Kaunitz, on the other hand, was playing for time, entertaining overtures, but raising difficulties, leaning towards France, but professing faith in the old alliance. With Spain, however, Newcastle was successful, and an agreement made with that country stood out as a solid result of his policy, immensely lightening the load of European complications. At the same time he was bringing to completion an understanding with Russia which was to prove of incalculable advantage and exert a decisive influence on the new grouping of the Powers which, if not already in progress, was certainly in the making.

Lord Albemarle, the British Ambassador in Paris, popular with the Ministry and welcome at Versailles, but not altogether adequately equipped for reading the signs of the times or interpreting French intentions, continued to send reports from his embassy which did little to discourage hopes of peace. Rouillé, the new Minister, had said to him in conversation that, so far as North America was concerned, " if it were referred to two persons only such as the Earl of Holdernesse and the Duc de Mirepoix, they might finish the whole affair d'un seul coup de plume." Albemarle also drew favourable inferences from the attitude of Louis XV and Madame de Pompadour, who he said was at this period " toute puissante."[*] On this, Newcastle became assiduous in the exchange of courtesies with the favourite. In August he wrote:[†]

The King is delighted with your account of M. Pompadour's sense of His Majesty's regard for her. I ought not

[*] Add. MS. 32736, f. 76, Albemarle to Newcastle, Aug. 14, 1754.
[†] *Ibid.*, f. 4, Albemarle to Newcastle, Aug. 1, 1754.

to mention myself at the same time, but she has vouchsafed to send me the prettiest present imaginable and all our heads and hands are at work to send something proper in return. I took the liberty to thank her by a letter. I wish you could find out how it was taken.

Apparently it was taken in the way Newcastle desired. Within a few days he was able to write: * "I have had a most gracious letter from La Marquise which I shall keep with reverence and gratitude." It is a matter for regret that, as an exception to the documents which passed through the Duke's hands, this letter finds no place in the Newcastle Papers, and that we are therefore unable to form an idea of the terms which excited his reverence and gratitude. Thenceforward the barter of amenities between the Duke and the Marquise proceeded apace. From the fair hand of the Mistress came notes and compliments, offerings of liqueurs and elegant products of the craftsman's art from Paris; in return there reached her pineapples and others of the fruits of the earth from the famous garden at Claremont, adulatory letters inspired perhaps as much by the tickled vanity of the Duke as by the larger motive of peaceful relations, and promises of the produce of India in the shape of " spotted deer, antilopes and pheasants " for which she had expressed through the intermediary of Albemarle a strong inclination, while on another occasion a telescope figured among the marks of civility which the Duke was at pains to show.

The lighter side of the Duke's feverish activity also intrudes at this time into the diplomatic correspondence with Albemarle, in the shape of discussions about a chef for the Duke's table at Claremont and Newcastle House. Albemarle declared that there were not more than thirty chefs of the first order in the whole of Paris; but one of these he had secured for Newcastle, and had arranged that a dinner was to be cooked, half by his own chef, reputed the most famous in Paris, and half by Fontenelle, the aspirant to the Duke's employ, a tribunal of guests to determine to which should be awarded the palm. Newcastle had a well-grounded belief in the efficacy of turning

* Add. MS. 32736, f. 49, Newcastle to Albemarle, Aug. 8, 1754.

wine and cooking to political account, and in the shaping of party opinion at his dinner-table. A study of his lists of guests in the Newcastle Papers shows how judiciously he combined waverers with staunch supporters in the range of his hospitality.

In October the cause of peace had received a check. "A most ill-judged advertisement," wrote Newcastle to Albemarle on October 16,* "from the War Office has set all the foreign Ministers on fire and made them believe that we are going to war which is I hope the furthest from our thoughts." † The advertisement in question was a statement with regard to the measures to be adopted in North America. The matter had arisen in this way.

By September 1754 Newcastle had made up his mind that assistance must be sent to the Colonies. Shortly after news of the defeat of Washington had reached London he had written:

> All N. America will be lost if these practices are tolerated, and no war can be worse to this country than the suffering such insults as these. The truth is the French claim almost all N. America except a Lisière to the sea to which they would confine all our Colonies and from whence they may drive us whenever they please or as soon as there shall be a declared war. But that is what we must not, we will not, suffer.‡

Nor could the most ardent militarist have looked for a stouter declaration of imperial faith. The proposal subsequently formulated was to send "the Highland regiment and to raise Independent Highland companies." This proposal was sub-

---

* Add. M.S. 32851, f. 51, Newcastle to Albemarle, Oct. 10, 1754.

† Albemarle replied to this, October 28: "By the nature of our Constitution nothing is kept from the knowledge of the whole world, even intentions and thoughts are guessed at and made publick by those abominable writers of Daily papers. In this country I experience every day the reverse, secrecy is recommended everywhere and nothing transpires till the King their Master's will is put in execution."

‡ Add. MS. 32850, f. 218, Newcastle to Albemarle, Sept. 5, 1754.

mitted to Cumberland, who at once negatived it, his opinion being that

> It would be better to send immediately two Regiments upon the Irish Establishment and upon their present low footing, to be compleated in America,* and that, not in Virginia only, but from the other Colonies too, who should furnish instantly their quotas of men, that the sending Highlanders already regimented would be but losing the corps, were the men to remain in America, and the raising new independent companies of Highlanders would be so much loss of time.†

But, added Cumberland, none of your preparations, none of your military measures are of any effect till the Government has fixed the bounds of the French in America.

> *How far they shall come and no further,* which being once done, he continued, and laid down as a permanent measure whether of War or of Peace, the most express and distinct instructions should be drawn for the Commander-in-Chief that he may not be liable to future reproaches from one or the other colony or be sacrificed, one day or other, to the clamour of merchants at home, or their interested correspondents abroad: otherwise it would not be dealing fairly with an officer of His Royal Highness' nomination. His Highness imagined that Governor Shirley was gone with 1800 men to attack Crown Point. I explained the present Expedition up the Kennebeck; His Highness thinks the operation must be in several parts particularly Crown Point, the regaining of a footing on the Ohio, and building forts there to cut the French chain from Quebec to the Mississippi, and still more particularly attacking the French forts upon the neck of the Peninsula at the head of the Bay of Fundi, all which His Highness thought we were authorised to do as the French had so notoriously infringed the convention for making no encroachments during the negotiations of the Commissaries.‡

* A little later Cumberland appears to have favoured the idea of completing the two regiments to full strength, and sending sergeants and corporals from the guards as instructors to America. Both proposals were negatived by the King.

† Add. MS. 32736, f. 563, Robinson to Newcastle, Sept. 22, 1754.

‡ Add. MS. 32851, f. 564, Robinson to Newcastle, Sept. 22, 1754.

Thus we see for the first time that the strategy which has been the subject of so much favourable comment, was the work, not of the Ministry as hitherto supposed, but of Cumberland. What he here proposed was adopted in its entirety, and became the substance of the orders issued to General Braddock.   Sir Julian Corbett has described this plan as " true defensive strategy," * the plan of operations being such that it enabled the defensive to pass into the offensive the moment the opening came.   Here again the credit must be assigned to Cumberland. The problem of the moment was to drive the French from the positions they had taken up contrary to the convention between France and England.   Solving that problem in the way suggested might or might not mean war—Newcastle himself certainly thought it consistent with the maintenance of peace †—but Cumberland's task was to provide the best means of turning out the French.   That was the situation with which he had to deal.   Incidentally, if his plan was successful, it placed the English in a more favourable and the French in a less favourable position for carrying on the struggle, and for passing from a purely military to a political objective.

Cumberland was at the same time sharply impressed with the want of co-ordination between the several Colonies, and to bring about the desired degree of union he proposed to create an office somewhat similar to that of Viceroy, and " to send some great person of quality and distinction after the manner of the Spaniards to carry such a plan [i.e. Union] into execution, by skill, management and all the arts of conciliation, and that such a person should have with him and under his direction the officer now wanted for the military command." ‡ The proposal was rejected by the King § and the Ministry. It seemed the doom of the Government to do nothing which might tend to prevent the ultimate defection of the Colonies. It was indeed in the first half of the century that the seeds of disruption were sown.

Cumberland's military plan, on the other hand, received the

* J. Corbett, *England in the Seven Years' War*, I, p. 25 et seq.
† Add. MS. 32851, Newcastle to Albemarle, Oct. 10, 1754.
‡ Add. MS. 32736, f. 554, Newcastle to Hardwicke, Sept. 20, 1754.
§ *Ibid.*

highest commendation from the King, who showed " surprise and the utmost satisfaction that His Royal Highness should have made himself so entirely master of the subject," * and was for pushing all preparations and "sparing all sorts of arms, furniture, ammunition, artilery and engineers." †

Robinson declared he had "never seen His Majesty so entirely pleased." Moreover the Ministry were greatly taken with the idea of fixing some territorial limit in America. That was an idea which, incredible as it may seem, appears not to have entered into their calculations till suggested by Cumberland. Now they were provided with a definite point of departure. They had been stumbling in the dark, and suddenly light had dawned. "There would, I should humbly presume," wrote Robinson after his interview with Cumberland, "be no difficulty in fixing secretly and in one's own breast, an ultimatum for both *operation* and *negotiation,* for *Political* not imaginary Boundaries, for *solid* and not *Charter* Limits. Such a principle once resolved upon and adhered to will surmount everything." ‡ The policy of banking on peace and leaving defensive measures very much alone was at an end. Thenceforward, although the definition of territorial limits is only partially carried out, there is a new note of decision in the handling of affairs, and this we may fairly attribute to the appearance on the scene of Cumberland as official adviser. Final arrangements were made at a meeting on September 25, when Newcastle, Hardwicke, Lord Anson, Sir Thomas Robinson, Fox, and Lord Granville "attended His Royal Highness at St. James's Palace." Cumberland expounded his plan and pointed out that "it enabled operations to be carried on afterwards, as future circumstances and future events may make advisable." "This consultation," Newcastle went on to say, "has put the Duke in a very high light as an Officer and I must do His R.H. the justice to say that he behaved with great Ability, Decency and Moderation and particularly upon the Article of Expense, where I have [sic] and shall stick as close as I can." §

* Add. MS. 32736, f. 569, Robinson to Newcastle, Sept. 22, 1754.
† *Ibid.*
‡ Add. MS. 32735, f. 569, Robinson to Newcastle, Sept. 23, 1754.
§ Add. MS. 32736, f. 592, Newcastle to Albemarle, Sept. 27, 1754.

Subsequently Cumberland's plan was drawn up for transmission to the general destined for the command in North America. It was an indication of this plan which had formed the subject of the " ill-judged advertisement " so grievously embarrassing to Newcastle. Four points of attack were included in the plan of operations: Monckton * in the north was to operate against Fort Beauséjour, and thus secure contact between Acadia and the mainland of Canada; a second force was to advance from the northern colonies of New Jersey, New York, and New England against Crown Point, a post held by the French south of Lake Champlain; a third column was to drive the French from Niagara; while the southernmost advance was to have as its objective Fort Duquesne, the capture of which would secure possession of the headwaters of the Ohio.

The officer chosen for the supreme command of these operations was Major-General Braddock. He was suggested by Cumberland † as the " properest " person for the position, and being approved of by the King, who had " a good opinion of Braddock's sense and bravery and had heard that he had become very stayed [sic]," ‡ he was cordially accepted by the Ministry and duly appointed.

Braddock was at this time fifty-nine years of age. Having entered the Coldstream Guards in 1710, he had a long record of regimental service to his credit. But beyond taking part in the attempt to raise the siege of Bergen-op-Zoom in 1746, he was without experience of service in the field. Cumberland has been blamed for selecting him as commander, and if Horace Walpole, who " loved to give " to his correspondents " an idea of our characters as they rise upon the stage of history," is to be believed, contemporary opinion was apt to regard Braddock as first and last a disciplinarian. Walpole describes him as " a very Iroquois in disposition," and relates that " when told that his sister having gamed away her little fortune and hanged herself in her lodgings in Bath with a truly English

---

* It was the orders to Monckton which were published in the *Gazette*. Add. MS. 32736, f. 536, Robinson to Newcastle, Aug. 2, 1754.

† Add. MS. 32736, f. 563, Robinson to Newcastle, Sept. 22, 1754.

‡ *Ibid.*, f. 569, Robinson to Newcastle, Sept. 22, 1754.

deliberation leaving only a note upon the table with those lines ' To die is landing upon some silent shore etc ' : Braddock only said, ' Poor Fanny, I always thought she would play till she would be forced to tuck herself up.' " Elsewhere the same authority says of him : " Desperate in his fortune, brutal in his behaviour, obstinate in his sentiments, he was still intrepid and capable." Few of those, however, who had been brought up in the tradition of the Marlborough wars, and had seen service under George I and during the early years of George II, and been inured to the habit of Prussian military punctilio and discipline by regimental service under those monarchs, could escape the charge of severity and harshness. It was a rough school and it produced rough pupils ; but so far from brutality developing under the rule of Cumberland, it is to be noticed that the officers notorious for their severity were officers of the old tradition, officers of the stamp of Hawley and Braddock. It is among the contemporaries of Cumberland that there is to be observed a new enlightenment. Wolfe, Monckton, Amherst, Murray, Conway—these were reared in the Cumberland school ; and while we need not attribute the spirit they developed directly to the influence of Cumberland, it is only fair to point out that it was under him that the new order of things was able to mature, and that captains who were to spread the fame of British arms to every quarter of the globe received their early training. In the case of Braddock the portrait which has become standardised is that of a man incompetent as a general and habitually " menacing death and hell " to all with whom he came in contact. That he was of a coarse and robust disposition may be admitted. Even his protégée Mrs. Bellamy, who regarded him " as a second father," is driven to vindicate his memory from the charge of brutality by an anecdote which reflects more credit perhaps on her own humanity than the general's.

> As we were walking in the Park [she writes] we heard a poor fellow was to be chastised, when I requested the General to beg off the offender. Upon his application to the general officer, whose name was Drury, he asked Braddock, how long since he had divested himself of his brutality and the insolence of his manners? To which the other

replied, " You never knew me insolent to my inferiors. It is only to such rude men as yourself that I behave with the spirit which I think they deserve." *

On the other hand, in the testimony of Wolfe, which we may take as indisputable authority, we find no word of Braddock's brutality; on the contrary, after Braddock's defeat Wolfe is found writing: " I do myself believe that the cowardice and ill behaviour of the men far exceeded the ignorance of the chief, who though not a master of the difficult art of war, was yet a man of sense and courage." † Elsewhere Wolfe writes: " I have some letters from Braddock's army, giving a very favourable account of the General's proceedings, and of his good behaviour to the People under his command." Even Walpole is constrained to admit another side to his account; writing on August 28, 1755, he says: " However with all his brutality, he [Braddock] has lately been Governor of Gibraltar,‡ where he made himself adored, and where scarce any Governor was endured before." While Dinwiddie wrote from America: " He is I think a very fine officer, and a sensible considerate gentleman. He and I live in great harmony." Clearly he did not appear alike to all men. There were other aspects to his character than those which it has been the fashion to commemorate. The situation to which he was appointed proved to be one requiring high qualities of judgment, powers of conciliation and tact, and a mobility of mind capable of dealing with new and totally unexplored conditions. Here was where he failed. Here his good sense, his integrity, and his inexhaustible personal valour were of very little avail. Accustomed to regular troops and the parade movements of Europe, he under-estimated the merits of Americans and Indians, and failed to adjust his ideas with sufficient rapidity to savage warfare. But when it is said, " Braddock took his troops through the American bush as if they were marching

* *An Apology for the life of George Anne Bellamy: written by herself* (1785), III, p. 56.

† Beckles Willson, *Life and Letters of Wolfe*, p. 274.

‡ This is incorrect. At the time of his appointment to North America Braddock held a command in Gibraltar but was not governor.

from London to Windsor," * less than justice is done to the dispositions made by the General. His order of march was as follows:

> Guides with six Virginian light horsemen led the way. Then, a musket shot behind, came the vanguard; then three hundred soldiers under Gage; then a large body of axemen under Sir John Sinclair, to open the road: then two cannon with tumbrils and tool-wagons; and lastly the rearguard, closing the line, while flanking parties ranged the wood on both sides.†

But no precautions could make up for the want of spirit in his regular troops. What Wolfe said of the regiments ‡ with Braddock proved, when the day of trial came,§ to be true.

> I have [he wrote] but a very mean opinion of the Infantry in courage. I know their discipline to be bad and their valour precarious. They are easily put into disorder, and hard to recover out of it. They frequently kill their officers through fear and murder one another in their confusion. ‖

Twenty-five officers killed and thirty-seven wounded ¶ in the panic which beset the regular troops on the banks of the Monongahela (July 9, 1755) made a toll to justify the fears of Wolfe. George Washington, who acted as aide-de-camp to Braddock, in a report to Dinwiddie bears out Wolfe's view of what occurred.

> In short the dastardly behaviour [he wrote] of the English soldiers exposed all those who were inclined to do their duty to almost certain death, and at length in despite of every effort to the contrary (they) broke and ran as sheep before the hounds, leaving the artillery, ammunition, Provisions and every individual thing we had with us, a prey for the enemy, and when we endeavoured to rally them in hopes of regaining our invaluable losses it was (with) as much

---

* Lord Rosebery, *Chatham: His Early Life and Connections*, p. 398.

† Parkman, *Montcalm and Wolfe*, I, p. 222.

‡ The 48th and 44th Foot.

§ July 7, 1755.

‖ Beckles Willson, *Life and Letters of Wolfe*, p. 274.

¶ Out of a total of eighty-six.

success as if we had attempted to stop the wild bears of the mountains.

He goes on to say that the men gathered themselves into a body of ten or twelve deep contrary to orders, and declares that two-thirds of the casualties were caused by our own men.* This confirms in a remarkable way the explanation of the defeat given by Wolfe, who at the time of writing had no details before him. Moreover it is to be observed that Washington in his report has not a word to say by way of criticism of the general's tactics. But if Braddock was one of the first to experience savage warfare and to fail, he was certainly not the last. It was his fate to be matched with conditions that were foreign to every tradition of the army, and for which the battle-fields of Europe were the worst possible training. To these conditions he succumbed, but owing rather to the panic which they engendered in his troops than to the faultiness of his own dispositions. Enough has perhaps been said to show that Cumberland, in choosing Braddock to command the North American expedition, acted not so grossly without reason as the popular view would suggest.

* Add. MS. 32857, f. 218, George Washington to Dinwiddie, July 18, 1755.

CHAPTER XIII

ALBEMARLE, when requested by Newcastle to allay the disturbance likely to be caused at Versailles by the Braddock expedition and to explain that it was an ordinary peace measure requisite for the protection of the Colonies, replied: " I must own that it requires a better head than mine to distinguish with proper nicety what we are now doing from hostile preparations." * Posterity may well sympathise with the ambassador's difficulty. On the whole the news made less sensation than was to be expected. At any rate it gave no visible check to the active negotiations between Versailles and St. James's. Albemarle notified Newcastle that the quota of " convicts and vagabonds " who were annually " transported " for military service to Louisiana, to the number of 1200, might also as a peace measure and a necessary precaution be increased this year.† To which Newcastle at once replied in effect: " That only shows what the French have been doing—if they send 1200 men every year, that means over 6000 since the Peace of Aix-la-Chapelle: here is another proof that they are the aggressors."

A survey of international relations at the beginning of 1755 would have shown little apparent ground for anticipating the diplomatic revolution which was pending. Outwardly the broad features of those relations remained the same. France and England, it was generally felt, were drifting into war. That was the central fact. Frederick the Great thought the chances were ten to one in favour of war.‡ " Je crois qu'il serait à parier dix contre un qu'il s'ensuivra la guerre, et que d'armement en armement des deux côtés on viendra à la rupture, sans avoir eu le dessein et sans savoir comment."

* Add. MS. 32851, f. 81, Albemarle to Newcastle, Oct. 23, 1754.
† Ibid., f. 119, Albemarle to Newcastle, Oct. 30, 1754.
‡ Frederick to Michell, March 22, 1755; quoted R. Waddington, Le Renversement des Alliances, p. 95.

An entirely exact forecast of what was actually to occur. It was round and by reason of this central fact that a readjustment of the interests of the various Powers in Europe was taking place. Events were leading quickly to a new orientation. Each Government was considering the best means for its own particular end. The end which Austria had in view was the recovery of Silesia. That end, as we know, Kaunitz believed could best be achieved by an alliance with France. This meant dallying meanwhile with England, and such was the procrastination of the Court of Vienna in the negotiations over the Barrier Treaty that Newcastle, after receipt of Keith's account of his interview with Kaunitz in November 1754, wrote in despair: "I see the great system upon the point of being dissolved. The conduct of the Court of Vienna is astonishing, they act as if they had no occasion for us and in return we are too prudent to act as if we did not want them." * But much had to occur before the actual dissolution of the alliance could be brought about. Till the opportunity arose, that is till a rapprochement with France was assured, it was necessary to keep up the forms and pretences of the old system, of the alliance with Britain; to make the delays over the Barrier Treaty palatable by protestations of friendship, and from time to time perform good offices towards England, as when Kaunitz transmitted to the British Ministry news of the Young Pretender, and of Frederick's intrigues with the Jacobites, and of the plot afoot for a landing in Ireland.

Meanwhile France was to all appearance on good terms with Frederick, whose sole concern for the moment was the retention of Silesia and the frustration of Austria's desire to recover that province. It was true that the treaty between France and Prussia expired in 1755, but there was good reason for supposing it would be renewed. Frederick was constantly tendering good advice to the French Ministry upon the question of her attitude to England, recommending even in April 1755 an attack on Hanover; † while France was

---

* Add. MS. 32851, f. 326, Newcastle to Hon. Mr. Bentinck, Dec. 17, 1754.

† Broglie, *L'Alliance Autrichienne*, p. 106, quoting letter of La Touche to Rouillé, April 1755.

endeavouring to further Frederick's ambition for a treaty with Denmark. * The most acute observer in fact might have counted on the continuance of friendly relations between Versailles and Potsdam.

Spain had entered into a definite treaty with Austria (Treaty of Aranjuez), guaranteeing their respective possessions in Italy. Spain moreover had established cordial relations with England, thereby frankly drawing away from her former ties with France.

Russia was lending a willing and artful ear to the solicitations of Newcastle, driving a hard bargain and manœuvring for better terms as the price of her assistance; while between Russia and Austria an understanding had been arrived at, induced by a common policy with regard to the Turk, and the hatred felt by the two Empresses for Frederick.

The uncertain factor in the situation was Frederick himself, though hitherto there was no evidence of his approaching defection from France. But Russia, "that great cloud of menace in the north," was a constant anxiety to the King of Prussia, and in the rapprochement between St. Petersburg and Vienna there lay a source of great uneasiness for Frederick and at the same time a threat to his hold on Silesia.

England was still vigorously trying to bolster up the old system, to galvanise Holland into activity, induce her to order her finances and push forward military preparation, while at the same time pressure was applied to the Court of Vienna to make her fulfil the obligations of the alliance. On the sea and in North America England could deal with the French, but if France elected to march her troops on Hanover, and if Frederick still remained friendly to French pretensions, what then? Here lay the real difficulty for Newcastle. Hanover, with its Continental consequences, its implied commitment to a land war, and its repercussion on home politics, was going to prove itself the most intractable of the war problems.

Thus at the beginning of 1755 the old orientation was ostensibly unaltered. It was only on the circumference and the fringes that visible changes were taking place, first in Spain and secondly in Russia—changes which were to react on the

* Add. MS. 32851, f. 152, Scheffer to Höpken, Nov. 7, 1754.

Central Powers entirely to the advantage of England. Here was seen the sagacity of Newcastle's foreign policy. While apparently a slave to the old system, he saw its weakness, and he sought elsewhere for further and not inconsistent securities. So that eventually, at the moment when the diplomatic revolution was imminent, he had secured the neutrality of Spain, he had formed a treaty with Russia by which that Power engaged to march troops for the protection of Hanover, he had signed the Convention of Westminster with Frederick the Great, and he had subsidised the principality of Hesse and obtained the call on a force of 8000 men for service in England. Newcastle had in fact set the stage after his own manner with both ingenuity and skill, and though by general agreement he proved but a weak and faltering actor when the drama was once in motion, in his preliminary work he had performed an invaluable service for the country.

Newcastle has been handed down from one generation to another in a blaze of derision. As if in anticipation of such a destiny, he left in the Newcastle Papers a documentary record of his life and actions which for completeness and volume has no equal among biographical material. He seems to have been determined that, from the reader who was disposed to uncover it, no secret should be hid. He has revealed himself with a frankness that has no reservations. For better or worse, and with absolute candour, he has in his manuscripts submitted himself to the inspection of the world. And from these papers the tendency to revalue the character and attainments of the Duke must continue to draw its inspiration. It is in them that modification, if such is to be found, of the portrait of him drawn by Macaulay and many others must be sought. It has been said of Macaulay "that he seeks truth, not as she should be sought, devoutly, tentatively and with the air of one touching the hem of a sacred garment, but clutching her by the hair of the head, and dragging her after him in a kind of boisterous triumph, a prisoner of war, not a goddess."

Macaulay himself was seldom as boisterous as when he turned his attention to Newcastle. It is thus that he writes of him:

No man was ever so unmercifully satirised. But in truth he was himself a satire ready made. All that the art of the satirist does for other men, nature had done for him. Whatever was absurd about him stood out with grotesque prominence from the rest of the character. He was a living, moving, talking caricature. His gait was a shuffling trot: he was never in time: he abounded in fulsome caresses and tears. His oratory resembled that of Justice Shallow. It was nonsense effervescent with animal spirits and impertinence. . . . Under the disguise of levity he was false beyond all example of political falsehood. All the able men of his time ridiculed him as a dunce, a driveller, a child who never knew his mind for an hour together; and he overreached them all round.

Newcastle was, it is true, an expert in the less reputable manifestations of human nature. He knew by heart the vanities and jealousies, the aversions and ambitions, the fears and venality of those within the radius of his personal influence, and on these he could play with a master hand. Moreover it may be said with truth that he never knew England, and never understood his countrymen. He did not realise the spirit which was latent in the country he served for so many decades, and never apprehended that he was dealing with a nation capable of being touched to fine issues, and ready to respond generously if an appeal were made to its patriotism and zeal. Quebec, Trafalgar, Waterloo were the product of forces that Newcastle had neither the genius to measure, nor the gifts to evoke. It is indeed instructive to compare the King's Speeches delivered during the ministries of Newcastle with those addressed to Parliament when power was in the hands of Pitt. In the one, the spirit of the nation finds no place; in the other, the language glows with patriotism and a new fervour of faith in the moral resources of the people.

Newcastle was not framed to advocate generous causes. Great events found him hesitating and often bewildered. But (and it is fair that he should be), if he is judged by his diplomatic successes on the eve of the Seven Years' War, it must be admitted that he deserved well of his country. The situation was one of extraordinary difficulty. All Europe was involved. In every Court from St. Petersburg to Madrid, from Constantinople to Stockholm, rival intriguers were negotiating for alliances.   In every quarter there were the signs of military preparation.   Nor could any man foretell what combination of Powers might be forming below the surface. Nervousness and hesitation had penetrated into the chancelleries of Europe.   Apprehension and perplexity were troubling the outlook of princes and rulers.   A struggle was impending— that at least was clear—but where the challenge would be flung and by whom it would be taken up, outside the immediate clash between England and France, was yet in doubt.   A faulty diplomacy might cement the alliance between Frederick and France—alienate Russia—leave Hanover open to immediate attack—and find England isolated with Austria as its sole and incompetent ally.   Newcastle avoided these pitfalls and, as will appear, kept in his hands the diplomatic initiative in Europe.   It was the heyday of the opportunist in foreign politics.   It was essential that every door should be kept open till the last moment.   This Newcastle did.   Indeed it was the success in his negotiations that was the proximate cause of the final grouping of the Powers.   The course which his policy took was guided, if not controlled, by his determination to protect Hanover.   And it is worthy of note that, often as the incubus of Hanover had reacted to the embarrassment of England, in this case it was to be the indirect and unconscious cause of a policy wholly advantageous in the end to British interests.

Newcastle recognised that it was on the high seas and in North America that the war must be won, that so far as the Continent was concerned English commitments must be reduced to a minimum, and that Hanover must if possible be secured by diplomacy and alliances.   To this end he applied his sleepless industry and his unrivalled knowledge of foreign affairs.   The despatches he penned to the various embassies on the Continent, and the letters with which he deluged George II when in Hanover, contain expositions of the politics of Europe which carry enlightenment on every page.   Nor can it be said that, once convinced of the end to be achieved, he faltered in the exploitation of the means to be adopted.   The despatch of Braddock, the orders to Boscawen, the building up of a naval superiority in home waters, the continuance of negotiations with

Mirepoix—these, having regard to his policy, were sound measures. But he was badly served. The failure of Braddock, the ill success of Boscawen, and later the incompetence of Byng, were frustrations which there was no reason to expect but which upset every calculation. Reverses like these he had not the necessary genius to retrieve. They needed the gifts of Pitt, and the vision, which Newcastle lacked, to understand the nation and gauge the effort of which it was capable.

While striving for power and place, Newcastle made no pretence of not coveting what he sought. In this respect he and the Lord Chancellor were a congenial pair. Neither of them had any idea of relinquishing the authority he had once held, or even suffering that authority to be infringed. On the other hand, they served the King through a long period of years with exemplary loyalty, and maintained the influence and prestige of the country at a high level in the Councils of Europe. And in those days the business of statesmanship had little other concern.

As time went by Newcastle seemed almost to acquire the status of a permanent official without the liability to superannuation. For half a century he held office with a degree of continuity that has never been approached, and in the end died poorer by £300,000. His personal integrity at a time when corruption was very general is unquestioned. In home politics he is not associated with any measure of improvement or reform, and in that he resembles the other statesmen of his time. There was a placid acquiescence in things as they were, and as long as they got no worse there was no very obvious reason for trying to make them better. But Newcastle was responsible for a change in the political conceptions of the time: he was largely the creator of the Party System. It is all very well to say that his idea of party was keeping himself in power, but it can be put in another way, it can be said that Newcastle and his colleagues had certain principles in common which in their view could only prevail if they had sufficient backing in Parliament. He had learnt his lesson under Walpole, in whose school he was an early disciple, and though in the management of a party he very rapidly outstripped his master, he was in that branch of politics carrying on and expanding the Walpole tradition.

Newcastle therefore used means, not always very decorous but still thoroughly characteristic of the time, to build up a strong party in Parliament, and by a system of rewards and deprivations to stimulate its activity. The system he established has in varying form been adhered to. The direct consequence of Newcastle's method of governing was an increase in the power of Parliament and a diminution in the power of the Throne. From this the responsibility of Ministers to Parliament emerged as a direct and definite relation. Each year it became more essential for the Cabinet to act in harmony with the views of the party to which they looked for support. Each year they became slightly more independent of the Crown. Later years were to witness a temporary set-back under George III to this constitutional progression, but Newcastle's political faith contained the origins from which subsequent developments have proceeded.* That was the mark which he left on the political practice of the country.

Newcastle was true to his principles, as his subsequent association and influence with the Rockingham Whigs shows. It was then that his political sagacity and firmness of purpose showed to greatest advantage. Indeed it may be said that the further he got away from the alliance with Hardwicke, the more independent and spirited he became. The Lord Chancellor was his confessor. To him he could pour out his woes, before him he could expose his difficulties, from him he was always sure of sympathy and sound advice. Cut off from that source of strength, he mobilised a new set of forces of his own, and at the end of his career in opposition presented an altogether more admirable figure on the political stage.

Personally he was of a kindly disposition, genial, devout, and hospitable, with a particular care for the pleasures which were to be derived from the excellence of his wine and cooking. His fidelity as a friend, the romantic constancy of his domestic devotion, the ease with which he could be placated, and his unfeigned delight in the successes of those whom he trusted, amply atone for his absurdities—his fussy ways, his morbid

* See Winstanley, *Lord Chatham and the Whig Opposition.* Mr. Winstanley and Sir Julian Corbett have been the first among historians to combat the accepted view of Newcastle.

care for his health, his sudden trepidations, and his presages of disaster. He was mercurial in temperament, at one moment apprehending death and damnation, at another basking in the sunshine of a cloudless sky. That he should have realised that Cape Breton was an island only after its conquest, that he should have declared Annapolis must be defended without knowledge of its whereabouts, and that he should have besought Lord Chesterfield to let the calendar alone—these and other illustrations, slenderly attested, of a certain side of his character, the side most vulnerable to the satirist, are very difficult to reconcile with the knowledge displayed in his private and public correspondence. But it was his fate to number Lord Hervey and Horace Walpole among his most pitiless opponents, and that was to give everlasting hostages to fortune.

When on his temporary retirement (May 26, 1762), the bishops, nearly all of whom owed their preferment to his patronage and hitherto had been found among the most faithful of those paying court at his levées, withdrew entirely from his circle, he observed, " Even fathers in God sometimes forget their Maker." He had no illusions after his long course of political experience, but he knew how to be good-humoured in adversity.

At the beginning of the year (1755) hope of peace received some support from the return to St. James's of the French Ambassador, the Duc de Mirepoix. He had left London in the autumn of 1754, and it was considered ominous that in France he had made a point of avoiding Albemarle. The English Ambassador had busily pursued him, rattling in his chaise along the great roads, now to Versailles, now to Compiègne, or again to Meudon, or nearer at home in Paris calling at the Duke's hotel in an attempt to defeat his evasive dodges of ill-health or pretended absence. " I don't like things nor Mirepoix's Put-offs," wrote Newcastle on hearing of these evasions. " For God's sake prevent a quarrel if you can. We must do ourselves right in North America. They are the aggressors." * Mirepoix, now † one of the dignitaries of France, was little qualified except by his station for the delicate

* Add. MS. 32851, f. 162, Newcastle to Albemarle, Nov. 7, 1754.
† He had recently been made a Duke.

task of Ambassador in London. Walpole, who on one occasion met him walking in Brentford "with a brown lap dog with long ears, two pointers, two pages, three footmen, and a vis-à-vis following him," had a poor opinion of his capacity, and complains that he could "not learn even to pronounce the names of one or two of our games at cards, which, however, engaged most of the hours of his negotiation." Much less was he master of the details of the situation in America. With only a nebulous apprehension of the facts, he was little qualified to bring about definite results in his negotiations, or even to send to his Government accurate reports of the situation or of his interviews with Ministers. But his return to London was at least taken as a symbol of goodwill on the part of France; he was known to be an ardent apostle of peace, his integrity was unquestioned, and while recognised as a fervent patriot he was justly credited with a lively sympathy for the English nation. Hitherto there had been great want of precision in the demands made on either side, there had been no serious attempt to discover an exact modus vivendi, or to specify a formula which would meet the growing difficulties of the situation. Cumberland's advice in September 1754 had never been given effect; since then much had occurred to impair the prospects of peace. Negotiation had brought Versailles and St. James's no nearer; while the activities of those in America, necessitating corresponding movements at home, had tended to drive them further apart. "Hostile intercourse" beyond the Atlantic was narrowing week by week the profitable area for diplomacy in Europe. Facts were displacing arguments—with the result that discussion at home had gradually changed its character, and was now directed to a consideration of how much of what had been done in America should be undone. An exact definition earlier in the day might have avoided this and given a basis to go on. Meanwhile the will to war was steadily rising, and the desire for peace which was equally shared by both Governments was steadily receding. A more illuminating illustration of the manner in which negotiations ought not to be conducted would be difficult to find. Had Cumberland's voice been listened to earlier, a different turn might have been given to the sequence of events.

CHAPTER XIV

THE course of the negotiations after Mirepoix's return assumed
an unexpected air of smoothness. Mirepoix produced a proposal from the French Court that hostilities should cease in
America for two years, that during that period the *status quo*
should be maintained, and that a Commission should in the
meantime settle all questions in dispute. The proposal was
at once and firmly rejected by the British Ministry. Then,
greatly to the surprise of Newcastle and Robinson, Mirepoix
stated that he had been invested with full powers to "negotiate the accommodation of all points in dispute," and "that
with regard to the Ohio in particular all the Forts and Establishments which had been built there should be demolished, and
that the whole Territory from the Appalachian Mountains to
the Great Lakes and the River Oubache should be evacuated
by the French forces and restored to the natives in its former
state, reserving only a free passage to both the English and
French, with a liberty for them to trade with the French." *
This involved concessions startling in their compliance. It
was as though the French had said, " We are in the wrong;
we will return to the *status quo ante*; we will undo all that
we have done." The papers embodying these transactions
were at once forwarded to Cumberland, who wrote on February
11 the following reply to Robinson:

> I return you many thanks for the communication of the
> Papers you sent me this morning. If France consents to
> the Paper marked Points I shall think we have got very
> well out of our present difficulties and indeed there is some
> appearance of it, as France seems both by the full Power
> and the Projet de Replique to be full as desirous as we can
> be of preserving the peace: But as no natural enemy ought

* Add. MS. 32853, f. 179, Robinson to Keene, March 11, 1755.

to be trusted I hope the King's Ministers will not neglect the little time that is left for Preparation.

I am your affectionate friend,
WILLIAM.*

Within a few days the word of caution at the end of Cumberland's letter found its justification. Mirepoix had communicated his account of what had passed between himself and the Ministry to Paris. The reply from Rouillé left no doubt that Mirepoix's desire for peace had outrun his discretion, and certainly his authority. The terms of the " Project of a Preliminary Convention " which the courier brought back from Paris were more inadmissible than any terms yet put forward. Briefly they were as follows: the stipulations in the Treaty of Utrecht with regard to the acknowledged subjection of the Five Nations to the Crown of Great Britain were to be regarded as " vain and nugatory "; all grants of land to British subjects since the date of that treaty were to be considered as " void and ineffectual "; the *status quo* was to be preserved; and as regards Acadia the proposals of the French implied that they were not prepared to allow British subjects quiet possession of even half the peninsula. †

To this the British Ministry replied with great firmness, at the same time defining with precision the limits within which the French must retire. The divergence between the two projects appeared no longer capable of adjustment; almost *pari passu* at Versailles and St. James's the psychology was changing. The intention to seek another form of arbitrament was simultaneously forcing its way to the front and displacing the belief in the efficacy of negotiation.

March 11 saw Newcastle and the Secretaries of State immersed in a voluminous correspondence, sending exhaustive accounts of the negotiations to the British representatives in Madrid, St. Petersburg, Vienna, and the Hague, each account adjusted to the palate of the Court for whose consumption it was designed. Newcastle followed it up with a long and con-

* Add. MS. 32582, f. 420, Cumberland to Robinson, Feb. 11, 1755.

† Add. MS. 32853, f. 179, Robinson to Keene, March 11, 1755; f. 193, Newcastle to Bentinck, March 11, 1755; f. 205, Holdernesse to Keith, March 11, 1755.

fidential communication to Bentinck. "What would Holland do?—could she spare six to eight thousand men to be taken into British pay for the defence of England? could she provide any number from six to ten ships of war? would she be prepared to assist in the defence of Hanover?"* Newcastle was afraid that the reply of the British Ministry to the French Project of a Preliminary Convention would lead to negotiations being broken off: there was the more reason to anticipate this as France was pushing forward her preparations; fleets were fitting out at Toulon and Brest, at Rochfort and La Rochelle; active measures were being taken to augment her marine and land forces. Moreover, owing to the death of Lord Albemarle (December 1754), England was without an Ambassador in Paris. The situation was embarrassing. It seemed hardly the moment for despatching Lord Hertford, who had been nominated for the post. His recall, if he went, might well synchronise with the moment of his arrival.

And through these critical days of discussion in February and March, Braddock at Williamsburg in Virginia was in counsel with Governor Dinwiddie and Shirley, settling the scheme of operations, appealing to the Colonies for men and money, urging on them the obligations of patriotism, holding parleys with the Indians, and searching north and south, high and low, for the means of transport for his troops. Here there was no question of negotiation, none of peace: it was war without disguise—a rude enough commentary on the proceedings in Paris and in London.

On March 25 a message from the King was delivered to Lords and Commons acquainting them "that the present situation of affairs makes it requisite to augment his forces by sea and land: and to take such other measures as may best tend to preserve the general peace of Europe and to secure the just rights and possessions of his crown in America." A grant of one million was voted without opposition. Ten thousand men were added to the army by the creation of seven new regiments, the addition of 1472 men to the Guards, and the raising of regiments on the Irish establishment to full strength. Five thousand marines were embodied and, in ac-

* Add. MS. 32853, f. 205, Newcastle to Bentinck, March 11, 1755.

cordance with the suggestion of Cumberland, placed under the jurisdiction of the Admiralty.

The war temper was rising. But negotiations went on, and despatches that bore all the semblance of ultimatums were sent and received, and then robbed of their finality by further conversations. The press kept the public informed of every step taken in the way of warlike preparation. Of censorship there was none, of leakage of official secrets there was a great deal. Frederick's forecast, " D'armement en armement des deux côtés on viendra à la rupture," was nearing its fulfilment. But the cloud of war was throwing no shadow over social life. " Balls, masquerades, and diversions," wrote Walpole, " don't trouble their heads about the Parliament or the war; the righteous who hate pleasures and love prophecies are finding out parallels between London and Nineveh and other goodly cities of old, who went to operas and ridottos when the French were at their gates." Nor was it without political significance that the King and the whole of the Royal Family should attend the ball given by the Russian Ambassador at Somerset House. No fewer than 1000 guests were present, an almost fabulous number for those days. The King arrived soon after 8 dressed in a black domino, tye wig and gold-laced hat. Cumberland showed to advantage " in a Turkish dress with a large bunch of diamonds in his turban." The scanty attire of a noble lady " who shone in the habit of a nymph studded with brilliants to the amount of £100,000," suggesting " the spangled canopy of heaven," did not fail to excite criticism and discussion. " The desert was the most elegant that expence could furnish," and the whole entertainment presented a scene of unparalleled magnificence. Gambling too, that abiding manifestation of human optimism, seems to have received a momentary acceleration, for we read of Sir John Bland * losing £32,000 in one evening to an impecunious Captain at White's Club.

The citizens [wrote Walpole] put on their double channeled pumps and trudge to St. James's Street in expectation of seeing judgments executed at Whites—angels

---

* He subsequently committed suicide.

with flaming swords and devils flying away with dice boxes, like the prints in Sadeler's Hermits.

These were the evils, masquerades and gaming, that were exciting the denunciations of the clergy, and the antagonism of the Puritan spirit.

> Pleasure always has been and always will be the principal business of persons of Fashion and Fortune. . . . Let them have their Plays Operas and Oratorios: their Masquerades and Ridottos, their assemblies, drums, routs, riots and hurricanes, their Ranelagh and Vauxhall, their Bath Tunbridge Bristol Scarborough and Cheltenham. The business of the Politician is only to prevent the contagion from spreading to the useful part of mankind.*
>
> The fury after licentious and luxurious pleasures is grown to so enormous a height that it may be called the characteristic of the present age. . . . Diversion is no longer the recreation or amusement but the whole business of their lives. They are not content with three theatres, they must have a fourth: where the stage is reduced back again to that degree of licentiousness which was too enormous for the corrupt state at Athens to tolerate.†

Thus did the author of *Tom Jones* denounce the habits of "the Upper part of mankind," when putting aside the role of a delineator of life he donned his magisterial office and charged the Grand Jury at the Sessions of the Peace. "Decadence" was not a word in current use; but it would sufficiently describe the state of society as seen through the eyes of those who in every age are found to despair of their own generation.

No rumours of war at any rate could stay the hand of the law, and we find that in January, February, and March the capital convictions in the provinces alone amounted to 75. The problem of man power had not as yet arisen. Fielding was even pleading against any remission of capital sentences, and as a greater security against robberies was for erecting a gallows at the Old Bailey and executing those who were con-

* Henry Fielding, *An Enquiry into the late Increase of Robbers* (1751).
† Henry Fielding, *Works* (1821), Vol. x, p. 171.

victed in the presence of the judges within as short a time as possible of the sentence being delivered.*

Meanwhile beyond the Atlantic Cumberland's plan of operations was well under way, Braddock was beginning his march on Fort Duquesne, Monckton was getting ready to sail from New York with his expedition to Acadia for the capture of Fort Beauséjour, Johnson was collecting men in New England for his attack on Crown Point, Shirley was laying plans for the advance on Niagara. At home the resolution of the Ministry was hardening. They were now deeply committed in North America. The naval preparations of France called for a practical answer. On March 24 the inner Cabinet resolved that seven ships should be sent under Admiral Boscawen to cruise off Louisbourg, and " fall on any French ships of war that shall be attempting to land troops in Nova Scotia or any other parts of the King's dominions, or to go to Cape Breton or through the River Lawrence to Quebec." † On April 17,‡ news having in the meanwhile reached the Cabinet that a squadron was about to sail from Brest, it was resolved that three more ships of the line and a frigate of fifty guns should be added to Boscawen's command. Negotiations still dragged on, but the character they had now assumed made it imperative that the Ministry should pursue their preparations with vigour and despatch. Orders were given to the press-gang to redouble their activities. Boscawen's fleet was increased to eleven ships of the line and one frigate, and it was resolved " that 1200 land forces should be immediately put on board the remaining fleet till a sufficient number of Marines can be raised to replace them." § On April 27 Boscawen put to sea.

In spite of the apparent imminence of war George II was determined to visit Hanover. The inconvenience of such a course was so obvious, the difficulties that might arise therefrom so considerable, that no effort was spared to induce him

* Henry Fielding, *An Enquiry into the late Increase of Robbers* (1751).

† Add. MS. 32996, f. 57, Cabinet Memoranda, March 24, 1755.

‡ *Ibid.*, f. 77, Cabinet Memoranda, April 17, 1755.

§ Add. MS. 32966, f. 89, April 22, 1755.

to remain in England. Earl Poulett, who had recently been dismissed from the office of Stole of the Chamber, even tabled a motion in the House of Lords that His Majesty would be pleased to lay aside his intention of visiting his Electoral Dominions. All parties combined in deprecating the indecency of airing such a topic in debate. After three adjournments the motion was finally brought on. A division was taken, and Earl Poulett found himself in a minority of one. Cumberland deplored the obstinacy of the King; but it was a tenet of his filial creed never to oppose a decision of his father. Privately the Ministerial protest was made, but the King resembled the dying Gladiator:

> He heard it but he heeded not—his eyes
> Were with his heart, and that was far away,

turned to Herrenhausen and his German Ministers, and the ease and delights of his Hanoverian environment. Besides, Hanover was in danger—was not his place among his own people? would he not be in a better position to negotiate for the protection of his kingdom by being there in person? Ministers were even afraid that the frustration of his desire would produce a serious illness. On April 28 accordingly his post-chaise with its escort of Lifeguards might have been seen by early risers crossing Westminster Bridge at 5 a.m. to take the Harwich road.* It was to be the last occasion of his leaving England. The same night a ball was given at Bedford House which was attended by Cumberland. Seen " at hazard with a great heap of gold before him somebody said he looked like the prodigal son and the fatted calf both." But whatever his appearance, he was now a formidable power in the State and a serious factor in the European situation.

The Duke of Devonshire had proposed that, in the absence of the King, Cumberland should be sole Regent.† This did not at all suit the Duke of Newcastle, who pointed out that should the King die abroad Cumberland would then have to

---

* *Gentleman's Magazine.*

† Walpole, *Memoirs of the Reign of George II* (ed. 1846), II, p. 22.

descend from being sole Regent to being merely a member of a council to advise the Princess of Wales, and persuaded the King that a more appropriate position for his son would be that of Head of the Regency.* " The Duke is at the head of the Regency," wrote Walpole; " you may guess if we are afraid! " † It meant a notable accession of power. Not only were all military appointments still in his hands, but as titular head of the executive he had now acquired a new and dominant influence in the direction of affairs. Thenceforward he was active in urging that the means adopted by the Ministry should be adequate to the execution of their policy. Mirepoix regarded the appointment as fatal to the chances of peace. " Here," said Pitt to Fox, " is the Duke King, and you are his Minister." " Whatever you may think," replied Fox, " the Duke does not think himself aggrandised by being of the Regency, where he has no more power than I have." Fox's reply, however, was far from representing the actual facts.

On May 9 Cumberland attended at Whitehall to preside over the Regency for the first time. At this meeting a report was read from Captain Taylor of H.M.S. *Seaford,* one of the cruisers of observation between Ushant and Land's End, to the effect that a fleet of twenty-five French ships had been sighted steering W.N.W.: upon this it was resolved " to give immediate directions to the Lords of the Admiralty that they should forthwith send to N. America six ships of the line and one frigate under the command of Francis Holbourne, Esq., Rear Admiral of the Blue, to reinforce Vice Admiral Boscawen." ‡

The fleet which had been sighted was the fleet that had been preparing at Brest, and whose sailing had been the subject of such varied rumour during the preceding four weeks. But now rumour had been translated into fact. Nineteen ships of the line and six frigates with lights extinguished had put

* *Ibid.*

† Walpole, *Letters,* iii, p. 304.

‡ Add. MS. 32996, f. 97, May 9, 1755. There were present at this meeting: Archbishop of Canterbury, Lord President, Lord Chancellor, Lord Privy Seal, Lord Chamberlain, Duke of Argyll, Duke of Newcastle, Lord Anson, Sir Thomas Robinson, Mr. Fox.

to sea from Brest Harbour on the evening of May 3. They had been followed to a point 120 miles W. of Ushant, and " were carrying a great press of sail day and night." Their destination was clearly America. The orders given to Holbourne were to rendezvous with Boscawen at Scatery Island. On May 11 Holbourne put to sea. Thus, with their course set to America, there were at this time on the waters of the Atlantic: Boscawen with eleven ships and one frigate, some 100 leagues in rear of him the French admiral Dubois de la Motte with nineteen ships of the line and six frigates, and starting eight days later than la Motte, Holbourne with six ships of the line and one frigate.

It was anticipated that part of the escorting French fleet, eight ships under Admiral Macnamara, might return when once they had passed the area in which they were most likely to be challenged and intercepted. Anson indeed, so Robinson stated, " had given Holbourne a private hint behind the Inner Council's back that he was to return immediately if he saw Macnamara returning, or had certain knowledge that he had returned."* Anson had no wish to see his superiority in home waters diminished. As a matter of fact Macnamara did return, but Holbourne, unaware of this, held on his course to North America. His orders † were more guarded than those of Boscawen. If he met a superior force he was to avoid action, but in the event of insult or attack he was ordered to fight as best he could. It will be remembered that Boscawen's orders were to fall on " any French ships of war " under specified circumstances.‡

On May 9, after the council presided over by Cumberland, the Lord President, Lord Granville, and Henry Fox dined with Mirepoix. Negotiations were as usual in a critical stage. It was of vital importance to Mirepoix to be certain as to the orders given to Boscawen: it was equally vital to British Ministers that he should remain ignorant. His secret information had led him to believe that at the last moment Boscawen, when about to sail from Plymouth, had received

* Corbett, *England in the Seven Years' War*, I, p. 49.
† Add. MS. 32854, f. 419, May 10, 1755.
‡ See ante, p. 149.

instructions to attack the French fleet "partout où il la pour-rait joindre." Was this correct? The dinner gave an opportunity of sounding the English Ministers. Confidences were exchanged in an atmosphere of hospitality, and when Granville and Fox left Mirepoix's house,* the Ambassador was satisfied that Boscawen's orders were to attack only in the event of the French undertaking hostilities in Acadia or any of the other colonies. Casuists must decide how far the English Ministers were justified in conveying this impression, and how far what would have been an accepted code of conduct in war was applicable to the middle state which involved war in America but the maintenance of friendly relations in Europe. Mirepoix, at any rate, was completely reassured. The French Ministry were duly informed. On May 16 Newcastle had the satisfaction of being able to write to Holdernesse, who was the Minister accompanying the King to Hanover, "Mirepoix has taken a house near St. James's Square, which does not look as if he soon intended to leave England." † Thus was further time gained for preparation. Another indication that France had no immediate intention of going to war, was found in an enquiry whether it would be agreeable to the King that the Court of Versailles should be represented in Hanover by Bussy. François de Bussy had during the War of the Austrian Succession occupied a responsible position in the French Foreign Office, and been zealous during that period in supplying information to the English Ministry in consideration of adequate money payments. In the archives of the Secret Service he had been known as No. 101. It was now a question whether an attempt should be made to resume the former intimate terms with him.‡ Before that point, however, could be determined a change had come over the relations of the two countries, and both Mirepoix and Bussy had been recalled to Paris.

For the moment things looked well. Everything was work-

---

* Waddington, *Le Renversement des Alliances,* p. 97.

† Add. MS. 32854, f. 544, Newcastle to Holdernesse, May 16, 1755.

‡ Add. MS. 32855, f. 2, Newcastle to Holdernesse, May 16, 1755. At the end of the Seven Years' War he was sent to London as one of the plenipotentiaries for the negotiation of the peace.

ing to plan. Boscawen was well ahead of la Motte, with an adequate superiority in naval force. High hopes were entertained of the military expeditions in North America. In home waters, even after the departure of Holbourne, there were seventeen ships of the line, and would shortly be twenty-three or twenty-four.* Negotiations were continuing, and there was little likelihood of France attempting any move in Europe for some time. The King could with reason say that "his affairs had never been in a more flourishing condition." † The greatest harmony prevailed amongst the Lords Justices. Recruits were coming in beyond expectation.‡ Lord Anson was so confident of his superiority at sea that he proposed that the home fleet under Hawke should cruise at the mouth of the Channel to convince the French of their readiness. Cumberland was completely reconciled with Newcastle, and about to visit him at Claremont on his way to Windsor Great Lodge, where he was now residing. All was for the best.

Even the Princess of Wales had been soothed into momentary equanimity on the subject of the Regency and her jealousy of Cumberland by the ministrations of Lord Hardwicke. Secretly too at this time she had entered into an agreement with " Pitt and his friends " through the mediation of Lord Bute and Sir George Lyttelton. The agreement was in the nature of an offensive and defensive alliance, with Cumberland and Fox as the objective of the attack, the interests of herself and son as the subjects for defence. It was to form the basis of a readjustment of political interests, far-reaching in its effects. And here the fluidity of international relations was finding a counterpart in the changes and intrigues among politicians at home. The retention of power by those who had it, the search after it by those who lacked it, were bringing about strange collisions and alliances.

---

* Add. MS. 32855, f. 112, Newcastle to Holdernesse, May 20, 1755.
† *Ibid.*, f. 44, Holdernesse to Newcastle, May 17, 1755.
‡ *Ibid.*, f. 112, Newcastle to Holdernesse, May 20, 1755.

CHAPTER XV

CUMBERLAND, surveying the military situation on the Continent, was chiefly concerned for the safety of Ostend, which he regarded as the key to British communications. Twenty thousand pounds, Ligonier had calculated, would put it in a state of stable defence.* But the idea of the Dutch was to concentrate on the defence of Namur. They could not be brought to consider a general concert of defence for the Low Countries. They would not incur the expense of strengthening Ostend. As usual they were asking for money.† Cumberland, with memories of Fontenoy and his campaigns with the Dutch as allies, regarded any such expenditure as pure waste of money. Namur must either be abandoned or made part of a general scheme. "Without some army," he wrote, "assembled in Flanders it matters but little how one or two fortresses are defended." ‡ This view was endorsed and forcibly expounded by Newcastle in his representations to the Hague.§ But the Dutch had no intention of adopting what appeared to them a quixotic policy. Their Ministers very politely in effect refused to budge. The States of Holland, mindful more of their frontier than of the Continental system, were disposed to neutrality.‖ The Princess Royal with tears and protestations upbraided Yorke for the coldness of the English Ministry. If money, she said, was not forthcoming from England, nothing could be done. Nothing in fact was done. But even here Newcastle did not believe that the danger was imminent. He thought it in the highest degree improbable

* Add. MS. 32855, f. 256, Newcastle to Yorke, May 30, 1755.
† The sum demanded was £60,000. Add. MS. 32856, f. 464, Newcastle to Yorke, July 4, 1755.
‡ Add. MS. 32855, f. 530, Cumberland to Newcastle, June 15, 1755.
§ Ibid., f. 113, Newcastle to Holdernesse, May 20, 1755.
‖ Add. MS. 32856, f. 243, Yorke to Newcastle, June 27, 1755.

that the French would move till they knew the fate of those vessels which were even now under press of canvas beating their way across the Atlantic.*

On May 23 news reached Cumberland at Windsor Great Lodge from the Admiralty that a portion of the French fleet had returned to Brest. He therefore called a meeting of the Regency † to consider the bearing which this might have on the relative strength of naval forces in home waters. The assurances given by Lord Anson were convincing and complete. The policy of the Government therefore remained unaltered. Their aim was to speed up their warlike preparations, maintain a preponderating superiority in the Channel, prolong the negotiations with Mirepoix, complete the subsidiary treaty with the Landgrave of Hesse-Cassel, bring persuasion to bear at St. Petersburg to induce the Czarina to agree to the loan of a Russian army, and make Austria and Holland play their part by sending troops to defend the Low Countries—and then, in due season, Braddock victorious in America, and the defeat of the French fleet by Boscawen off the shores of Acadia, would change the face of things. France would realise the futility of a general war if in North America and on the high seas she was at the mercy of England. That was the situation as it presented itself to Newcastle. It was true that France was forming artillery parks, and magazines of hay, corn, and other provisions, and concentrating troops on the line Givet, St. Omer, Valenciennes, Lille, Mézières, Charleville; ‡ but the contemplated British victories would in all probability paralyse these landward activities.

One cloud, however, was creeping above the horizon, was indeed already casting a shadow and dulling the lively colours of Newcastle's fancy. On May 28 Holdernesse informs Newcastle " that the *Court of Vienna flatly refuse sending any succours to the Low Countries* till the treaty to be made with

* Add. MS. 32855, f. 119, Newcastle to Holdernesse, May 20, 1755.

† The Regency appear to have met generally at 7.30 p.m., either in the Cockpit or more often at Cumberland's apartments in St. James's Palace.

‡ Add. MS. 32855, f. 370, Andrew Mitchell to Newcastle, June 6, 1755.

Russia is concluded and signed: " I never saw the King more uneasy than at this event." * Here was a condition totally unacceptable, menacing in its extravagance, and quite inconsistent with the spirit of the old alliance.† Here at last was the true mind of Austria revealing itself. The King was indignant, Holdernesse deeply perplexed, Newcastle instinctively suspicious. Had they known that in the archives of Vienna there lay that momentous treatise ‡ which, written in 1749, had so profoundly influenced the tone, the temper, and the secret aims of Austrian policy, suspicion would have displaced all else. Was not the writer, one of the foremost minds of Europe, now First Minister to the Imperial Throne? Had he not in that review of national policy shown that in the next war the aims of England and Austria would be no longer similar but divergent, that Austrian troops would be demanded for the defence of the Low Countries, and that England, engrossed in maritime warfare, would be in no position to give direct help to the recovering of Silesia? and had not his conclusion been that it was with France that an alliance must be concerted? § And so during these intervening years the genius of Kaunitz had been directed to achieving the seemingly impossible, to recasting the broad framework of European relations.

Placed in 1750 at the Court of Versailles as the representative of Maria Theresa, Kaunitz had, till he was recalled two years later to occupy the position of Minister at Vienna, devoted himself to the task of conquering the Parisian world. His efforts were not confined to Ministers and the entourage of the King and Madame de Pompadour, but among men of letters, among the " philosophes," among the clergy and the financiers, throughout in short the whole social fabric, he sought to combat the prejudice which existed against things German, against German thought, German manners, and German absence of refinement and grace. It was not only by his astonishing perspicacity and his intellectual finesse that he set

* Add. MS. 32855, f. 236, Holdernesse to Newcastle, May 28, 1755.

† Add. MS. 32856, f. 464, Hardwicke to Newcastle, July 5, 1755: " They [the Austrians] will send 20,000 men into the Netherlands provided certain things are done which they know never will be done."

‡ See ante, p. 9.

§ Duc de Broglie, *L'Alliance Autrichienne* (1895), p. 18.

out to accomplish his end, but by the employment of every art that could add stature to his personality or lustre to his presence in the world of Paris. Of a tall and striking figure, with regular features, with eyes that radiated intelligence, and manners that at once denoted the highest degree of natural courtesy and distinction, he was well framed to show that elegance was a game at which Germans as well as French could play. He could with as much facility charm the King and lift from that weary presence the sense of ennui, as insinuate criticisms of Frederick and advocate the cause of the Imperial Crown in his diplomatic discourses with Ministers. Affecting in his dress and his perruques a degree of fantasy which seemed to bring him into rivalry with the *petits maîtres* of the capital, he was at the same time able to win the admiration of soldiers and statesmen by the force and culture of his intellect. Just as at Brussels and the Congress of Aix-la-Chapelle his entertainments and concerts had eclipsed all others and been the envy of the assembled plenipotentiaries, so in Paris his hospitality outshone that of rival embassies, and yielded nothing in brilliance to the great houses of the Faubourg St. Germain. In his habits he was eccentric. To dinner parties he would bring his own dessert. Fresh air was an object of dread to which he exposed himself as little as circumstances would allow. Even while passing from his carriage to a palace door his mouth would be covered. No etiquette was permitted to detain him even in the presence of his sovereign after eleven at night. In his discourse he was fluent and illuminating. In his judgments and portraits of men he was unerring. No discouragement could deflect him and no difficulty deter him in the pursuit of the policy which he had conceived for the advantage of his country and the Empress-Queen to whom his endeavours were dedicated. At the conclusion of his embassy he had to confess that no proposals which Austria could make would change the system on which the policy of Louis rested. "That," he said, "can only be brought about by some alteration of circumstances which will show France where her real interests lie. Hitherto no circumstance of that kind has presented itself." * In 1755, as we have seen, he was still

* Add. MS. 32855, f. 354, Newcastle to Holdernesse, June 6, 1755.

carrying on the old tradition with England. Not yet had he reached his goal.

But that lucid mind, looking forward and calculating the strains and stresses which were disturbing Europe, saw that his hope might yet mature. With a perceptible stiffening of his attitude towards English demands, there went an extension of friendly offices to France, a greater freedom in communicating views, a wider search for avenues of approach. By June 7 Newcastle's suspicions had deepened. He expressed alarm. The evidence which was coming in showed a change in the relations between Paris and Vienna.* By June 28 Holdernesse found it necessary to write a note of warning to Keith. " It is not," he said, " the first time that Count Kaunitz has been observed to affect a disobliging and unnecessary mystery even in Trifles. . . . And I must not conceal from you that suspicions have arisen in other Courts of some duplicity in the Court of Vienna on the present occasion." †

It was not the only sign of change in the politics of Europe. In May 1755 Frederick was making a voyage to Holland, in the incognito of a Polish officer, accompanied by Prince Ferdinand ‡ of Brunswick passing as a Dresden merchant. In December 1754 he had written to his representative in London one of those letters which were habitually intercepted and deciphered, in which he declared that he did not believe the agreement negotiating between England and Russia, " sous le Prétexte frivole de me brider par là et de m'empêcher d'attaquer le Pais d'Hanovre," § would come to anything. Had he changed his view? Because here in May he was suggesting an interview with George II. The proposal came through the Duke of Brunswick. The meeting could take place when he was on his way through Hanover to Holland. Newcastle and Holdernesse welcomed the suggestion. ‖ It might have a significance of the deepest import. Only in April Frederick had been giving aggressive advice to La Touche, the French

---

* Add. MS. 32855, f. 354, Newcastle to Holdernesse, June 6, 1755.
† Add. MS. 32856, f. 29, Holdernesse to Keith, June 28, 1755.
‡ *Ibid.*, f. 262, Holdernesse to Newcastle, June 27, 1755.
§ Add. MS. 32851, f. 340, Frederick to Michell, Dec. 21, 1754.
‖ *Ibid.*, f. 354, Newcastle to Holdernesse, June 6, 1755.

representative at Potsdam, and speaking of his uncle George II in terms which La Touche thought it more decent in his letter to Rouillé not to repeat: " invade Hanover," said Frederick, " c'est le moyen le plus sûr de faire chanter ce —— Ici le roi de Prusse qualifiait le roi d'Angleterre son oncle d'une épithète cavalière qu'il est inutile de vous rendre." * But the hatred of the nephew for the uncle was as water unto wine in comparison with the hatred of the uncle for the nephew. This *volte-face* affected George not at all. Nothing would induce him to see the King of Prussia. His personal animosity was stronger than reasons of State; besides, were not the Russian negotiations a better argument than any he could produce at an interview with so formidable a nephew as Frederick? George, however, did agree that if Frederick took the shortest route, which lay actually beneath the ramparts of Hanover, he should be received with a salute from the guns of the city.† But the Prussian King passed a " German mile away " from the walls : the guns were silent : George remained invisible at Herrenhausen. Later the King so far yielded to the solicitations of his Ministers that he agreed to the firing of a salute from one of the forts within earshot of which Frederick would pass on his return journey; and so it came about that, as the King of Prussia " in cinnamon coloured coat with gold buttonholes; in black wig : his face and coat considerably dusted with Spanish snuff," passed with his attendants along the burning summer roads towards the end of June,‡ there broke on his ear the sound of a Hanoverian salute. It was a sound that must have been not without suggestion to that restless brain. And as he leant back in the shadow of his great coach the roll of the cannon may have carried to his mind some hint that the menace of Russia was perhaps not so near, his tenure of Silesia perhaps more secure. It was a sound well calculated to bring a smile across those vivacious lips. For no man knew so well or had proved so faithfully the frailty of a treaty obligation. None had so proclaimed that the word of Kings

* Waddington, p. 163.

† Add. MS. 32856, f. 38, Holdernesse to Newcastle, June 18, 1755.

‡ Holdernesse writes that it was the hottest summer within the memory of man.

and rulers was of small account. How far, if at all further, an interview would have carried matters at this juncture, it is impossible to say. Holdernesse could only write: " Les pour-parlers avec le Roi de Prusse se sont dissipés en fumée." *

Meanwhile the French fleet under Dubois de la Motte, sailing with instructions that imposed on the admiral the necessity of avoiding combat so long as it did not compromise the honour of the flag, had sighted on June 9 the British ships under Boscawen off the banks of Newfoundland. True to their orders the French ships, under a crowd of sail, endeavoured to evade an engagement. On June 10 the rearmost ships were overhauled. Le Lys and L'Alcide were forced to surrender; the remaining fourteen vessels succeeded in reaching their goal. Four hundred soldiers and 200,000 livres in specie remained in the hands of the British. But the result was a meagre fulfilment of British hopes. Everything had been compromised, nothing in reality had been achieved.

On the mainland Braddock was pursuing his arduous march. On June 5 he had written from Wills' Creek complaining of the skinflint policy of the authorities, the difficulties of transport, the obstacles he had encountered in the lethargy and avarice of the colonials and the physical features of the country. " I know not whether to express a greater surprise at the supineness and unreasonable œconomy of the Governments and people of the southern colonies or at the general falsehood and dishonesty that prevails among them." †

Preaching his last sermon to the people of Savannah in 1741, Whitefield had told his congregation that they were the " scum of the earth, and that God had only sent them to prepare the way for a better set of men." ‡ Fifteen years had, in Braddock's opinion at any rate, wrought no change in the character of the Colonists. They were doing little to assist and much to embarrass the British commander. They were exploiting to the best of their opportunity the mercenary side of the situation.

* Add. MS. 32856, f. 38, Holdernesse to Newcastle, June 18, 1755.
† Add. MS. 32855, f. 336, Braddock to Newcastle, June 5, 1755.
‡ *Diary of the First Earl of Egmont,* III, p. 230 (His. MS.).

11

It was in January that Braddock had left England: at the beginning of June he was still one hundred and ten miles from his objective. On June 10 with his army he began the last stage of his fatal march, winding along the narrow trails of the forests, "sprawling and staggering" up paths nearly perpendicular in some places, moving sometimes at the rate of not more than four miles a day, sickness invading his force, the fatal Indians hovering on his flanks. But it was not till August that the full tale of the Braddock disaster was to reach the ears of the Ministry in London. Before that, a momentous decision had been come to by the Regency.

The question had definitely to be settled—what orders were to be given to Sir Edward Hawke, who with his fleet of twenty-one ships of the line was now ready to put to sea? Cumberland, more than ever convinced that France was only waiting her own opportunity to commence hostilities,* was for giving orders to Hawke which would involve attacking the French fleet and harassing their commerce. British superiority in home waters was, so Lord Anson assured the Lords Justices, decisive. The French trade ships would shortly be due on their homeward voyage from the East and West Indies, and the capture of these would be a serious blow to the finances of France and at the same time lessen the number of her men available for sea service. A victory in the Channel at such a moment might have a paralysing effect on French activities, might in fact lead at once to a reasonable peace. This was why "the D.," as Newcastle wrote, "certainly wishes nothing but war." † A further consideration present to the mind of Cumberland was the impossibility of taking any active steps on the Continent during the remainder of the year. ‡ If as everybody now seemed to agree war must come, then in Heaven's name let it begin under the circumstances most favourable to England—that is, on the sea, and while England had such a marked superiority of naval force.

Newcastle, on the other hand, who was beginning to show all the hesitancy and timidity with which he has been credited,

* Add. MS. 32856, f. 448, Newcastle to Holdernesse, July 2, 1755.
† *Ibid.*
‡ *Ibid.*

now that the need for great decisions had arisen, reasoned that it was one thing to pursue hostilities in America, another and very different thing to commence them in Europe: to do so would make the British the aggressors, saddle them with a charge of breach of faith, tend to turn Spain from her promise of neutrality to supporting France, and in any case precipitate a general war on the Continent.

Cumberland and Newcastle therefore were now divided in opinion. They respectively represented the two extremes of policy suggested by an exceedingly difficult and complicated problem. Newcastle was able to command a majority on the Regency, and thus to avert an immediate decision. He manœuvred to secure delay and avoid responsibility. First the question of orders for Hawke was referred to Hanover. On June 22 an answer was received from Holdernesse. The King was of opinion * that Hawke should forthwith put to sea to exercise and discipline the crews, but without instructions for the present to fall upon the French fleet or to intercept their trade. The King desired that the Cabinet should be summoned at once, and furnish advice as to what should be done if France sent no answer or an unsatisfactory answer to the last communication of the British Government (of June 6): should negotiations be broken off? should hostilities be commenced either with or without a declaration of war? Here was a demand for definite advice. How was it met? On the evening of Sunday, June 29,† the Regency assembled in Cumberland's rooms. Of what took place, there is no clear account, but from the resolutions come to it is evident that Newcastle had once more ensured postponement. It was resolved in the first place that, as no definite instructions could be given to Hawke, his sailing with any part of the fleet should be suspended. Then in lieu of giving the King the advice asked for, the resolutions went on to ask counter questions of the King. If a reply came from Mirepoix, should it be sent to Hanover to ascertain His Majesty's pleasure thereon, or "would he be pleased to permit his servants to determine how far it might be proper to break off negotiations?" If

* Add. MS. 32856, f. 95, Holdernesse to Newcastle, June 22, 1755.
† Add. MS. 32996, f. 149, June 29, 1755.

no reply came, might Mirepoix be told that negotiations must be considered at an end? If it was found necessary to give hostile orders to Hawke, might they be framed without reference to His Majesty? * In the same way, might the question of war with or without declaration be left to His Majesty's Ministers? Thus responsibility was being bandied about between Hanover and London without finding shoulders strong enough to bear it, and all the while opportunity was receding and precious time being lost. Newcastle in one of his letters to Holdernesse in reference to this meeting wrote: " If we openly opposed a measure of vigour in appearance, proposed and supported by the Duke †—and this is the unhappy situation in which we are in—the only way to prevent the ill effects of it was to gain time to get powers to act." ‡

Here then was a frank confession of the means which the Newcastle party were adopting to outwit Cumberland and his supporters. Newcastle wanted time. He deemed it essential for the maturing of his Continental schemes to hold Hawke in check, and avoid any action which would precipitate the crisis in Europe. He was playing for safety, and handling the situation very much as he would if it were a party question at home. He was the wary huntsman. He wanted every earth stopped. He wanted in fact to see France isolated and European opinion as far as possible on his side before taking action. On the other hand, it can equally well be argued that the judgment which Cumberland had formed was right. He brought to bear on the problem not only a massive common sense, but a power, formed and tempered in the fire of military experience, of estimating factors which could only be surmised as well as those which were known. The War of the Austrian Succession had taught him much—above all that England's power for effective action on the Continent was cramped and even sterilised by the inefficiency and unwillingness of the Dutch and the Austrians, and that her true sphere of operations under such conditions was the sea. No one knew better than Cumberland that the Peace of Aix-la-Chapelle was rendered

---

* Add. MS. 32996, f. 149, Cabinet Memoranda, July 2, 1755.
† Cumberland.
‡ Add. MS. 32856, f. 448, Newcastle to Holdernesse, July 2, 1755.

possible less by the gallantry of his soldiers in the Low Countries than by the success of the fleets which England had been able to equip. On land everywhere and on every occasion either the Dutch or the Austrians, and generally both, had failed him. Marshal Saxe had been uniformly victorious. And yet during the course of the war France had been reduced to a point of complete exhaustion. Her commerce had been destroyed, her treasure depleted to the verge of bankruptcy, her fleets sunk, captured, or rendered powerless to act, and her mercantile marine conducted into English ports. Sea power had brought about this result. And now in 1755, with the naval superiority of Britain again present, there was a chance of epitomising the experiences of the previous war and of inflicting at once and at the outset a blow which might cripple the power of France, and bring about a favourable peace. To Cumberland the risk of alienating Spain was a political risk which the military situation rendered it necessary to take. A naval victory would infuse a new spirit into the allies, and resolve many hesitations in Europe, give pause to Frederick in his friendship with France, and bring Russia warmly to the side of England. Cumberland was right in thinking war could no longer be avoided. British action in America and the orders to Boscawen had made it morally certain. That was the assumption on which he proceeded. If further we take into account that, as we now know, Austria was leaning towards France, the States of Holland towards a neutrality, and Frederick towards a break with Louis, and that Russia was only waiting the occasion to act with the Maritime Powers, we have a series of factors which, though not revealed at that time, tend very much to support the correctness of Cumberland's judgment. In his opinion the moment to strike had come. A naval victory in that summer of 1755 would have resounded through Europe and brought about, so he considered, reactions on the whole decidedly favourable to the British cause. But it was not to be. At every turn Cumberland was frustrated, whether by the King in respect of the military preparations which he proposed for America, or by Newcastle in the larger strategy involved in the question of peace or war.

CHAPTER XVI

On July 9 Holdernesse replied to the communication of the Lords Justices dated July 2.* The King, he stated, desired that the Regency should exercise a discretionary power, and act in the matter of peace and war according as circumstances might require.† The delegation of authority was therefore constitutionally complete. Responsibility was once more shifted to London. At the moment that Holdernesse in Hanover was writing his despatches to London, Braddock on the continent of America was drawing near to Fort Duquesne. On that day (July 9) the British soldiers in their scarlet coats, loaded with the full weight of their equipment ‡ and sore tried by a summer of unusual intensity, were for the second time in company with the blue-coated Virginians fording a bend of the Monongahela river. It was towards one o'clock that the rearmost portion of the long column had reached the opposite bank. No cloud was visible in the sky. It was a moment impressive in its pageantry. The passage of the river had been effected with all the picturesque ceremonial of a parade. Colours had been unfurled. Bands had broken with their music the heavy silence of the surrounding forest. Guns, howitzers and waggons, packhorses and cattle had squelched and rumbled through the shallows, and were now at rest on the opposite bank. The brilliance of the scene, the order with which it had been executed, the halt which followed in the cool shade of the trees, had given fresh heart to the troops. The prospect of an end to that unwonted march had heightened their spirits. It was with a

* See ante, p. 164.

† Add. MS. 32856, f. 589, Holdernesse to Newcastle, July 9, 1755. *Ibid.*, f. 594, Holdernesse to Robinson, July 9, 1755.

‡ Add. MS. 32857, f. 216, Adam Stephens to John Hunter, Fort Cumberland, July 18, 1755: "You might as well send a cow in pursuit of a hare as one of our soldiers loaded as they are against naked Indians or Canadians in their shirts."

Earl of Holdernesse

D'ARCY ROBERT, FOURTH EARL OF HOLDERNESSE (1718-1778).

From the Portrait by Knapton in the possession of the Dilettante Society.

new though shortlived confidence that towards three o'clock the advance was resumed. Barely had the long line uncoiled its length, and the flank guards disposed themselves parallel to the line of march, when the guides at the head of the column fell back to give warning that the enemy were on all sides in the forest, fronting the line of advance. It is no part of this narrative to trace the events that followed. Suffice it that before sundown, the British force was in rout,* the General mortally wounded, the guns abandoned, the scene of the action strewn with the dead and dying. Every horror with which the dreaded infamy of the Indians had terrorised the settlers was associated with the defeat. It was a mere remnant of the force which, as evening fell, recrossed the Monongahela † and began its retreat towards the distant borders of a civilised world.

Meanwhile at home the Newcastle party, as we have seen, had gained another step in their policy of retardation. But a chronic apprehension, now taking a more than usually lively form, was forcing itself on the attention of Newcastle. Reviewing the financial resources of the country, he was dismayed at the prospect which faced the Government. The estimate of supply for 1756 was £4,641,535. This allowed for 40,000 seamen, 26,089 " Guards and Garrisons," 8,000 marines, and a sum of £236,420 " for forces in the Plantations." ‡ Five millions could be raised by 4d. in the pound on land and by the malt tax, by one million from the Sinking Fund, and by one million from a lottery. Beyond this Newcastle considered it impossible to go. " From this state of the case," he wrote, " it appears that it will be impracticable to raise above five millions without new and most burthensome and probably insufficient taxes, and without increasing very considerably the National debt." § All this was an additional argument for

---

* See ante, p. 132.

† A suburb of Pittsburgh known as Braddock occupies the site of the battle. Pittsburgh itself is built on the site of Fort Duquesne, which later became Fort Pitt.

‡ Add. MS. 32857, f. 34, Estimate of Supply for 1756, from which the above figures are taken.

§ Add. MS. 32857, f. 2, Newcastle to Holdernesse, July 11, 1755.

keeping clear of Continental warfare. This Lilliputian idea of British finance was supported by Sir John Barnard, the financial adviser of the Government, who considered that to incur further "expenses on the Continent would be fatal to this country." * Indeed Sir John was for leaving Hanover to fish for itself, meanwhile forcing a peace in America and on the sea, when the restoration of Hanover, if that state had been invaded, would naturally be a term of any arrangement come to.† He even went so far as to say that the raising of six millions in the last year of the War of the Austrian Succession had been "a mad project and that we could not have gone on with a war at that expense." Newcastle's own conclusion was that Britain must cut her strategy according to her financial cloth, a conclusion which coincided with but admitted of no extension of the scheme he had already formed and was putting into execution. No wonder George II was apprehensive and insistent for precise information as to what the Ministry intended to do for his kingdom. It was all very well to say that he "need not doubt having the assistance of this country," but what form was the assistance to take? Newcastle could only point to the Russian negotiations, the Hessian treaty, an undertaking to pay for an augmentation in the army of Hanover, and a proposal, if the Dutch would contribute, to renew the Bavarian and Saxon treaties.

On July 14 news reached London of Boscawen's engagement off the coast of Newfoundland. Though Walpole wrote gaily to Mann, " Our correspondence will revive: the war is begun," disappointment prevailed in Ministerial circles. " What he [Boscawen] has done," wrote Hardwicke,‡ is either too little or too much. The disappointment gives me great concern." The City, however, took a favourable view. They welcomed the signs of vigour manifest in the orders to Boscawen, § thereby giving great comfort to Newcastle. There was a very marked

---

* Add. MS. 32857, f. 4, Newcastle to Holdernesse, July 11, 1755.

† *Ibid.*, f. 45, Newcastle to Holdernesse, July 11, 1755. This was the view subsequently entertained by Pitt, both in his interview with Hardwicke on August 8, 1755, and in his famous speech.

‡ *Ibid.*, f. 91, Hardwicke to Newcastle, July 14, 1755.

§ *Ibid.*, f. 185, Newcastle to Holdernesse, July 18, 1755.

increase in the deference paid to City opinion at this period, synchronising as it did with the growth of the industrial spirit and commercial influence. The French Ministry, not altogether without reason, expended themselves in outbursts of indignation against the conduct of England. Every Court in Europe was circularised with diatribes against the action of the British. Rouillé in his letter to Mirepoix said the King of France " se revancherait par tout pour l'insolente Pyratterie de cette nation et la Fausseté de ses Ministres." * And it was in such a sense that the Chancelleries of Europe were instructed. Bussy was given orders to leave Hanover unless Holdernesse " could give assurances that Admiral Boscawen had not received orders to attack his Most Christian Majesty's Ships."† The Duc de Mirepoix was abruptly withdrawn from London. " Voilà la danse commencée, le Duc de Mirepoix parti par ordre de sa Cour sans prendre congé," wrote Newcastle on July 24.‡ Mirepoix, with his train of lap-dogs, his pedestrian accompaniment of footmen, and his cabriolets, had already ceased to be anything but a faint symbol of a fading peace. But now the " house near St. James's Square "§ was empty : and all its significance had vanished.

The advent of war was so gradual, the footfall of its approach was accompanied by so little sound or fury, that popular enthusiasm and even interest was scarcely stirred. It was essentially at the outset a war of commerce—a matter for the trading world—the lately risen portion of the community whose concern was industrial. It was in due time to change its character, but for the moment it had no affinity with the emotions of the mob. Knots of idle spectators would gather in the evening about St. James's Palace to watch the members of the Regency arrive. There they would see Cumberland in his scarlet coat and cockaded hat and high military boots stepping out of the chaise which had brought him from Windsor; Lord Hardwicke in his chancellor's wig and robe arriving from Powis House in Lincoln's Inn; Newcastle, who

* *Ibid.*, f. 295, Newcastle to Holdernesse, July 22, 1755.
† *Ibid.*, f. 310, Holdernesse to Newcastle, July 23, 1755.
‡ *Ibid.*, f. 330, Newcastle to General Wall, July 24, 1755.
§ Ante, p. 153.

would post from Claremont, or come in his coach from New-castle House, or stroll across the Park from "his lodgings in the Cockpit"—a tall, upright figure, in full white wig and three-cornered hat, clothed in sombre velvet and ruffles, the diamond star of the Garter adding prestige to the distinction of his appearance; and Fox and Robinson, and the veteran Lord Granville also adorned with the blue ribbon and star. There were grave enough decisions to be made within the Palace doors; but these were wanting in such dramatic quality as would find a response in the public mind. Probably never in history was the normal life of the nation less disturbed at the prospect of hostilities than on the eve of the Seven Years' War. In August Walpole was writing, "The war which began with such a flirt of vivacity, is I think gone to sleep;" and yet to those who had ears to hear there was the hum of armies moving and the stir of nations gathering strength for war.

If Cumberland was for war abroad, he was far too conscious of the disadvantage of the Royal House divided against itself at such a moment not to make an effort to establish peace in his family at home. In June he is found visiting the Princess of Wales at Carlton House, and suggesting that the young Prince of Wales and his brother Prince Edward should accompany him to Portsmouth to review the fleet. The Princess was not of a conciliatory disposition; her jealousy of Cumberland as head of the Regency, of his rising popularity, of his influence in the counsels of the nation was not to be overcome. She was secure in her new alliance with Pitt and her more than friendly relations with Lord Bute. Newcastle and Hardwicke discussed the possibility of inter-vention, but considered it too dangerous: "How difficult it is," wrote Hardwicke,* "to carry the knife between the Paring and the apple in such cases." If they interfered they would only burn their fingers. The Princes therefore remained in London. Cumberland proceeded alone to Portsmouth. Here he was received on July 2 with an enthusiasm which showed him to be once more a popular favourite. It was a reception reminiscent of the days of Culloden, when as a young prince twenty-five years of age he had in 1746 returned in triumph

* Add. MS. 32856, f. 270, Hardwicke to Newcastle, June 27, 1755.

to London. Among those who came to witness the review and pay homage to the Captain General was one of Cumberland's most consistent and faithful admirers.* And the cordiality which Cumberland extended to Lieutenant-Colonel Wolfe, now twenty-eight years of age, made it clear that he still entertained the high opinion which he had formed of that officer on the battlefields of Flanders, and endorsed by early and rapid promotions.

The Ministry had now nothing further to expect from the King. The responsibility had been fixed once and for all. Decision rested with the Lords Justices. On July 21 Cumberland summoned a meeting to decide on the orders to be given to Hawke. Again there was a cleavage of opinion. Cumberland at the outset said: " If they had any prospect of a peace, he had nothing to say; but if they were convinced it must be war, he had no notion of not making the most of the strength and opportunity we had in our hands." † Assuming it was to be war, he was in favour of falling on every ship flying the French flag, whether of the navy or the merchant marine. Newcastle ‡ was for limiting hostile action to ships of the line, Lord Granville for extending it to all vessels carrying the King's flag, " but he was absolutely against meddling with trade—he called it vexing your neighbours for a little muck." §

Granville's proposal, though it has received the qualified support of the highest authority,|| was a compromise adjusted to a state of things which in substance did not exist. Our neighbours had already been sufficiently " vexed " by the action of Boscawen; any day news might arrive from Braddock; how was it possible any longer to hope for peace? Then again, instructions to attack vessels carrying the King's flag were instructions to make war—neither more nor less. To spare commerce at the same time, was to make that war imperfectly. Nevertheless the proposal was carried. Newcastle and Granville have both stated their reasons. Newcastle's guiding

---

* Beckles Willson, *Life of James Wolfe,* p. 268.
† Dodington, *Diary,* p. 344.
‡ Add. MS. 32857, f. 298, Newcastle to Holdernesse, July 22, 1755.
§ Dodington, *Diary,* p. 345.
|| Julian Corbett, *England in the Seven Years' War,* I, p. 61.

preoccupation was to avoid a charge of beginning a European war.* If orders were given to Hawke to fall upon any little frigate, it would probably mean war in forty-eight hours: ships of the line were not so easily to be found. Besides, it would never do to begin the war before the King could get notice of what the instructions to Hawke actually were. In any case France had behaved in such a " very violent manner " over the Boscawen affair, that they were sure to begin hostilities themselves. Granville † thought that the result of attacking French trade would be to antagonise Prussia and Spain and cause Holland to take up a neutrality, but, as his proposal showed, he was quite ready to fall on any vessel carrying the King's flag. It is difficult to believe that such a splitting of hairs in face of the enemy could have done much to calm the susceptibilities of other nations.

But as if this were not compromise enough, the next day, July 22 (the day moreover on which Mirepoix was recalled), Lord Anson, who during the interval must have been " got at " by Hardwicke or Newcastle, was for further modification of the instructions. A night's reflection, so it was said, had brought him round to the view of Newcastle, and by the morning he was in favour of limiting Hawke's orders to hostile action against ships of the line only. With so weighty an authority on his side, Newcastle had then to obtain the assent of Cumberland; but his own words best describe what occurred:

> It has always been my opinion that the beginning of hostilities in Europe should depend upon the nature and consequence of the object. . . . H.R.H. has been as invariable for taking everything of every kind. My Lord Granville was of a third opinion. To fall upon no merchantmen but upon every the least considerable vessel with the King's flag, and so notwithstanding all I could say It was determined last night at our meeting with His Royal Highness. But my Lord Anson reflecting upon what I had said (which in regard to the Men of War he thought should be confin'd to Ships of the Line) did this morning desire that that part of the Instructions might be reconsidered. I

* Add. MS. 32857, f. 295, Newcastle to Holdernesse, July 22, 1755.
† *Ibid.*, f. 266, Granville to Newcastle, July 20, 1755.

persevered in my opinion. H.R.H. seem'd to acquiesce tho he professed his Opinion to be the same as it always had been.*

The politician had won. The soldier had reluctantly been argued into formal acquiescence. Can there be any doubt that Cumberland was right? that the time for compromise was past? and that to issue instructions for hostile action and at the same time circumscribe the effectiveness of that action was wrong? Newcastle was at least consistent in his policy of temporising and postponing, because he did not believe that any ships of the line would be encountered.† But the reasoning of Lord Granville and Lord Anson could lead neither to the maintenance of peace nor to the effective prosecution of war. It was as though a footpad about to deprive his victim of his money should propose to leave him his purse in the hope of escaping a charge of theft. Everything that Cumberland was urging in May and had been urging since he became head of the Regency was given effect at the end of August and the beginning of September. Then it was that the orders which he was in favour of issuing to Hawke were despatched to the commanders on all the naval stations of Britain—to Boscawen and the captains on the coast of Newfoundland, Virginia, and Carolina, to the Admiral in the Mediterranean, and to the commanders off the Leeward Islands and Jamaica and in the Downs, all of whom were ordered " to seize and take by all means in your power all French ships, as well as men of war and privateers as merchantmen, and to send them into port without embezzlement till his Majesty's pleasure be known." ‡ Exactly the measure that Cumberland pleaded for in May.

Between July 22 and the end of August little change had occurred. Spain, it is true, had intimated the likelihood of her observing an attitude of neutrality, Wall going so far as to write to Newcastle that the Court of Spain considered " that what Boscawen did in America was the suite of hostilities begun by the French: § and that the repair of the Fortifica-

* Add. MS. 32857, f. 298, Newcastle to Holdernesse, July 22, 1755.
† *Ibid.*, f. 295, Newcastle to Holdernesse, July 22, 1755.
‡ Admiralty Secretary In-letters, August 27.
§ Add. MS. 32858, f. 353, Newcastle to Holdernesse, August 30, 1755.

tions of Dunkirk * authorised anything that Hawke may do here "—on which Newcastle's comment was: " I think this is a great point and those who were not immediately for beginning war in Europe for the sake of a Prize of a cockboat from a regard to Spain are now fully justified by the event." But were they? Was the policy of Spain in reality based on niceties of such a character? Expediency is seldom at a loss, above all in the case of international affairs, for a plausible and even high-principled explanation. But there is little reason to doubt that a defeat of the French fleet would have disposed Spain to a neutral attitude no less effectively than so debateable a point as the initiation of hostile action. With that exception the arguments which were good at the end of August were the arguments which Cumberland had used throughout. But there was a further consideration on Cumberland's side. In the meanwhile a large portion of the East and West India trade ships had passed into the safety of French ports, and the opportunity of striking a serious blow at French commerce had gone. Had Cumberland prevailed earlier in the day, la Motte might never have reached Newfoundland, the commerce of France might have received a vital injury. According to information received, during the two months preceding July 26 " the value of eighty millions " † (livres) had arrived from the French Indies. In August more ships were expected from the West Indies, and so lively was the fear for their safety when it was known that Admiral Hawke had sailed (July 28) that the insurance rose 25 per cent. at Antwerp.‡ In Paris the greatest alarm was felt, troops were moved with all haste to the coast, war was considered certain, every effort was made to strengthen the defences of Dunkirk; while Louis XV, at last aroused to a sense of what was pending, embarked on severe economies, the building of residences and châteaux for himself and Madame de Pompadour, including alterations at the Louvre, was stopped, his hunting establishments were curtailed

---

* By the Treaty of Aix-la-Chapelle Dunkirk was to be dismantled.

† Add. MS. 32858, f. 55, Information from Compiègne, July 26, 1755.

‡ Add. MS. 32857, f. 320, Andrew Mitchell to Newcastle, August 5, 1755.

and cut down to two in number; it was also announced that his journeys with Madame de Pompadour, which had made such a drain on the exchequer of France, would in future be limited to Choisy and Fontainebleau.* When it was found in August that there was no attack on trade, it was assumed that England had no desire for war. France meanwhile was able to go forward with the strengthening of her armaments and the development of her strategic plans.

If we examine the course of British policy and the influences at work during the critical year 1755, it is clear that Cumberland, as military adviser of the Government, must be acquitted of responsibility for the ill success which attended the opening of the Seven Years' War. He and those who acted with him held views which were not allowed to prevail. They were outvoted and not infrequently outmanœuvred by the Newcastle faction. And while much may be said in defence of Newcastle's conception of the political and military situation, little can be urged in defence of the decisions which were ultimately taken. On the other hand, had Cumberland's advice been followed, a very different turn might have been given to the initial phase of the war, France might have been cut off at the outset from the continent of America, and British supremacy at sea allowed a decisive opportunity to declare itself.

* Add. MS. 32858, f. 55, Information from Compiègne, July 26, 1755.

CHAPTER XVII

On July 22 news arrived in England that Fort Beauséjour had fallen to Monckton on June 16. This, it will be remembered, was one of the four objectives in Cumberland's plan of operations. By this stroke the French were hemmed in to the mainland of Canada, and their communications with Cape Breton and Louisbourg through Acadia severed. It was a partial set off to the disconcerting action under Boscawen. The fate of the two remaining expeditions may here be noticed. Johnson by the first week of September had reached the southern end of Lake George in his advance on Crown Point. There he met and defeated the French under Count Dieskau, who, learning from papers captured on the occasion of Braddock's disaster the intentions of the English, had pushed south from Crown Point with a force of regulars and Indians. The encounter was an incident little more than local in its effect. Johnson * was unable to exploit his success. Sickness, indiscipline, and the shortage of supplies kept him in the vicinity of the scene of his victory, and in November he withdrew, after constructing Fort William Henry at the southern point of Lake George. He had, however, performed a valuable service in negotiating successfully with several powerful tribes among the Indians.

By no means the least important of the four expeditions was that under the command of Major-General Shirley and destined for the capture of Fort Niagara. Shirley was Governor of Massachusetts and now more than sixty years of age. His life had been spent at the law, but the successful practice of his profession had done nothing to hinder him from a belief in his aptitude for a military career. He had sat as one of the members of the Boundary Commission in Paris, and had there married a young Catholic French girl. Neither of these

* He was subsequently knighted.

experiences had shaken him in his policy of dispossessing the French from North America. He had propounded many plans and conceived many military schemes for effecting the purpose, and was regarded alike by the Home Government and in the colonies as an able and zealous leader. At the council held at Alexandria on Braddock's arrival in America, Shirley had readily agreed to the suggestion that he should take command of the force intended for Fort Niagara. It was recognised that the possession of that fort by the English would cut the communications of the French with the Ohio and their southern posts. But the expedition was a failure. It achieved no more than the planting a garrison of seven hundred men at Fort Oswego. Early in November Shirley was back in Albany.

Thus, of the four expeditions, Monckton's alone entirely achieved its object: Braddock's had ended in disaster; Johnson's had failed in its main design, but could count a victory to its credit; while Shirley's had accomplished no part of its programme. The tactical successes had done little to retrieve the complete failure of the strategical purposes aimed at. At home, as the summer progressed and the urgency of affairs increased, the Ministry found themselves, not for the first time, in the difficulty of requiring the presence of the King in England and of having no available means of persuading him to forsake the allurements of Herrenhausen. Holdernesse was directed in July to make representations on the subject. After his first effort in that direction he wrote: " J'ai été reçu ce matin comme un chien dans un jeu de quilles; quand on envisage de près le moment de partir on devient d'une humeur terrible. . . . We say that this being the part of our dominions which is in the most danger it is necessary we should not desert them." * One cannot deny a measure of sympathy to the old King, called on to forsake his native home, and exchange the peace and autocracy of Hanover for the clamour of party strife and the comparative servitude of constitutional monarchy in England. " There are Kings enough in England," he exclaimed; " I am nothing there. I am old and want rest, and should only go to be plagued and teazed there about that damned

* Add. MS. 32857, f. 313, Holdernesse to Newcastle, July 25, 1755.

12

House of Commons." * But he was being plagued already. A storm in England was beating up over the Russian and Hessian proposals. Pitt was hostile. Legge, the Chancellor of the Exchequer, had refused to sign the warrant for the levy money for the Hessian treaty. † Newcastle was fearful that if Pitt took action the difficulties in the House of Commons would be immense, might even prove fatal to the policy of subsidies. The King therefore must be brought to accept and countenance Pitt. Lady Yarmouth was consulted. She was easily persuaded as to the expediency of conciliating so formidable an opponent. As usual, her influence was on the side of peace and common sense. The King was at first unapproachable on the subject, and spoke with violence and ill humour against Pitt. Lady Yarmouth persevered. Holdernesse expounded the situation with tact. Newcastle wrote skilful and convincing documents on the state of home politics. The combined effort was successful, and by July 20 ‡ an undertaking to "accept the services of Pitt and Lord Egmont and countenance them" was wrung from the reluctant King. That was the first step in the vain attempt to muzzle Pitt, but by no means the last. With this accomplished, more direct pressure was applied to induce the King to return to London. Lady Yarmouth advised that a formal appeal should be addressed to him. Cumberland, who had deprecated the King's departure and was as eager for his return, readily assented to the suggestion; and a letter was accordingly forwarded from the Regency humbly urging the difficulties which would be created by a further prolongation of the King's residence in Hanover. It was rightly thought that Cumberland's signature to the appeal would be effective. Holdernesse was able to reply that the "yachts" would be ordered for the second week in September.

Before that date two events of capital importance had changed the outlook on foreign affairs. On August 12 the first overtures were made to the King of Prussia. All through the summer George had been industriously scraping Europe

* Add. MS. 32857, f. 553, Holdernesse to Newcastle, Aug. 3, 1755.
† *Ibid.*, f. 354, Newcastle to Holdernesse, July 25, 1755.
‡ *Ibid.*, f. 256, Holdernesse to Newcastle, July 20, 1755.

for troops to protect Hanover. The Elector of Cologne, the Bishop of Wartzberg, the Duke of Wolfenbüttel, and Prince Waldeck, amongst others, had all been approached in turn: the policy, as Hardwicke called it, of " picking up handfuls of men from little Princes by subsidies," had been exploited to its utmost limits; but the treaty with Russia had not yet been signed, and it was felt in Hanover that these efforts might prove vain unless the formidable and detested nephew at Potsdam could be brought into some general arrangement. Newcastle had urged that steps should be taken in this direction.* Early in August † the King, acting on his own initiative, had despatched Holdernesse to invite the Duke of Brunswick to act as intermediary, and convey to the Prussian King certain tentative suggestions and a pious hope that Frederick would limit the conflagration threatening in Europe by preventing his allies from attacking Hanover. The Duchess of Brunswick, Frederick's sister, had assured ‡ Holdernesse that her brother would " never take part in the present quarrel; he had got what he wanted [Silesia], and all he cared for was to keep it." That was gratifying as far as it went. But every Court in Europe knew that no matter what his obligations, no matter what his undertakings, Frederick when the time came would be guided solely by expediency. It was universally realised that, if he thought it would help him to keep Silesia, he would overrun his uncle's dominions without hesitation or notice. Frederick replied with evasive circumspection. § He deplored the quarrel between France and England over such an insignificant cause, and declared that they had already spent more money than the territory which they were fighting about in North America was worth. Why couldn't the matter be adjusted by proper mediation? To that

* Add. MS. 32857, f. 348, Newcastle to Munchausen, July 25, 1755: " Could it not be represented to the King of Prussia that if he takes no part in the war and undertakes that the King's German dominions are not attacked, then the troops from Russia shall not be requisitioned? " (trans.).

† Add. MS. 32858, f. 140, Holdernesse to Newcastle, Aug. 14, 1755.

‡ *Ibid.*

§ *Ibid.*, f. 226, Frederick to the Duke of Brunswick, Aug. 19, 1755.

end he would be prepared to use his good offices. He neither rejected nor acquiesced in the suggestions made. It was in fact too soon for him to make irretrievable decisions of policy. He could not yet tell what would be the fate of the treaty negotiations between England and Russia. Meanwhile he was closely watching France, with a growing uneasiness at the dilatoriness of her Ministers, the corruption of her Court, the inefficiency of her administration, and the state of her finances.* At any rate he could not commit himself for the time being. But the ice, thick as it was, had been broken. Negotiations had been opened, and, in spite of his uncle's refusal to see him so lately as June, had been initiated by England. The memory of the salute fired in his honour in that month as his coach rumbled through his uncle's dominions suddenly assumed a new significance. Evidently it had meant something more than a flutter of smoke and a gesture of parade.

The other event which created a profound and painful impression in England was Braddock's defeat, the news of which reached London on August 22. The utmost confidence had been felt in England as to the outcome of Braddock's expedition. Cumberland, with his usual desire for a precise and definite policy, had been urging on the Ministry as recently as August 4 † the necessity for making up their minds " whether or not Braddock should attempt Quebec and the French settlements." He said to Newcastle, " You can and ought to take and hold the whole of North America; you command the sea; you can send troops, and it is in America that the war must be won." For the moment, however, visions of conquest were blurred by the consternation caused by Braddock's defeat. " Our piratic laurels," wrote Walpole, " with which the French have so much reproached us have been exceedingly pruned." But at last that steady pressure which Cumberland had exercised in favour of forward measures was allowed to prevail, and the orders already referred to ‡ were issued, not confined, as Newcastle proposed, to Hawke, but extended, as Cumber-

* See *Political Correspondence of Frederick the Great,* Vol. XI, especially the letters to Knyphausen.

† Add. MS. 32857, f. 568, Newcastle to Holdernesse, Aug. 4, 1755.

‡ Ante, p. 173.

land urged, to all commanders on all stations of the British navy. Of this proceeding Newcastle wrote, " This new act of vigour immediately after the arrival of the bad news, will shew spirit "; * and then with a stab at Cumberland added, " You know who recommended Braddock and pick'd out these two regiments." The good relation between Newcastle and Cumberland was wearing very thin. A steadily growing divergence of opinion on the measures to be taken was once more driving them into opposite camps. The lightest challenge to Cumberland's authority was welcome to Newcastle; he could even pause to note with satisfaction that Granville had attended a meeting of the Regency after having obviously " din'd," and been very noisy, and had frequently and sharply contradicted Cumberland. Newcastle was nothing if not vindictive.

On Tuesday, September 16, the King landed at Margate. He had returned to England to find a formidable opposition to the policy of subsidies. Often as the situation has been described, the part played by Cumberland renders it necessary briefly to refer to the transactions which ensued. The Captain General was little disposed in favour of the policy. His view was that the old system was dead, and that in the absence of new alliances " we were cut off from the continent not only for the present but for his time." † He had discussed the matter with Fox, and declared that " the bent of the nation was strong against subsidies for Germany, and that it would be brought to endure them with much reluctance." ‡ There is nothing, however, to show what may have been his alternative; we may rather suppose that his personal view was that Hanover ought to be defended, but that till the feeling in England declared in favour of such a policy, it was not politically desirable or even practicable to attempt it. Certainly he was not prepared to go as far as Pitt, and say that he would rather pay five millions by way of *dédommagement* to Hanover at the end of the war than embark on subsidies at such a moment. On the contrary, if the temper changed, if the defence of Hanover showed itself as an obligation which

---

* Add. MS. 32858, f. 291, Newcastle to Holdernesse, Aug. 26, 1755.
† Add. MS. 32857, f. 182, Newcastle to Holdernesse, Sept. 18, 1755.
‡ Dodington, *Diary*, p. 362.

the nation thought it should fulfil, then he would welcome subsidies as a means to achieving that end. Till then, he was in sympathy with the "almost universal language": * "Sea War, No Continent, No Subsidies." Fox was still hesitating. Pitt and the Leicester House group were definitely hostile. Some, including Pitt, were for opposing the Russian treaty without compromise while prepared to accept the Hessian treaty; others were for rejecting all traffic whatsoever with the Continent by means of subsidies. Newcastle and Hardwicke were therefore using all their ingenuity to disorganise the opposition. It was a difficult task. Negotiations were opened with Pitt. He was interviewed by Hardwicke. This was followed by a meeting with Newcastle, at the prospect of which Newcastle probably understated his apprehensions when he wrote, " I cannot say I have much Glee in seeing Mr. Pitt." † But Pitt was not to be shaken in his resolution to oppose the Russian treaty. That skilful and protracted negotiation by which the King in Hanover had been induced to agree to accept Pitt's services was in consequence rendered abortive. It became imperative as an alternative to make sure of Fox. " In view of the conduct of the Princess of Wales, Mr. Pitt, Lord Egmont, and Sir George Lee, it was absolutely necessary either to take Mr. Fox or go out." Newcastle offered to resign. The King would not hear of it, and Newcastle himself recognised that he would have been exposed for the second time in his career ‡ to all the odium of deserting the King at a crisis.

All this had a great deal of significance for Cumberland. He had worked for ten years with Fox in close friendship. In every measure which he had proposed he had received the political support of the Secretary at War. They had seen eye to eye. They were joint leaders of a definite body of opinion in the State. They held identical estimates of those in power. They had shared a common interest in the welfare of the Army. Together they had passed through the dark days preceding the Peace of Aix-la-Chapelle, and all the political changes and intrigues which had since developed, and never had Fox failed

* Add MS. 32857, f. 362, Newcastle to Holdernesse, July 25, 1755.

† Add. MS. 32858, f. 242, Newcastle to Hardwicke, Aug. 22, 1755.

‡ See *William Augustus Duke of Cumberland*, p. 257.

in the sincerity of his attachment or the constancy of his admiration for the Duke. Now there was in prospect a severance of this alliance. The Army was the passion of Cumberland's life, and in Fox he had a proved and certain ally. But Fox Secretary of State would mean an end of that harmonious understanding which had existed for so long in military matters. Fox as usual sought Cumberland's advice: the Duke's first consideration was his friend's advancement. He advised agreement with Newcastle's terms; and on September 24 Fox accepted the post of Secretary of State with the leadership of the House of Commons. "What I have done," wrote Fox to Lady Hervey, "is in consequence of the deliberate express and concurring advice of the *Duke,* the Duke of Marlborough, Lord Granville and Lord Waldegrave." * On receiving the news Cumberland wrote as follows: †

Mr. Fox, I received your two letters last night the second of which gave me all the satisfaction imaginable for it is no matter to us how bitter the pill was for them nor how much they show'd it since at last the King has put you at the head of the House of Commons. You know my love and the sence I have of your behaviour towards me well enough to conceive the share I take in the success you have gain'd which is much more agreeable as it is a thorough vindication both of the judgment and honesty of the part you have acted ever since Mr. Pelham's death, as to your successor it is a flee bite and no more now—you have had justice and dispel'd the cloud that hung over you so long . . . but how the Duke of Newcastle can bring himself to give you power I still doubt.

Your very sincerely affectionate friend
WILLIAM.

Cumberland had better reason than he knew for "still doubting." On September 26 ‡ Newcastle wrote a letter to Lady Katherine Pelham, which betrays the inner working of his mind and certainly does little to embellish his reputation.

. . . The King will not suffer Mr. Fox to do anything

* Holland House Papers, Fox to Lady Hervey, Sept. 29, 1755.
† Holland House Papers, Cumberland to Fox, Sept. 25, 1755.
‡ Add. MS. 32859, f. 213, Newcastle to Lady Katherine Pelham, Sept. 26, 1755.

even in the House of Commons without previously consulting me: and I am persuaded Fox sees it in this light. I told the King Fox said we must stand and fall together. The King said he [Fox] may very well fall without you. This being the state of the case, the making Fox thus Secretary of State was the best thing for me. He has an office which the King told me he would do ill in. He can seldom see the King without my Lord Holdernesse. He is removed from Secretary of War and so far removed from the Duke. But above all it has given me an opportunity to show the world that the King would put into that office (as he has done) the man the most declared friend of mine My Lord Barrington *without consulting the Duke*. This is a great circumstance.

Whatever Newcastle had intended at the outset, he could now boast that in exchanging the amenable Robinson for the disquieting personality of Fox as Secretary of State, he had seen to it that due limitations were set to Fox's position. He could fortify himself with the opinion of the King that Fox "would do ill," and he could reckon with complacency that he had broken up the Cumberland-Fox combination, and slighted Cumberland with the ingenuous connivance of the King by appointing Barrington as Secretary at War without consulting the Captain General.

Cumberland acted with the magnanimity he never in any crisis or at any time failed to show. He received Barrington "very civilly" and at his first interview told him, with all generosity, that he had no one in view whom he would have preferred for the place. Newcastle had played his parliamentary cards with his habitual skill, and now with Fox as Secretary of State he could feel safe with regard to his subsidies. On September 30, 1755, the treaty with Russia was signed. The substitution of Sir Charles Hanbury-Williams for Colonel Guy Dickens as representative at the Court of the Empress Elizabeth had led to a quick conclusion of the negotiations. They were of the first importance. Indeed, we may fairly point to the treaty with Russia as one of the outstanding features of the eighteenth century. More than any other single circumstance it was responsible for what is known as the diplomatic revolution. To the influence of this treaty can be traced the rupture between Prussia and France, the Convention between Frederick and George II, the alliance between Austria and France, and the preservation to the Low Countries of the coast-line on the North Sea.

If one of the results of the diplomatic revolution was that ultimately it facilitated the conquest of Canada, and the expulsion of the French from North America and India, then the credit due to Newcastle for persisting in his Russian negotiations and bringing them to a conclusion in spite of Pitt and a clamorous opposition must be regarded as far outweighing his many subsequent failings during the progress of the war.

In 1755 the key to the situation was Frederick. That was the basic idea of Newcastle's foreign policy. When once that pact so laboriously brought into existence at the Winter Palace was in Newcastle's hands, the situation in Europe was revolutionised. Hanover for the moment was safe. Hanover, with the obligations it connoted, no longer clogged British policy. The treaty in fact restored freedom of action, and emancipated for the time being the political and military force of Britain, enabling it ultimately to develop on proper strategic lines. It became possible to concentrate on North America and the sea. It became possible effectively to treat with Prussia. Newcastle held the winning suit. He could talk in terms which Frederick would understand. And just how much Frederick was affected, intimidated, and even overborne by the Russian treaty we can learn from his *Political Correspondence* and from the intercepted letters between Bunge and Höpken * now in the Newcastle Papers. These make it clear that as far back as January Frederick was watching for any signs of pourparlers between England and Russia. Later, when aware of the nature of the negotiations, his concern was aroused. As the negotiations progressed his anxiety deepened. He was even found writing in September to enquire of his Ambassador in London whether he thought the King and Ministry " pourraient faire quelque Démarche pour gagner ma neutralité ou

---

* Bunge at this time was Swedish Minister in Paris; and the recipient of the confidences of the French Ministry. His despatches to Höpken, the Minister at Stockholm, were intercepted by British agents and forwarded to Newcastle with great regularity.

s'ils ne feront rien à cet égard et paraîtront ne pas beaucoup se soucier de moi." * With the deepening of his anxiety there grew in his mind a corresponding mistrust of France and a doubt as to the capacity of the French Ministry to deal with the situation. He was impatient at their timidity in negotiation, saying that they acted as if they were made of cotton.† He had offered advice and it had not been followed. He had urged vigorous and immediate preparation, and he saw only dallying and lethargy. He was alarmed at the state of their finances, the extravagance of the Court, the influence of Madame de Pompadour. Why did they not declare war, invade Hanover, and overrun Flanders? Was there no policy, no plan? could they not see that England was merely negotiating to gain time? Feebleness, in his opinion, could go no further.

In November France determined to send the Duc de Nivernais as special envoy to Frederick. The Duke's instructions were immediately known in London by means of the intercepted correspondence between Bunge and Höpken.‡ His orders were to invite Frederick to march on Hanover; and as Frederick had long since made it known that he could not stir in this direction without adequate security from France against the Russian menace, the Duc de Nivernais was instructed to lay before Frederick certain proposals for dealing with this aspect of the situation.§ Frederick declined to entertain any such idea. The proposals were impracticable and worthless. All he could say to France by way of mitigation was that by entering into a neutrality with England he was keeping within their frontiers 60,000 Russians. Thus the treaty with Russia had done its work. It had paralysed Prussia. Newcastle's foresight had been rewarded. It was then but a short step to the Convention of Westminster, and from thence by a logical and inevitable progression to an alliance between England and Prussia with a common objective.

* Add. MS. 32859, f. 193, Frederick to Michel, Sept. 23, 1755.

† *Politische Correspondenz*, XI, p. 117, Frederick to Knyphausen.

‡ Add. MS. 32860, f. 217, Bunge to Höpken, Dec. 8, 1755.

§ These were: (1) to stir up the Porte to threaten the Russian frontier; (2) to form a confederacy in Poland to oppose the passage of Russian troops; (3) to form a confederacy in the Empire between all the allies of France.

CHAPTER XVIII

As time drew on, the association between George II and Cumberland became more and more cordial. In a world where so little was congenial to the King's taste, where so much was dull and even forbidding, his relations with his son stood in high relief. They made a streak of colour in the rather spiritless surroundings which hedged the existence of the King. Here at least was a stable element based on solid values, among the otherwise fugitive and ephemeral phenomena of a Hanoverian Court. Here at any rate were the indications of permanence; and yet within two years the relationship was to be dissolved, on the one side with an outbreak of bitterness and injustice, though on the other, it is true, with loyalty and good faith unimpaired.

In truth no one could look on the goodwill of the King as a permanent institution—at best it was a precarious investment, with uncertain returns. Neither Minister nor courtier could count on his friendship. Indeed his English Ministers never formed any part of his personal life; they were at best the " King's servants," here to-day and gone to-morrow, talking an always unfamiliar speech, concerned with a side of affairs that was distasteful to his habits and inclinations, a necessary infliction varying only in the bother they caused or relieved. His life when in England during his later years was one of semi-isolation. From the recesses of Kensington, where he resided during the spring and summer, he seldom emerged; there he held his levées, interviewed his Ministers, stormed at the perversity of politicians, strolled in the gardens of the palace, and spent the evenings in the sedulous routine of cards with Lady Yarmouth. These habits were seldom infringed.

In November he would take up his residence at St. James's.

Here the King was faithful to his custom of going to St. James's Chapel on Twelfth Night, attended by the principal officers of Court, to " offer frankincense, myrrh, and gold," and in the evening playing at hazard in the Palace with the Royal Family; on rare occasions he would show himself to the populace by walking in the Mall; otherwise to all intents and purposes he might have been a state prisoner, with his itinerary circumscribed by the confines of his palace gardens. His recreation was the transaction of business. Industry was his passion; reviewing capital sentences of the Courts of Justice or the penalties inflicted by courts-martial, a function of the prerogative which he exercised with indefatigable zeal—but seldom with advantage to the condemned. The course of the law was rarely interfered with. Soldiers condemned to death had little to hope for. Sentences of one thousand lashes were not infrequently reduced to six hundred, but his general rule was to confirm whatever sentence had been given. In any case, as Lord Tyrawley * declared that no man could endure more than three hundred lashes, the mitigation provided by the King was more a question of arithmetic than mercy.

He scarcely ever entertained; informality was unknown to him. Ministers never wrote or spoke of him except as an individual remote and apart, whom it was their function and often their misfortune to be obliged to conciliate and humour. Hanover, Cumberland, and Lady Yarmouth were the lodestones of his solicitude and affection. In England he was an exile. His home was elsewhere. The formal gardens of Herren-hausen, the broad well-proportioned façade and the spacious rooms of the palace, the summer-houses where he would sit with the favoured of his subjects, the trim lawns and hedges of yew, the wide paths glowing in the July heat where he could walk with the gait and uncriticised assurance of a Louis Quatorze, the neighbouring forests where he could hunt with all the ceremonial of an autocrat—these were the real solace of a spirit that chafed in the alien environment of England. It was in England that Queen Caroline had died. It was here that his quarrels with his family had become a byword. It was England with its politics which had stood between him

* See post, p. 207.

and the scenes of his youth. It was England with its entanglements which was now jeopardising his native country. It was
Pitt, already one of the foremost of Englishmen, who was for
allowing Hanover to be overrun and left to its fate. And then
again it was England, saved from the Stuarts by Cumberland,
which had shown such deep ingratitude to his son. Ever and
again he would reveal the bitterness in his heart: as when
he said of the Princess of Wales that " she was angry with
Fox for being against the Regency Act, and he was in the
right to be for my son rather than for her. It was the lies
they told and particularly this damned Egmont against my
son for the services he did this Country which had raised this
clamour against him." * The wonder is not that George II
blustered and fretted at the bonds of his English connection,
but that he bowed to the dictation of its needs, and carried
out his constitutional duties with such singleness of purpose.
Certain it is that the presence of Cumberland in England was
his mainstay, and that without him his kingship would have
held an intolerable irksomeness. What Cumberland's feeling
was for the King there is no sort of evidence to show. Whether
at the back of that resolute and disciplined character there lay
a measure of affection for his father, whether in that rigid and
unfailing loyalty there was mixed an element of devotion, can
only be a matter of conjecture. It is at least highly probable;
Cumberland's love for Fox, his lifelong friendship with his
sister Princess Amelia, his gratitude to those who had served
him, and his generosity to his dependents, at any rate show
that he had a deep fund of humanity in his composition. And
something more perhaps than loyalty was needed to bear him
with such dignity and resolution through the crisis which, as
will subsequently be seen, was to arise before the end of the
reign between father and son.

Parliament met in November. Pitt, as we have seen,
had been approached by both Hardwicke and Newcastle.
To Hardwicke Pitt had said of the subsidy treaties:
" Subsidy Treaties would not go down, the Nation
would not bear them, that they were a chain and a connection and would end in a general plan for the Continent

* Add. MS. 32860, f. 19, Newcastle to Hardwicke, Oct. 12, 1755.

which this country could not possibly support." * It was clear
that Pitt had no intention of letting Ministers have their own
way. He felt strong enough to make claims which Newcastle
considered exorbitant. He was threatening in his attitude.
Now too the King was getting old, and Pitt had the backing of
Leicester House. Pitt was becoming a formidable menace.
" Mr. Pitt," wrote Walpole in September, " is scouring his old
Hanoverian trumpet, and Mr. Legge is to accompany him with
his hurdy gurdy." But there was no immediate cause for
alarm. The debates on the Address at the beginning of the
session (November 15) showed that Newcastle was secure by
an overwhelming majority on the question of subsidies. Pitt's
eloquence, and never had he been heard to such advantage,
could persuade no more than 105 members to vote against the
treaties, while Newcastle's followers, led by Fox and William
Murray, numbered 311. Early in December, Pitt, Legge, and
Grenville were dismissed from their Ministerial posts. They
had at least shown that it was possible for a considerable time
to carry on an embittered opposition to the Ministry of which
they were members without surrendering the emoluments of
office. Sir George Lyttelton succeeded Legge as Chancellor
of the Exchequer, Lord Darlington and Lord Dupplin became
joint Paymasters in the place of Pitt, and " that so often
repatriated and reprostituted prostitute " Bubb Dodington
became once more Treasurer to the Navy.

On one proposal all parties were united, namely to grant
£100,000 in relief of the distress caused by the Lisbon earthquake (November 1). That catastrophe had deeply stirred
the public sympathy. Nor did the gesture of benevolence with
which Britain came forward with succour lose at all in sincerity from the recollection of the panic which had been created
in London by a tremor of the earth in the year 1750. Now,
in the hope of averting a similar visitation to that of Lisbon, a
day of fasting was prescribed by Royal Proclamation, to be
observed on February 6 throughout the country. All de-
nominations except the Quakers seem to have accepted the
expediency of the demonstration, and contributed to it with
decorum. But the Quakers, who insisted on keeping their

* Add. MS. 32858, f. 76, Hardwicke to Newcastle, Aug. 9, 1755.

shops open, became the target for bitter attacks by the populace, and caused the solemnity of the fast day to be marred by rioting.

When it was a question of military ways and means, what was known as the Inner Cabinet continued to meet from time to time, under the presidency of Cumberland, at St. James's Palace. The Inner Cabinet or Conciliabulum was one of those improvisations which hostilities and a state of war tend to bring about. It had no place in the Constitution, but was the outcome of the emergency, and largely corresponded to the War Cabinet of more recent days. Cumberland, as acting head of the Regency and as Captain General, had a dual claim to form part of its constitution, but even Cumberland was not always present at the deliberations. It had no recognised status, nor has there come down to us any Cabinet minute dealing with its formation. It was a body which may be said to have been carved equally out of the Lords Justices, the Cabinet Council, and the Privy Council, and to have exercised to some extent the authority of all three. Nominally its decisions required confirmation by the Cabinet, in practice the confirmation was on occasions dispensed with. Thus a decision of the Conciliabulum would become the subject of a resolution by the Lords Justices, in whom lay the executive, without reference to the Outer Cabinet. Hardwicke and the two Secretaries of State were the permanent members, and met sometimes without, more often with, Cumberland, Anson, and Lord Granville the Lord President. Later on Lord Mansfield, who had no connection with the Government, was called in to act as a member. He appears at first to have taken a strictly constitutional view, and wrote in answer to the invitation: " Nobody can see the scene blacker than I do. I don't understand from anything in your Grace's Request how or in what shape or with what view I am to be called to any Meeting. . . . But I shall not wish to attend where I have no right to be, only to be marked as present." * In the end, however, he consented, and Newcastle was able to write: " Lord Mansfield is called to the Cabinet Council . . . this is a great proof of Mr. Pitt's desire to go on with us and that the King should

* Add. MS. 32873, f. 119, Mansfield to Newcastle, Aug. 16, 1757.

have the assistance of able and honest men though they have not any particular connection with him." *   In time of war therefore the tendency, which had been so steadily growing, to regard the Cabinet as a Parliamentary institution, responsible to Parliament, was suspended.

But at these meetings, if the policy of Cumberland was one thing, the temper of the Government was quite another.   The aim of Cumberland was to give coherence, vigour, and consistency to the national policy; the aim of the Government was to do the least which might in their fluctuating judgment be consonant with the defence of the country and the prosecution of the war, above all to pursue economy to the point of parsimony, and trim their sails to the choppy breezes of Parliamentary favour.   Cumberland made frequent representations as to the insufficiency of the forces of the Crown. †   Like Pitt, he believed in developing British resources and in organising the country for war.   But he could do little with Ministers in their then disposition.   He was constantly overruled.   Yet we may fairly attribute to Cumberland's influence the fact that there was some show of vigour in the resolutions come to at the meetings over which he presided.

In September he had urged that new regiments should be raised.   This was categorically negatived by the King with the approval of Newcastle.   The Government decided that the increase ‡ to the land forces should be by way of augmentation only.   Even as to this there was hesitation, and a peremptory message was received from the Captain General.   "The Duke orders me to acquaint your Grace that he thinks the augmentation should begin at once," wrote Barrington. §

In November, ‖ Cumberland, alarmed at the inadequacy of the military preparations at home, had entertained a proposal made by one Prevost, a Swiss soldier of fortune, whereby commissions should be given to foreign Protestants with ex-

* Add. MS. 32874, f. 115, Newcastle to Hardwicke, Sept. 18, 1757.
† Add. MS. 32858, f. 440, Cumberland to Newcastle, Sept. 5, 1755.
‡ The land forces voted for 1757 were 47,449—£1,213,743 3s. 9d.; and for 1758, 53,777—£1,253,368.   Votes of House of Commons, 1756-7.)
§ Add. MS. 32861, f. 292, Barrington to Newcastle, Dec. 1, 1755.
‖ Cumberland Papers.

perience of active service. These officers were to be sent overseas to serve with battalions to be raised in America. The battalions were to be four in number. In February 1756 a Bill was introduced to give effect to the proposal. Pitt opposed. He described the measure as a breach of the Act of Settlement; he said * that the utility of the proposal was so small " that it was stabbing that Act with a bodkin." The constitutional objection, however, was probably less sincere than his habitual line of argument that a British war should be fought by Britons. " That state alone is a sovereign State qui suis stat viribus non alieno pendet arbitrio." † This was also Cumberland's opinion, but until the Ministry could be brought to the same way of thinking, it was folly to discard even secondary means of preparation. After many days of debate, the Bill passed by 198 to 69. Lord Loudoun was made colonel-in-chief of the regiment. Colonel Prevost was given command of the first battalion. Prevost soon found that he had volunteered for an uneasy post: " Les hommes," he wrote from America to Cumberland, ‡ " en général sont mauvais et l'écume de ces Colonies." Moreover he was having difficulties with Loudoun and the regular Army: he complained of " les humiliations et les dangers auxquels nous sommes continuellement exposés par la haine, l'envie et la jalousie du reste de l'armée contre nous." § The regular officer was in fact being true to his tradition, he was showing himself shy of innovation, and jealous of what seemed a departure from the accepted system. But recruiting went forward, chiefly in Pennsylvania. The four battalions were formed and known as the Royal Americans, a title which in due time gave place to that of the famous Sixtieth.

Prevost's were not the only complaints that came from America. Lord Loudoun, who had taken up his position as Commander-in-Chief early in the year (1756), was confronted with unexpected difficulties. The colonists were showing a lamentable indifference, refusing quarters to British troops,

* Walpole, *Memoirs George II*, II, p. 160.
† *Parliamentary History*, XV, p. 702.
‡ Cumberland Papers.
§ *Ibid.*

13

withholding money for carrying on the war, and charging double value for purchases on behalf of His Majesty's forces,* while among the men raised in America desertion and drunkenness were so rife that Loudoun, an early convert to Prohibition, declared that nothing short of "staving every drop of liquor in the country" † would effect a cure. In truth, and they can hardly be blamed, the American colonies were dead to any notions of imperialism. For the most part they were wholly taken up with their own political differences, which had no concern with either the quarrels of England or the beating of the distant drum in Europe. As to the progress of the French on the mainland, on the distant side of the mountains, or round the great lakes, and about the headwaters of the Ohio, this was a matter for Britain to deal with.

By December 1755 the clamour ‡ in the country for the strengthening of the Army had given Cumberland the necessary support for his demand, and on December 16 it was resolved by the Inner Cabinet "that 10 new regiments of Infantry as also such numbers of Light Dragoons be forthwith raised in such manner as His Majesty shall think advisable." § —the very proposal which Cumberland had urged in September. On January 20, again, it was resolved in the Duke's apartments to despatch £120,000 for the use of the four colonies of New England, to send a Lieutenant-General (Lord Loudoun) and two Major-Generals to America, to send two battalions from Ireland, to raise four battalions in Pennsylvania and colonies adjacent, and further to raise 2000 men as provincial regiments in New England and send them to Nova Scotia, and thus enable the Commander-in-Chief to draw some of the King's regular forces to the continent of America. This it was calculated would give a force in North America of 13,400 men. ‖ But the methods of the Ministry were ill adapted to the general situation. There was an almost total lack of co-

* Cumberland Papers.

† *Ibid.*

‡ Even in October Newcastle had written, "Augment the troops in any way the General Cry" (Add. MS. 32966, f. 257).

§ Add. MS. 32965, f. 321, Cabinet Memoranda.

‖ Add. MS. 32996, f. 355, Cabinet Memoranda, Feb. 16, 1756. The actual strength was very far short of this.

ordination. The broad strategy, as is now recognised, was correct, but there does not seem to have been present to the mind of any one Minister a definite idea of how that strategy should be executed and rendered effective. The action taken was piecemeal and spasmodic—one day a vote for money, another day an order to mobilise more ships, or again to make a small increase in the number of the land forces. Here a resolution to supersede a general, there an order to court-martial an admiral; at one time a concentration of forces to repel invasion, at another the dispersion of those same forces to conduct an impotent offensive, or again an enervating endeavour to strengthen the defences at home with Hessians or Hanoverians—such was the history of Ministerial mismanagement during this period. Vagueness as to the immediate object, timidity as to the means to be employed, hesitation as to the expediency of what was proposed, vitiated the counsels and infected the plans of the Government, whether considered in relation to America or Germany, the Channel or the Mediterranean, the raising of money or the enlisting of recruits. They were unable either to estimate or evoke the spirit of the nation; they were ignorant, and in their ignorance deeply sceptical, of the financial resources of the country. Thus at every turn their strategy was hampered by their politics, and their military conceptions subordinated to considerations of party. Cumberland, clear in his views and emphatic in his methods, regarded with impatience this distracted scene. The military situation presented itself to his ordered mind as a definite problem, allowing room for neither vacillation nor deflection. He approved the end which the Ministry had in view, and he was tireless in urging that the means should be adequate to its execution. But at this time, save for the support of Fox, he stood alone. The Government went their way. The initiative fell from their grasp, and the advantage passed into the hands of France. In December 1755 extravagant demands were received from the Court of France, in which as the price of further peace negotiations it was stipulated that all ships and men captured by the English should be restored. To this a firm and spirited reply was sent. "I am glad," Cumberland was able to write to Fox, " the Government begin to show vigour; it is certainly strong enough to resent insults." * Even now there was no declaration of war.

Meanwhile during the winter of 1755–6 information, very definite and authentic in character, as to the plan formed by France, had been coming in through secret channels. The French were raising an army of 180,000 men.† Marshal Bellisle had been appointed as Commander of the land forces on the coast from Dunkirk to Bayonne. An invasion of England was intended, with simultaneous feint attacks on Scotland and Ireland.‡ The Young Pretender was to be dished up again and used as a makeweight in the general movement. Minorca was to be seized, and for this purpose an expedition was to be formed at Toulon. At the Channel Ports barges for the conveyance of troops were being built. Dutch ships were being purchased with the same end in view. At Brest, Rochefort, and La Rochelle, the dockyards were working at full pressure and reinforcements preparing for Canada. But which was the true objective? Was the threatened invasion merely a means of tying the British fleet to home waters? Was Minorca the real aim? or again, was it Canada? In any case the preparations along the French coast could not be disregarded. The display of military force and the concentration of shipping constituted a threat that had all the appearance of passing into action. Thus to the Ministry at home the paramount consideration during the winter 1755–6 was the fear of invasion. Troops were concentrated on the coast. Orders were given for the conduct of the civil population, for the lighting of beacons, the driving inland of horses and cattle, the removal or destruction of forage. Under the influence of this same fear an undue proportion of the fleet was kept in the vicinity of the home ports, nor was it till April (1756) that Byng with ten ships was despatched to the Mediterranean. Then, in May, news that the long-rumoured descent on Minorca had taken place reached London. The real objective so skilfully masked was now revealed. A meeting of the Inner

* Holland House Papers, Cumberland to Fox, Dec. 20, 1755.
† Add. MS. 32859, Intelligence, Fontainebleau, Sept. 24, 1755.
‡ Add. MS. 32861, f. 383, Bunge to Höpken, Feb. 6, 1756.

Cabinet was summoned, when, with Cumberland presiding, it was resolved to send four large ships * to reinforce Admiral Byng and three or four battalions to relieve the garrison of Fort Mahon in Minorca, and if His Majesty should concur to declare war against France.†

Byng sailed from England on April 6, 1756. On May 2 he reached Gibraltar. There he received news that the French had effected a landing at Minorca, and there he wasted a week of invaluable time, his mind hovering among the possibilities which were presented by the new situation. A positive order had been sent to General Fowke, Governor of Gibraltar, to embark a battalion from the garrison ‡ of that fortress. In the fortress a Council of War was held. It was decided that Gibraltar was not in such a military state that a battalion could be spared. The order was accordingly disregarded.§ On May 8 Byng, reinforced by three more ships from the force in the Mediterranean, sailed from Gibraltar. The instructions which he had received before leaving England were to use all means in his power to relieve Minorca if the French had landed, or alternatively to blockade Toulon if the expedition under the Duc de Richelieu had not by that time left that port. At 9.30 on the morning of May 20 Byng was in touch to the S.E. of Minorca with the French fleet under La Galissonière. A light mist lay over the Mediterranean. Little wind was stirring. Byng had under his command thirteen ships of the line, La Galissonière only twelve, but the heavier armament was with the French. The condition of their ships was slightly superior: they were better manned, cleaner, and faster. La Galissonière had obtained possession of the code signals in

* Cumberland calculated rightly that the garrison of Fort Mahon would be able to hold out a month or six weeks. He proposed to send an order to Vice-Admiral Boscawen immediately to detach a portion of his fleet for the reinforcement of Byng, thereby saving time. The proposal was negatived by Lord Anson. (Holland House Papers, Newcastle to Fox, May 6, 1756.)

† Add. MS. 32966, f. 419, Minutes of Cabinet Meeting, May 6, 1756.

‡ Add. MS. 32865, f. 428, Barrington to Fowke, March 21, 1756.

§ Cumberland called this Council "an infamous Council of Warr [sic], infected with terrors and void of obedience." (Holland House Papers, Cumberland to Fox, May 31, 1756.)

use by the British fleet.* These were to prove of service to the French. The morning was passed in manœuvring for the "weather gauge." Nor was it till 2.30, seven hours after the French fleet had been first sighted, that the signal to engage was given. The action was indecisive. At about 5.30 it ceased. For two days Byng remained in the vicinity. No attempt, however, was made by the French to renew the action. On the third day La Galissonière was sighted, but Byng decided that the condition of his ships did not permit him to attack. On May 24 a Council of War was held, when it was resolved to return to Gibraltar. Byng had failed in every particular. He had failed to land troops on the island. He had left the French fleet practically intact. He had done nothing to interfere with the French communications and the transport of reinforcements between Toulon and Minorca. On June 19 he was once more under the guns of Gibraltar. The Council of War had been his undoing. On June 28 the fortress of St. Philip, the key position of Minorca, surrendered. Before Byng was ready again to sail from Gibraltar,† the order recalling him had arrived. On July 9 he sailed for England, arriving at Portsmouth, where he was placed under close arrest, on July 27. It was not till March 14, 1757, that with unshaken fortitude the admiral met his end at the hands of a firing party on board the *Monarque* in Portsmouth Harbour. For eight months his case had been the battle ground of politicians; but while it is probably true to say that if there had been no political considerations at work his life would have been spared, it is also true that his trial was fair, his condemnation in accordance with the letter of the naval code, and that only the exercise of the prerogative of mercy could have saved him from his tragic destiny.

The news of Admiral Byng's indecisive fleet action and intended return to Gibraltar reached London on May 31. On June 3 a meeting of the Inner Cabinet was held in Cumberland's apartments, when it was decided that Lord Tyrawley

* A. de Boislisle, *Mémoires du Maréchal de Richelieu* (1918), p. 129.
† "If Byng has lost one day at Gibraltar, he is the most damnable of traitors," wrote Wolfe to his mother, July 26, 1756. See Beckles Willson, *Life and Letters of Wolfe,* p. 300.

of Versailles. France was to regard the Austrian Netherlands as inviolable; the Empress was to refrain from assisting England. A further convention provided for mutual defence. Secret stipulations carried the matter further, and gave an entirely different character to the alliance. By these stipulations the Empress undertook to join forces with France, should France be invaded by any ally of England, a reciprocal guarantee being given by France. Thus any attack by Frederick was provided against. Kaunitz had scored. The recovery of Silesia had been brought within range of practical achievement. The change which since 1749 he had laboured to bring about was an established fact. Now at last on the one side were ranged France and Austria, on the other Prussia and England.

The full effect of these negotiations on Russia was not altogether foreseen. Clearly if, as proved to be the case, Russia had made her subsidy treaty with England largely because she desired an opportunity of falling upon Frederick, the Convention of Westminster would thwart that object of her policy. But this ingredient of Russia's diplomacy was not so immediately apparent. Newcastle, it was true, was quite aware of the embarrassment that negotiations with Frederick might cause at the Winter Palace. But neither Newcastle nor anyone concerned in the transaction estimated correctly the strength of the motive by which Russia had been impelled towards agreement. In December 1755 Newcastle had written to Sir Charles Hanbury-Williams pointing out the difficulty in which the Ministry now found themselves. The Russian treaty, he said, had been revealed to Frederick in order to keep him quiet; now a pact with Frederick was imminent, and it must be kept secret from the Czarina, unless Williams had reason to believe that Frederick had already communicated the fact to the Russian Court, which he was quite likely to have done, in order to cause ill feeling between London and St. Petersburg.*

Russia, however, was to learn soon enough, first of the Convention of Westminster (January 1756) and then of the Treaty of Versailles (May 1756). The effect was immediate and dramatic. Frederick was the first to realise what was in-

* Add. MS. 32861, f. 441, Newcastle to Williams, Dec. 26, 1755.

volved. Very few secrets in the Chancelleries of Europe were
hid from the Prussian King. His own vigilance was only
equalled by that of his agents. His suspicions about Russia
were early aroused. Within a week of the signing of the
Treaty of Versailles he was saying to Mitchell, the representative of George II at Potsdam, " Are you absolutely sure of the
Russians?" * By June his suspicions were confirmed. He
had learnt that negotiations were proceeding between France,
Austria, and the Czarina, that Russian troops were massing in
Livonia and Courland and armies being formed in Bohemia
and Moravia, and that Newcastle's efforts to keep Russia on
the side of England were likely to fail. His own preparations
were well advanced. What then was to be the policy of the
Most Christian King and their Imperial Majesties of Austria
and Russia? What significance was Frederick to attach to
the military camps and depots forming in Bohemia and
Moravia? to the armies gathering in Livonia and Courland?
What assurance could the Court of Vienna give that these forces
were not for aggression? " We have one foot in the stirrup,
and I think the other will soon follow," he wrote to his sister
in the early days of July. Before the final answer from Vienna
was in the hands of Frederick, he had resolved to act. At
dawn on August 26 couriers were speeding from Potsdam
with the order to march. On August 29, 1756, the Prussian
army crossed in three columns into Saxony. It was the
beginning on the Continent of Europe of the Seven Years'
War, and the prelude to events in which Cumberland was to
play a notable and much debated part.

---

* *Political Correspondence*, XII, p. 328. Frederick was at this
time unaware that a secret article of the Anglo-Russian Treaty provided that the Russian troops should only be used against him.

CHAPTER XIX

CUMBERLAND was residing at this time (1756) principally at Windsor Great Lodge, returning to London at intervals for Cabinet Councils and the transaction of military business. At Windsor he was busy with his improvements, landscape gardening, planting, forming Virginia Water, directing the administration of the Forest and superintending his racing stud. George II had long ceased to visit the Castle. At Windsor Cumberland reigned in his stead.

The Cumberland Papers show the measures he found it necessary to take against invasion, the dispositions of the forces under his command, and the difficulties raised by members of Parliament whose constituents objected to the burden of having troops billeted in their area. The total forces * at his disposal were 34,283 British troops, 8,605 Hanoverians, and 6,544 Hessians. Cumberland was no believer in the French threats of invasion. Like Frederick the Great, he thought France would only make the attempt if invited to do so by neglect of precautions. But the country was panicky. Ministers were convinced of the likelihood of attack. Newcastle with his mercurial variability was subject to paroxysms of alarm. Walpole relates that, retiring to bed one night, Newcastle found a mysterious card with the words " Charles is very well and is expected in England every day "; his agitation was unbounded, the house was ransacked, enquiry made in every quarter, and peace only restored when it was discovered that it was a card from the Duchess of Queensberry to the Duchess of Newcastle relating to the prospective return of Lord Charles Douglas. The Jacobite bogey was still extant. The story illustrates the trepidation to be found in responsible quarters at this time. Apprehension was in the air. A spirit of serious-

---

* Cumberland Papers, Abstract of the Forces in 1756.

ness had begun to tinge even the habitual flippancy of the social world. " Nobody," wrote Walpole, " makes a suit of clothes but of sackcloth turned up with ashes."

Nor were public fears allayed by the unwonted movement of troops. Hessians in their blue uniform turned up with red, their hair plaited behind and hanging below their waists, on the march to Winchester; Hanoverians in their dark uniforms with the motto on their caps " Vestigia nulla retrorsum," which Dodington translated " They never mean to go back again," * garrisoning Maidstone and the coastal areas of Essex; Cumberland with his headquarters staff passing to and fro on tours of inspection; and the footguards in Hyde Park practising a new system † of Prussian drill; these, if they failed to restore confidence, were at least successful in keeping alive the fear of attack. Troops were disposed along the coast from Dorsetshire to Sussex: one of the principal concentrations being on Blandford Downs, where Wolfe, now a lieutenant-colonel, notes the improvement which had taken place under Cumberland, in the care of the men, their clothing, their food and equipment, their bedding, and even their medical attendance. The Army was small. It was easy for Cumberland to keep in touch with the several units of which it was composed, and to know the personal qualities of commanders and the military value of their respective battalions. A new spirit was undoubtedly awakening. The association of merit with promotion and command was becoming customary instead of merely accidental. To be absent from the regiment, to have avoided the initial step of even joining on appointment, hitherto normal perquisites of a commission in the Army, ‡ were offences no longer tolerated. Letters from the Secretary at War make it clear that Cumberland was determined to end such indulgences. He insisted that discipline was the basis of efficiency, and that discipline itself

* Walpole, *Letters,* III, p. 432.

† This may have tended to restore the public confidence, for whereas firing at 50 yards' range under the old system 50 men had scored only three hits on the target, under the new system approximately 50 hits were registered (*Gentleman's Magazine,* XXVI, p. 259).

‡ Cumberland Papers, Barrington to Cumberland, May 9, 1757, makes it clear that, in accordance with Cumberland's orders, officers who had never joined were being superseded.

was dependent on the character and personal gifts of the Commander. Preferment was to be given accordingly. He made it his business to familiarise himself with the details of every unit in his command, its records, its personnel, its *moral*. He encouraged officers holding positions in the Plantations to write to him personally, and thus to keep him informed first-hand as to the state of the garrisons abroad and the improvements which could be effected. A considerable portion of his correspondence consists of letters of such a character. There was probably more than formal compliment implied when the Secretary at War wrote: * " It has always been my wish that the whole kingdom might know as well as I do how much the country is served and obliged by the constant care and attention as well as ability with which the Army is superintended by your Royal Highness." He was all for giving such support as was possible or needed to officers on foreign stations. To Lord Loudoun commanding in America he wrote freely of the stumbling blocks to a war policy both at home and abroad:

My Lord Loudoun [he wrote on December 23, 1756],— I write this private letter to assure you of the thorough satisfaction your conduct has given me. I will not fail to support you to the utmost of my ability through the many difficulties you find in the executing of your orders and in opposition to the public service. Nothing can be worse than our situation here at home without any plan or even a desire to have one. Great numbers talked of to be sent to you, but without any consideration of how, and from whence, without considering what they should carry with them. But that you may know what can be done for you I write in my own hand trusting to your Honour that you will burn this as soon as read. †

At the same time he enclosed a plan of operations which involved an expedition up the St. Lawrence with Quebec as the objective, but added that it must be left to Loudoun finally to determine what was to be done. ‡

* Cumberland Papers, Barrington to Cumberland, June 7, 1757.
† Cumberland Papers.
‡ *Ibid.*

With Lord Tyrawley, who had been sent to supersede Fowke at Gibraltar, Cumberland was equally confidential. He was always for trusting "the man on the spot." Tyrawley was appalled by the unpreparedness of the fortress. A long report to the Secretary at War is minuted by Cumberland as follows: "All that has been done by Lord Tyrawley has been approved at home, and as he has had full powers he will no doubt do everything necessary without considering expense and do nothing unnecessary how little it may cost."

James O'Hara, second Baron Tyrawley (1690-1773), was a man after Cumberland's own heart. He had earned distinction on many fields in the wars of Marlborough, having received his first commission as lieutenant in his father's regiment at the age of thirteen. Scored with wounds and rich in military honours, he was sent in 1728 to the Court of Portugal, where he remained as Ambassador till 1741. Here he attained an astonishing popularity. The King offered him a permanent military position, and on his retirement bestowed on him fourteen bars of gold. From Portugal he returned with "three wives and fourteen children," and in 1743 was sent as Ambassador-extraordinary to Russia, where he remained for two years. At the time of his appointment to Gibraltar he was a Lieutenant-General and Colonel of the 2nd Coldstream Footguards. In 1763 he was made Field-Marshal. He was a man of much humour with an arrogant wit, a formidable and relentless opponent. Accustomed to the despotic Courts of Lisbon and St. Petersburg, he had little reverence for Parliamentary institutions and spoke of them as "the French do of the long robe." * As the result of his expenditure on works at Gibraltar in 1756, it was proposed that his action should be censured in the House of Commons. He affected not to know where that institution was situated, but claimed to be heard at the bar. At the bar accordingly he appeared. There he confronted those who had been ill advised enough to censure him with so much "art and frankness," and brow-beat his opponents with such "arrogant humour," that they were glad to cry off from such "tough game." He remained master of the field. The House declared itself satisfied of his integrity.

* Walpole, *Memoirs*, III, p. 108.

With his roughness of character and bluntness of method he was yet humane, indeed he is responsible for one of the very few protests on record against the savage brutality of military punishments. In a letter to the Secretary at War he treats the matter from a precociously humane point of view.

On May 13, 1757, he wrote to the Secretary at War as follows:

I beg leave to desire your Lordship to call for the proceedings of a General Court Martial held here the 9th May that goes over by this conveyance to the Judge Advocate General where your Lordship will see that I have approved of the Proceedings and sentences of that Court Martial and have dissolved it rather than call a Rehearing but am of opinion that such Corporal Punishments are not to be undergone by any man, that 300 lashes are as much as the strongest man can bear at one time by the opinion of the surgeons that attend these Punishments, more especially in hot weather. In this Court Martial some are sentenced to one thousand, others to fifteen hundred, and one to two thousand lashes.

Now my lord as no man can endure above three hundred lashes at a time, and that such criminal will be two months at least before he will be in a condition to be further punished, whether it might not be proper to reconsider the Articles of War at a proper time, as to Corporal Punishments, since a Criminal so sentenced will not have received his full Punishment at the end of a year and a half, during which time the man is lost to his Regiment, or perhaps dies in the Provost's hands contrary to all humanity, and to the great discouragement of the soldier. I only point out the Inconveniences, but leave the remedy to my Superiors. In the meantime much of these sentences in the present case must be remitted as circumstances may point out, which too is by no means eligible since it is playing with Punishments.

Nothing, however, was done. The punishments went on, and seem indeed to have increased, until under the Duke of Wellington they became one of the scandals of Europe. If in China the profession of a soldier was formerly regarded as the most degraded of pursuits, the view taken in England was little different. Thomas Pitt in 1750, when introducing a Bill to limit the period for enlistment, probably expressed the view generally entertained:

> A man's listing in the Army can never proceed from prudence or discretion or from a deliberate act of the mind: for no man in his right senses would ever bind himself for life to serve another man, and not only to be bastinadoed, whipt, and tortured whenever his master pleased to be angry with him, but also to be put to death if ever he left the service without his master's consent.

In the same debate Lord Barrington, subsequently Secretary at War, said: "We know that idleness, extravagance, and dissoluteness are the causes that send most common men into the Army." Posterity has chosen to indict Cumberland for brutality. What he did was to continue the military code as he found it. It took many years to persuade the military mind that discipline could be maintained and be of a higher quality without the infliction of inhuman penalties. Nor was it till 1881 that flogging in the Army was finally abandoned. The Duke of Wellington, who ruled the Army in days when more humanitarian views were beginning to prevail, far from mitigating the existing forms of punishment, insisted on their application and made them more general in practice. By that time Beccaria, Bentham, and Romilly had expounded to the world that it was not only desirable but expedient to be humane as well as just. The public conscience had begun to revolt against the criminal code of the country, and mercy was creeping into the administration of the law. Wellington was proof against such influences. Before the Commission to enquire into Military Punishments, as late as 1850, he said: "There is no punishment which makes an impression on anybody except corporal punishment. . . . I have not an idea what can be substituted for it." * In the time of Cumberland there were no fewer than two hundred offences† for which death was the penalty prescribed by the law of the land. It is small wonder

---

* See *William Augustus Duke of Cumberland*, p. 82 et seq.

† Coleman Phillipson, *Three Criminal Law Reformers*, p. 170. The author states that during the reign of George II sixty-three offences were added to those punishable with death.

that he failed to introduce modifications into the Mutiny Act. But he at least was grateful to the soldiers who fought under him, and showed solicitude for their welfare. He did not describe them as " the scum of the earth."

Walpole, writing in his earlier manner of Cumberland, said:

> He was as angry at an officer's transgressing the minutest precept of the military rubric as at deserting his post, and was as intent on establishing the form of spatter dashes, or the pattern of cockades, as on taking a town, or securing an advantageous situation.*

Though later Walpole formed a very different estimate of the Captain General, he here certainly makes the most of Cumberland's German prepossessions. Strictness, punctilio, and a narrow regard for the movements of parade and the design of uniforms, were caught from the Prussian model and infected alike George II and his son. The mechanical side of military efficiency was readily imitated. Other things, it is true, went with it, but they were less easily acquired. In spite of Oudenarde and Dettingen, the military ideas of George II travelled little beyond the barrack square. It was rather his habit to translate soldierly competence into terms of pipeclay and buttons. In such matters he was constantly interfering. It is to his influence rather than to that of Cumberland that we should attribute the frequent and minute variations in military dress and deportment. Cumberland had the larger sense of the Army's needs. His rule was for the most part wholly beneficial. He recalled the Army from its tendency to follow the French example of the day, and make campaigns, with their train of mummers and courtesans, as far as possible an extension and variety of social activity. His set purpose was to mould the Army into a compact and efficient fighting force—disciplined, trained, and imbued with a martial spirit. Gradually, by slow degrees and by steady pressure, he reduced the intrusion of political influence to its proper proportions. He had seen enough of it in his early years of campaigning. Preferment was no longer a reward for the political claims of a relative. Capacity and the performance of duty came to be recognised

* *Memoirs*, II, p. 102.

14

as a ground for promotion; * delinquents ceased to shelter behind Parliamentary patronage. Commanding officers were taught their responsibilities. It was an entirely new spirit which found expression in a letter from Cumberland to Loudoun in reference to the want of discipline in Otway's regiment: " I am afraid your letter convinces me of what I feared before, that it [the regiment] was composed of a set of ignorant and undisciplined officers, and till you make examples of the officers you will never make a regiment of it." † With so small a force to supervise one may hazard the conjecture that the ideas and personality of the Commander-in-Chief would count for a good deal, and would to some extent find themselves reflected in the genius and character of the Army. Here once more in fairness to Cumberland it should be remembered that the Marlborough tradition was exhausted, and represented for the most part by a few venerable and inadequate survivors. The Army of the Seven Years' War had come into existence under Cumberland, its officers had been trained under him, its soldiers had fought under him. Those whose names were to figure in history on the roll of military fame were contemporaries of the Captain General, issuing from the Army which he had controlled during the critical years of growth.

In the course of the winter of 1755-6 Cumberland inspected every unit stationed in Britain. Thus every colonel knew that he was subject to the personal supervision of the Captain General, whose approbation was to be won by deserving well.

When in 1757 Cumberland went for the last time to take command of an army on the Continent, he left the troops in England in a state of greater efficiency than at any time since the wars of Marlborough.. His subsequent resignation, as Wolfe declared, was a misfortune for the nation. ‡

Outside his military preoccupations he is little heard of at this time. He seems to have pursued his devotion to the beautiful Lady Coventry, is even seen in her company on the

---

* Many instances could be cited. Wolfe's testimony is sufficient. See, e.g., Beckles Willson, *Life and Letters*, pp. 125-256, etc.

† Cumberland MS., H.R.H. to Lord Loudoun, Oct. 22, 1756.

‡ Wolfe to Major Rickson, Nov. 5, 1757 (Beckles Willson, *Life and Letters of Wolfe*, p. 340).

MISS ELLIOT, "WHO LIVED UNDER THE PROTECTION OF THE
DUKE OF CUMBERLAND."

From a drawing in the Royal Library, Windsor.

causeway in Hyde Park, " the new office where all lovers now are entered." *

In May 1756, again, he is heard of as taking sides in the perennial squabbles in connection with the opera, and bestowing his patronage on the side of the Italian contralto Mingotti, in her quarrel with the manager Vanneschi. " To pass away his time, Mars is turned impressario," Walpole writes; " in short the Duke has taken the Opera House for the ensuing season " —the same opera house, built by Vanbrugh in the Haymarket, which had been the scene of such family discord in the early years of George II's reign, when the King and Queen would sit in an almost empty theatre listening to Handel's music, while Frederick Prince of Wales with fashionable audiences was applauding Buononcini in Lincoln's Inn Fields. Now Frederick was no longer there to applaud, and the King was playing cards at Kensington. Cumberland had the field of royal patronage entirely to himself. We hear no more of his youthful escapades in the bosquets and among the less reputable frequenters of Marylebone Gardens, nor of visits to Hockley in the Hole, nor, since his disastrous support of the pugilist Broughton,† of his patronising prize fights.‡ Time and responsibility have purged his tastes. He is all for the opera, and hazard and cricket, but chiefly and supremely for racing.

---

* Walpole, *Letters*, III, p. 419.

† See *William Augustus Duke of Cumberland*, p. 291.

‡ It was at this time that Miss Elliot was living under the protection of the Duke at Windsor. Nothing is known of her except the sketch by Paul Sandby which appears in a volume containing portraits of the Duke's household.

CHAPTER XX

CUMBERLAND first took to racing as a serious recreation some time after his campaign in Flanders. Thereafter he was a familiar figure on the post road to Newmarket. He would leave St. James's Palace in his post-chaise at four in the morning; his usual route would be by Epping, Bishop's Stortford, and Chesterford, at which places it was customary to change horses, the whole journey occupying seven hours. Each year his visits were more frequent, and towards the end of his life his residence was extended over more time than was covered by the actual race meetings. Walpole, who kept a vigilant eye on the movements of Princes, first writes of Cumberland at Newmarket in 1753. It may well have been Cumberland's first formal visit. It was at any rate the occasion of his first occupation of the Palace, a structure which has proved such an elusive feature to those dealing with the origins of Newmarket. Indeed a general uncertainty prevails about the nature of the buildings in the town at this time. Walpole in 1743 wrote: "How dismal, how solitary, how scrub does this town look; and yet it has actually a street of houses better than Parma or Modena. Nay, the houses of the people of fashion who come hither for the races are palaces to what houses in London itself were fifteen years ago." * Information which throws little light on Newmarket, but does a good deal to obscure our knowledge of residences in London, to say nothing of those in Parma and Modena. However that may be, we do know that the so-called Palace adjoined the existing Rutland Arms, but here again, contrary to what we should expect, there would seem to exist no positive information as to its character and dimensions. It was originally built in the reign of James I. After being destroyed by fire it was subsequently rebuilt by

* Walpole, *Letters*, I, p. 381.

Charles II. Evelyn, visiting it in 1670, found it "meane enough and hardly fit for a hunting house," and was much disturbed by the introduction of "chimnies in ye angles and corners" of the rooms, "a mode now introduced by his Majesty which I do at no hand approve of. . . . It does onely well in very small and trifling rooms, but takes from the state of greater." Nor did the situation of the house, "plac'd in a dirty streete without any court or avenue, like a common one, whereas it might and ought to have been built at either end of the towne, upon the very carpet where the sports are celebrated," escape his censure. Thereafter its repair and equipment were dependent on the whim of the Sovereign. William III and Queen Anne made use of it as a residence, but under George I its occupation became fitful, and with the advent of George II was discontinued. By the year 1753, at the time of Cumberland's visit, it had been so long out of commission that it had to be refurnished for the occasion. George II vainly imagined that the expenses of this undertaking would be paid by his son, but Cumberland, regarding the Palace as within the category of royal residences, arranged that the cost should be defrayed out of the Great Wardrobe,* an invasion of his personal resources which Walpole notes was very ill received by the King.

It had never been commodious, and accommodation for the guests of Royalty had usually to be found elsewhere. Cosmo the Third, Grand Duke of Tuscany, when the guest of Charles II, was lodged at the "Inn of Maidens" opposite the King's House. The Grand Duke has left perhaps the most complete picture of the life of Newmarket that has been handed down from either the eighteenth or seventeenth century.†

The account, though remote in time from the period with which we are dealing, presents fairly close resemblances to the manners and customs of 1750. Like the more leisurely frequenters of racing of the eighteenth century, Cosmo broke the journey between London and Newmarket at an excellent inn at Bishop's Stortford. At Newmarket, he kept, in accordance

---

* Walpole, *Letters*, III, p. 152.

† *Travels of Cosmo the Third Grand Duke of Tuscany during the Reign of Charles II*, ed. 1821, p. 205 et seq.

with the habit of his host, extremely early hours, and at sunrise issued forth to accompany Charles in hare coursing. Thereafter, dinner was at 12, and on the second day of his residence a match, the only race on the occasion of his visit, was run between two horses whose owners' names were Howard and Elliot. The horses, previously prepared with a beverage of " soaked bread and fresh eggs," were led from Newmarket to the course by their jockeys, who were dressed in taffeta of different colours, though, as will appear, it was not till 1752 that it was resolved that owners should declare and adopt specified colours. Charles and his guest took up a central position surrounded by the lords and gentlemen of the Court. As the competitors approached the station occupied by the King, the Duke of York and a crowd of courtiers set off after the competitors " at the utmost speed scarcely inferior to that of the racehorses." At the winning post the victorious horse was acclaimed with drums and trumpets. Drums and trumpets very soon fell into disuse. But the habit of setting out at the utmost speed after the competitors was continued till 1838, when it was put a stop to by an edict of the Jockey Club.

> See, like a routed host, with headlong pace,
> The *Members* pour amid the mingling race!
> All ask, what crowds the tumult could produce—
> Is Bedlam or the C——ns all broke loose?
> Such noise and nonsense, betting, damning, sinking,
> Such emphasis of oaths, and claret drinking!
>
> Like schoolboys freed, they run as chance directs,
> Proud from a well bred thing to risque their necks.
> The warrior's scar not half so graceful seems,
> As, at NEWMARKET, dislocated limbs.*

Racing, it will be seen, was little more than an incident of the visit. Hawking, coursing, the shooting of dotterel, hunting, and cock-fighting were long the diversions which claimed an attention at Newmarket little less in degree than

* Thomas Warton, *Newmarket* (1751). An exceedingly scarce poem which contains as much information about Newmarket as Gay's *Trivia* does about London.

racing itself. By Cumberland's time the Heath had become
pretty well restricted to its proper uses. The diversions had
altered in degree if not in kind, and there was less likelihood of
finding, as in the time of Evelyn, " jolly blades, racing, dancing,
feasting, and revelling, more resembling a luxurious and abandon'd rout, than a Christian Court." Gambling, it is true,
held its own—had indeed probably grown. On this very
occasion in 1753 Cumberland was accompanied " by half the
nobility and half the money in England," and while the Palace
may have witnessed greater state and louder revelry, it probably
never gave shelter to gambling as high or hospitality more
cordial. There was no organised or official " ring " at this
time, but the prospect of ruin through betting was quite as
realiseable as in subsequent years, at least if we are to believe
the poetry of Thomas Warton:

> Amid the lists our hero takes his stand;
> Sucked by the Sharper, to the Peer a prey
> He rolls his eyes that witness huge dismay;
> When lo! the chance of one unlucky heat,
> Strips him of game, strong beer, and sweet retreat.
> How awkward now he bears disgrace and dirt
> Nor knows the Poor's last refuge, to be pert.*

Contemporary references in fact point to Newmarket as the
principal racing resort of sharps and blacklegs.

Cumberland, now (1753) thirty-two years of age, played the
part of host with such ease and good humour, that his conquest
of the new world of racing was complete. If he had lost hearts
by his campaign in Scotland,† he certainly won them by his
hospitality at Newmarket. Racing was in the hands of the
few. Its votaries were probably no freer of prejudice and
convention than at other periods in the history of the sport. It
was no easy world to vanquish, even for a Prince of the Blood
with an unrestricted table, and it may be counted to the credit
of Cumberland's geniality and good fellowship that he made
himself so eminently welcome in so brief a space of time. The

---

* Thomas Warton, *Newmarket* (1751).
† Walpole, *Letters*, III, p. 155.

Goddess of dullness * who included racing among the pursuits to which her disciples were to give their attention, would have knocked in vain at the doors of the Palace in 1753.

The connection of the Crown with racing under George I and George II had become very slight; indeed the Palace at Newmarket and the office of " Keeper of the running horses "— a post worth £1,000 per annum—were the sole surviving symbols of that patronage of the Turf which had been so active under the Stuarts down to and including Queen Anne. Some attempt, however, was made during the reign of George II to improve racing by legislation. In the thirteenth year of that reign an Act was passed which is not without interest as showing the rapid growth of the sport. It is entitled " An Act to restrain and prevent the excessive increase of Horse Races." The preamble recites: " Whereas the great number of horses running for small plates, prizes or sums of money have contributed very much to the encouragement of idleness, to the impoverishment of many of the meaner sort of the Subjects of this Kingdom, and the Breed of strong and useful Horses has been much prejudiced thereby . . ." It was, however, rather the breed of strong and useful horses with which the Legislature was concerned than the fate of " the meaner sort of the King's subjects." The operative part of the Act in fact relates to matters of a purely technical character, such as the Jockey Club was subsequently formed to deal with. No one by this Act was to enter a horse for a race unless he were the bona-fide owner. No one was to start more than one horse in any single race. No plate or prize of a less value than £50 was to be competed for. No horse of five years was

---

* All my commands are easy, short and full:
My Sons! be proud, be selfish and be dull:
Guard my prerogative, assert my Throne:
This nod confirms each Privilege your own.
The cap and switch be sacred to his Grace;

  . . .

The judge to dance his brother Sergeant call;
The Senator at cricket urge the ball;
The Bishop stow (Pontific Luxury)
An hundred souls of Turkey in a pie.
    Pope, *Dunciad,* Book IV, line 381.

to run for any plate, prize, or stake unless he carried 10 stone, or if six-years 11 stone, or if seven years 12 stone. The penalty for a breach of any of these enactments was forfeiture of the value of the horse—half the value to be paid to the person laying the information and suing, and half to the poor of the district.

In the same Act we find Parliamentary recognition of the status of Newmarket. Section 5 says that no person is to start or run any match except at Newmarket Heath or Black Hambleton in the County of York, unless the prize is of the value of £50 or upwards. Section 7 provides that the entrance money is to be paid to the second horse. Five years later these provisions were repealed by 18 Geo. II, cap. 34. Here again the preamble is of interest. It is in these terms: " And whereas the thirteen Royal Plates of one hundred guineas each annually run for as also the high prices that are constantly given for horses of strength and size are sufficient to encourage Breeders to raise their cattle to the utmost size and strength possible . . ." Clearly therefore in these years racing was regarded as an institution which it was desirable that even Parliament should take cognisance of, and do its best to foster. Moreover, just as in later years it was the custom to adjourn for the Derby day, so in 1757 was it urged as a reason for the postponement of an important question in Parliament that it would clash with the date of a Newmarket meeting.* As for the King himself, his attitude was rather that of the Eastern potentate who received a suggestion that he should witness the Derby with the unanswerable retort, " No, why should I go to the Derby? It is already known to me that one horse can run faster than another." Anyway there is no record of George II visiting Newmarket or evincing any interest in the Turf.

There were at this time only two meetings at Newmarket, spring and autumn; but in 1753, the year of Cumberland's semi-state visit, a second spring meeting was instituted, and in 1762 a second October meeting, and again in 1765 the July meeting, all inaugurated during the lifetime of Cumberland. The cups and prizes were few. Racing consisted for the most part of matches, the usual stake mentioned in the Cumberland Papers

* Walpole, Memoirs, II, p. 380.

being 500 or in a few cases as much as 1,000 guineas.* Apart from Royal Plates and Matches, the most favoured form of contest was "Give and Take Plates," in which the weight carried was graduated by the inches of the horse. According to the scale given in Pond's *Sporting Kalendar,* if a horse of 14 hands carried 9 stone, the horse of thirteen and fifteen hands would respectively carry 7 stone and 11 stone. The matches made by Cumberland were run either over the Beacon Course or the Round Course; the terms were half forfeit, and in a few later cases "crossing and jostling" (which were still regarded as permissible) "barred." An example may be quoted:†

First Meeting 1759

The Duke's Spider weight 8 stone 12 pounds to run over the Beacon Course with Lord Rockingham's Remus weight 8 stone 7 pounds for 500 guineas half forfeit; crossing and jostling barr'd.

I have been unable to discover when "crossing and jostling" ceased to be a usual incident of racing. But by 1775 it had evidently fallen into disfavour, and if allowed was only allowed by the terms of the match. In that year Captain O'Kelly, the purchaser of Eclipse, when asked to take half share in the stake of a particular match, said: "No: but if the match had been made cross and jostle as I proposed, I would have not only stood all the money, but have brought a spalpeen from Newmarket, no higher than a twopenny loaf, that should have driven his Lordship's horse and jockey into the furzes, and have kept him there for three weeks." ‡

The Cumberland Papers contain several entries of matches with Rockingham. The future Prime Minister was serving his apprenticeship for a political career by achieving prominence on the Turf.—an example which has been followed with success in subsequent cases as well. As a boy of fifteen he had joined Cumberland's standard at Carlisle during the rebellion,

---

* The equivalent of approximately rather more than 6,000 to-day.

† Cumberland Papers. In the *Sporting Kalendar* for 1753 John Pond in the General Rules of Racing lays it down that "crossing and jostling" are permissible unless the contrary be stated.

‡ *Sporting Magazine,* II, p. 333.

a fact claimed as an early sign of his Whig faith, but more probably a manifestation of his gambling instincts. He was ready at any time to back a side or put up money for a match. Did he not in 1756 wager 500 guineas that, over a course from Norwich to London, he would find five geese to beat Lord Orford's five turkeys in a walking match? * With his horses he was on firmer ground. He owned Solon, Sampson, and Bay Malton. In 1770 he won a match of 4,000 guineas, beating Lord Bolingbroke's Paymaster with his horse Solon. He was in close association with Cumberland on the Turf, an association which was to be equally close when later they both turned their attention to politics.

Other owners with whom Cumberland matched his horses were Lord Sandwich, the Duke of Ancaster, the Duke of Bridgewater, Lord Portmore, Lord Gower, the Duke of Devonshire, Lord March, the Duke of Grafton, and Sir Richard Grosvenor, all of them original members of the Jockey Club. In 1761 appears the entry of a match at Ascot Heath:

> The Duke's Bay Colt got by Ishmael and Lord Sandwich's Colt got by Squirt; 8 stone each: to run one four miles Heat for 200 guineas: half forfeit.

Ascot, founded in the reign of Queen Anne, had fallen out of favour and fashion. Regular meetings were no longer held. Between 1750-60 Cumberland turned his attention to it, and by 1760 had brought it into a prominence second only to Newmarket. In 1751 there was a four days' meeting, one race taking place each day. The first day was for hunters only: the third for horses owned by huntsmen, Yeomen Prickers or Keepers belonging to the Windsor Forest.† By 1762 the Ascot meeting had expanded to five days, and was devoted mainly to matches between horses owned by " Noblemen and Gentlemen." ‡ In that year Cumberland ran horses in four races and paid forfeit in a fifth. Before Cumberland's death Ascot had become the resort of the fashionable world, and a

* Walpole, *Letters*, IV, p. 4; *Gent. Magazine*, 1756, p. 498.

† John Pond, *The Sporting Kalendar*, p. 24.

‡ Reginald Heber, *An Historical List of Horse Matches run in the year* 1762, p. 19.

social centre, with a standard of decorum more pronounced than that in vogue at Newmarket, the appearance of the Duke of Grafton with Nancy Parsons at the races in 1764 exciting the highest disapproval and being taken as evidence that he had lost all sense of propriety.*

In 1750-1, if not at the instance, certainly under the ægis of Cumberland, the Jockey Club was started and held its meetings at the Star and Garter in Pall Mall †—a well-known eating house and the recognised resort of Clubs. It was here that in 1765,‡ at a meeting of a Club of Nottinghamshire gentlemen, a dispute arose between Lord Byron and Mr. Chaworth as to which of their manors carried the largest stock of game: the question becoming of a nature too deep for words to determine, recourse was had to a neighbouring room, where swords were drawn and where by the light of a candle held by a waiter Lord Byron was successful in transfixing his opponent. The affair led to the arraignment of Lord Byron on a charge of murder, and his conviction by his peers on the count of manslaughter. §

There is nothing to show that the Jockey Club was formed with any idea of legislating for the Turf or reforming the sport of racing. In its early days it was merely an association of owners and others interested in racing, united by a common devotion to a particular branch of sport and bent on improving the quality of racehorses.

In May 1753 two Jockey Club Plates, open only to horses owned by members of the Jockey Club, were run for at Newmarket. Of one of these plates we find that Cumberland in 1754 was the winner with Marsk, sire of the famous Eclipse—the only other race, with the exception of matches, of which he is the recorded winner being the Challenge Whip in 1764 with a horse called Dumplin. But the plates to be won were few in number. Indeed at the time of the death of George II in 1760 there were only sixteen royal plates, 100 guineas each, to be competed for in the whole of Britain. These were all

---

* Walpole, *Letters,* VI, p. 116.
† Robert Black, *The Jockey Club and its Founders* (1891), p. 6.
‡ Walpole, *Letters,* VI, p. 180.
§ *Ibid.,* p. 216.

for five- and six-year-old horses, except the Royal Plate at Ipswich, which in 1751 at any rate was won by a four-year-old.*

Cumberland with his new-formed association took a lease about this time (1752-3) of the Coffee Room at Newmarket. As was to be expected, the Club soon outran the intention of its original foundation, and by degrees acquired a solid jurisdiction based on the acquisition of land which included the racing and training grounds at Newmarket. But in its early years, during the lifetime of Cumberland, the Club was feeling its way. Measures of drastic reform were no part of its programme. It gave occasional decisions, and from time to time settled internal differences between its members, but it was in no way an arbiter of general authority. Its prestige was a matter of slow growth. Its position as the legislature of the Turf was only evolved after many years of probationary attempts to dictate rules for the guidance of racing. Here reference need only be made to that which it accomplished under the presidency of Cumberland.†

In 1756 the Club abolished racing in heats for the Jockey Club Plates and substituted a single heat. In the same year it gave a decision as to the placing of horses in the Jockey Club Plate Race, which was quoted with approval and acted on in a similar dispute some years later. Before this date disputes as to the running of horses in the King's Plates had been determined " by such Person or Persons who shall be appointed by the Master of the Horse," an *ad hoc* organisation. On the other hand a tribunal already existed at Newmarket in 1751 for determining doubtful cases, as may be gathered from the poem of Thomas Warton:

> Thy sages hear, amid th'admiring crowd
> Adjudge the stakes most eloquently loud;

* John Pond, *The Sporting Kalendar* (1752), p. 84.

† The principal authorities are: Robert Black, *The Jockey Club and its Founders* (1891); Robert Black, *Horse Racing in England* (1893); Whyte, *History of the British Turf* (1840); J. P. Hore, *The History of Newmarket and Annals of the Turf* (1886); *Newmarket: An Essay on the Turf* (1771); Frank Siltzer, *Newmarket* (1923); The Cumberland Papers; Walpole's *Letters*; also *Encyclopædia Britannica*, art. " Horse."

> With critic skill o'er dubious bets preside,
> The low dispute or kindle, or decide:
> All empty wisdom, and judicious prate,
> Of distanc'd horses gravely fix the fate,
> Guide the nice conduct of a daring match,
> And o'er th'equestrian rights with care paternal watch,
>
> . . . . .
>
> And know no Rostrum, but Newmarket's Stand.

In 1758 the Jockey Club was firmer in the saddle, and published an edict the effect of which was to disqualify from riding at Newmarket any rider failing to declare, or cause to be declared for him, the fact that he was above the permitted allowance of two pounds overweight. This was the first effort in the direction of penal legislation. In 1759 the Club inaugurated the Weights and Scales Plate of 100 guineas to be paid for " out of the funds arising from the weights and scales," an indication that the Club had already established its jurisdiction over weights and scales. This race was open to any competitor and not confined to horses belonging to members of the Club. Here at any rate is enough to show the germ of later developments—a germ which one hundred years later was, under the direction of Admiral Rous, to find its structural form in a code of regulations, under which the racing of the present day is carried on and enabled to flourish.

It was also while Cumberland was President of the Club that racing colours became a settled feature of the Turf. We have seen that in the time of Charles II jockeys wore different colours, but it was in 1762 that

> To prevent disputes and as a convenience for distinguishing the horses in running it was agreed at a meeting held at Newmarket, Oct. 4, 1762, by the Dukes of Cumberland and Grafton, Lords March and Grosvenor, Mr. Vernon and Mr. Shafto, that certain colours specified and annexed to their names should in future be worn by the riders. This regulation was carried into effect in the second October meeting of the same year.*

The colours registered were:

* Heber, *An Historical List of Horse Matches Run* (1763), p. xxviii.

H.R.H. Duke of Cumberland . .	Purple
Duke of Grafton	Sky Blue
Duke of Devonshire . .	Straw colour
Duke of Northumberland . .	Yellow
Duke of Kingston . . .	Crimson
Duke of Ancaster . . .	Buff
Duke of Bridgewater . .	Garter Blue
Marquis of Rockingham. . .	Green
Earl Waldegrave	Deep Red
Earl of Orford	Purple and White
Earl of March	White
Earl Gower	Blue
Viscount Bolingbroke . .	Black
Lord Grosvenor . . .	Orange
Sir John Moore, Bt. . .	Darkest Green
Sir James Lowther, Bt. . . .	Orange
Mr. R. Vernon	White
Hon. Mr. Greville . . .	Brown trimmed with yellow
Mr. Jenison Shafto . . .	Pink

If the Club began its career on right lines, and such a claim for it can hardly be denied, it should be remembered that it was under the Presidency of Cumberland, one of the greatest and most devoted patrons known to the Turf, that the initial steps were taken. To the last days of his life Cumberland was faithful to his passion for racing, a passion which in his affections took second place only to his devotion to the Army. No failure of health would deter him from his expeditions to Newmarket, no physical pain would prevent his visits to the races or the training ground. He would be seen on the Heath, mounted on his charger during the first years of his attendance, or later—no longer in scarlet, his military appointments ended, when his immense weight, the constant recurring pain of his wound received at Dettingen, the gout, and disabling bodily afflictions had debarred him from activity—seated in a landau dressed in his blue coat and leaning from the window to follow the fortunes of his horses or exchange words with his colleagues of the Jockey Club.

Illness by this time (1758) had set its mark upon his features. The sight of one eye had gone. His complexion had become pallid. Increase of flesh had blunted the outline and added to the heaviness of his countenance, which already showed on one side a slight distortion. His form was, as we know, massive to excess but not ungainly. But in spite of growing physical infirmities he had retained his air of distinction; adversity had not shaken the resolution so conspicuous in his expression, nor weakened the grave and steady courage associated with his presence.

In October 1764 he had shown alarming symptoms in London. In spite of every remonstrance he insisted on going to Newmarket. The day after his arrival he had two seizures, his wound broke out, he was attacked by the gout, his life was despaired of. Yet in November of the same year Walpole is found writing:

> The Duke of Cumberland has a dangerous sore throat but is recovered. In one of the bitterest days that could be felt he would go upon the course at Newmarket with the windows of the landau down. I can conceive a hero welcoming death, or at least despising it: but if I was covered with more laurels than a boar's head at Christmas I should hate pain and Ranby * and an operation.

This was within a week of an incision of " many inches " made in his knee by the Surgeon Ranby—an operation in the middle of which Cumberland, who was holding the candle, exclaimed " Hold! " Ranby said, " For God's sake, let me proceed now; it will be worse to renew it." The Duke repeated " I say hold! " and then with complete calmness ordered them to give Ranby a clean waistcoat and cap, saying, " The poor man has sweated through these." " It was true," adds Walpole; " but the Duke did not utter a groan." † Within less than a year Cumberland was again dangerously ill. On March 26, 1765 Walpole writes:

> The Duke of Cumberland's state is less precarious, as his fate more certain and verging fast to a conclusion; yet he has ordered his equipages for Newmarket and persists in going there if he is alive: he seems indifferent both where he dies and when.‡

* Surgeon in Chief to the King.
† Walpole, *Letters*, VI, p. 136.
‡ *Ibid.*, p. 206.

In truth Cumberland was possessed of unquestioned bravery. He opposed an imperturbable front to the assaults of fortune, whether they took the form of cannon balls and bullets on the field of battle, the pain and disabilities of disease, or the strokes of adversity with which his career was chequered. He never capitulated. Nor was it merely brute courage by which he was animated and held. He entertained an almost romantic conception of duty—duty to himself, to the position he occupied, to the obligations imposed on him by his calling in life. He was resolute to hold his course. It was his creed neither to flinch nor turn aside. His flesh was heir to no common share of ills, but he ruled them out as factors in the scheme of life. On April 7, in spite of every entreaty, he set out as usual for the Spring Meeting at Newmarket. And it is satisfactory to know that on this occasion he should have seen his chestnut filly (the first descendant of Marsk to run) beat Lord Bolingbroke's bay filly for a stake of 300 guineas.

There is nothing to show in what year Cumberland first owned racehorses.* We know that in 1749 he was owner of a colt called Entrance, by the Godolphin Arabian out of Hobgoblin. In 1750 we know that he acquired Marsk—an event that was to prove a turning point in the history of thoroughbreds in this country. The horse at that time belonged to John Hutton, Esq., of Marsh, near Richmond, Yorkshire. The entry in Mr. Hutton's stud book sets out the transaction:

> In the year 1750 his Royal Highness the Duke of Cumberland gave me—John Hutton—a chestnut Arabian in exchange for a brown colt, got by Squirt, bred from the Ruby mare, and which his Royal Highness afterwards called Marsk.†

Horses in those days were not run before the age of four or five. And it was not till 1754 that Marsk was seen at Newmarket, when he won for the Duke the Jockey Club Plate of 100 guineas and upwards in one heat over the Round Course. Marsk's racing career was limited to five races, in three of

---

* A list of the horses owned by Cumberland in 1763 will be found in Appendix I.

† Whyte, *History of the British Turf,* I, p. 461.

15

which, run in April 1755 and April and May 1756, he was beaten. He was then kept in the Duke's private stud. The Duke's faith in him, despite his public form on the race-course, was to be justified. On Cumberland's death Marsk was sold at Tattersall's to a farmer in Dorsetshire. Later he was purchased for 20 guineas by Mr. Wildman. His fee as a stallion remained at the low figure of 3 guineas. About 1771 the horse was sold to Lord Abingdon for 1,000 guineas. The date is important. The great increase in the price paid for the horse, in the absence of evidence to the contrary, can only be attributed to the astonishing performances of his produce Eclipse during the years 1769-70. Indeed, if no other evidence existed as to the parentage of Eclipse, this fact alone would raise an almost irresistible presumption that Marsk, and not as has been suggested Shakespeare, was the sire of Eclipse. In the Cumberland Papers at Windsor Castle there is a list of mares with their stallions for 1761 and 1762. This list shows that, in 1761 at any rate, Cumberland believed in the combination of Marsk and Spiletta. What more probable than that he should have again renewed his faith in such a conjunction? So far, therefore, as it goes, the evidence from the Cumberland Papers may be said to confirm the common tradition that Marsk was the sire. Marsk remained in Lord Abingdon's stud at Rycot in Oxfordshire, at the then high figure of 100 guineas,* till his death at the age of twenty-nine.

In 1755 Cumberland acquired Cypron, and at about the same time Spiletta. Cypron became the dam of King Herod (1758), Spiletta of Eclipse (1764). Thus it will be seen that in the space of fourteen years Cumberland owned or bred horses that transformed the racing stock of England. No fewer than 95 winners of the Derby alone, between the years 1780 and 1924, trace their origin in the male line to Eclipse;† and if we add

---

* Ten guineas before that date was considered an exceptionally high fee. See List of Stallions for 1762, Heber, *Historical List of Horse Matches Run,* p. 120. Since the above was written I have found conclusive evidence in the Cumberland Papers as to the origin of Eclipse. See Appendix I.

† See Theodore Andrea Cook, *Eclipse and O'Kelly* (1907). By far the most exhaustive work on the subject of Eclipse and his origins.

Pommern, Fifinella, Gay Crusader, and Gainsborough—winners of the New Derby at Newmarket 1915-18 inclusive—we have a total of 99 winners of the great race whose direct descent is from Eclipse.* Of King Herod, whose sire was Tartar, it has been said that " he proved to be one of the best bred horses this kingdom ever produced, and as a stallion inferior to none, being sire of a larger number of racers, stallions and brood mares than any horse either before or since his time." † The produce of King Herod in nineteen years, 1771-89, won £201,505. ‡ King Herod carrying the Duke's colours ran six times in all. In October 1763, his first race, he beat the Duke of Ancaster's Roman for 500 guineas. In April 1764 he won a sweepstake of 300 guineas. In June of the same year at Ascot he was matched against Lord Rockingham's Tom Tinker by Sampson for 1,000 guineas, and was again successful, starting at four to one on. At Newmarket in October he defeated the Duke of Grafton's Antinous for 500 guineas, Antinous starting at six to four on. In May 1765 at Newmarket he won another 1,000 guineas stake for the Duke, for the second time defeating the Duke of Grafton's Antinous, the weights having been slightly altered in the meanwhile in favour of Antinous. In October 1765 he ran his last race for the Duke, and on this occasion suffered his first defeat. Carrying 9 stone, he lost to Sir James Lowther's Ascham, six years old, 8 stone; the stake being again 1,000 guineas.

Cumberland's more famous horse Eclipse was born in 1764, the year of the great eclipse of the sun. The evidence as to his birthplace does not exclude all doubt. But it is now generally accepted that he was foaled in the paddocks at Cranbourn Lodge,

---

* In the opinion of Mr. Arthur Portman, editor of *Horse and Hounds,* which opinion he has authorised me to state, there is not to-day a single thoroughbred throughout the world which has not in its veins the blood of Eclipse. It is also Mr. Portman's opinion that, although never beaten, and enjoying, as we know, a reputation for exceptional speed, Eclipse over a distance of two miles would stand no chance against thoroughbreds of to-day owing to his nearness to the Arab.

† Whyte, *History of the Turf,* I, p. 500.

‡ *Ibid.,* p. 501.

Windsor. * A contemporary advertisement of Eclipse at the stud contains the following:

ECLIPSE

was got by Mask † and bred by his late Royal Highness the Duke of Cumberland at Cranbourn Lodge and was sold when a foal for £45 and afterwards proved to be the best horse in the Kingdom.

Moreover local tradition is expressed by the following inscription set up in the paddock in which Eclipse is said first to have seen the light:

The celebrated Race Horse
ECLIPSE
By MARSKE out of SPILETTA
Was foaled in this Paddock
1764. He was bred by
H.R.H. WILLIAM
DUKE OF CUMBERLAND.

Cranbourn Paddocks then may reasonably be accepted as the birthplace of the famous horse. And it is at Cranbourn Paddocks that we must conclude Cumberland carried on his stud, near to his chief residence, Windsor Great Lodge, now known as Cumberland Lodge.

The question has often been asked, Where did Cumberland train his horses? There can, I think, be very little doubt that he trained on the Berkshire Downs, in the neighbourhood of Ilsley and Wantage. A house and stables are said to have been occupied by Cumberland at the foot of Gore Hill, and the uncontested tradition has been that he trained on Prestall Down.‡ At Midgham, situated in the locality, and the residence

---

* The matter is fully dealt with in Cook's *Eclipse and O'Kelly* (1907), where also will be found the arguments for and against the supposition that Shakespeare and not Marsk was the sire.

† Cook, *Eclipse and O'Kelly* (1907), p. 289. The name is spelt Maske in the Cumberland Papers.

‡ William Hewett, *The History and Antiquities of the Hundred of Compton, Berks* (1844).

of Stephen Poyntz, formerly the Duke's tutor, Cumberland was a constant guest in his youth, and when he took to racing no more favourable place for training than the Downs in question could have been present to his mind.

The first half of the eighteenth century was the great period of the Arab. In the reign of James I there had been introduced into this country a horse from Constantinople known as the Markham Arabian, a small bay horse, but he achieved success neither as a racer nor a sire. The Duke of Newcastle, who wrote on the management of horses in 1677, describes him as "a bay, but a little horse and no rarity for shape. When he came to run every horse beat him." * The time was not yet ripe, it would seem, for the infusion of the specialised characteristics of stamina and endurance.

Thereafter for a time the horse of Arabia was under a cloud. But in the reign of Charles II interest in the Eastern horse was revived. The horse master of the King was despatched to the Orient, and in due course returned with a number of mares. These, known as the "royal mares," like certain Flemish painters who, their names being unknown, have been given titles corresponding to their works, such as the Master of the Death of Mary, or the Master of the Sibyl, are identified by their produce, the most famous perhaps being the dam of Dodsworth. This mare was a Barb, a breed which was no novelty in England, or indeed on the Continent. They were "Barbarie horses" that ran in the Strada del Corso at Rome, riderless and with spurs hanging loose to their sides, when Evelyn was a spectator of the Carnival in 1644.† Nomenclature was not exact, and they may well have been Barbs that Evelyn later speaks of as "Turkish or Asian" horses, three of which were brought over in 1684 and inspected by the King and Duke of York in St. James's Park. Evelyn's description is worth quoting:

> I never beheld so delicate a creature as one of them was, of somewhat a bright bay, two white feet, a blaze; such a head, eyes, eares, neck, breast, belly, haunches, legs, pasterns

* Cited Cook, *Eclipse and O'Kelly*, p. 10.
† *Memoirs of John Evelyn*, ed. 1827, I, p. 274.

and feete, in all regards beautifull and proportion'd to admiration: spirited, proud, nimble, making halt, turning with that swiftnesse, and in so small a compasse, as was admirable. They trotted like does, as if they did not feele the ground.*

The Barbary horse must have been a well-accepted type in Britain in the time of Shakespeare. His references to the Barb are not infrequent. It is in fact the only type which he specifically names:

> Oh! how it yearned my heart when I beheld
> In London streets, that coronation-day,
> When Bolingbroke rode on roan Barbary.

Again, in the match between Hamlet and Laertes, that "card or calendar of gentry," the stake was "six Barbary horses against six French swords, their assigns, and three liberal-conceited carriages." And it will be remembered that, to "poison the delight" of Brabantio, Othello was represented by Iago as a Barbary horse, with the probability that Brabantio would have "coursers for cousins and gennets for germans."

It is, however, when we come to the advent to this country of the Byerley Turk in the reign of William III, of the Darley Arabian in the reign of Queen Anne, and the Godolphin Barb, which was imported some twenty-five years later, that it is possible to trace the foundations of the thoroughbred of to-day. The Darley Arabian was brought to Buttercramb, the seat of Mr. Darley in Yorkshire, about 1710, having been purchased by his brother, a merchant at Aleppo. Aleppo, as Sir Theodore Cook has pointed out, is still one of the regular markets for the horse-dealers of Najd. It is therefore probable that the horse was of the "Keheilan" breed, the most numerous and the most esteemed of Eastern horses, and found at their best in Najd. The predominant colour in the Keheilan breed is bay, a fact not to be lost sight of in considering the prevalent colour among thoroughbreds of the present time. It is no wild assumption that it was a horse of Keheilan breed, "whose neck was clothed with the quivering mane," who pawed in the valley, rejoiced in his strength and leaped as a locust, "who mocketh at fear and is not dismayed," who "smelleth the battle afar

* *Memoirs of John Evelyn*, ed. 1827, III, p. 123.

off, the thunder of the captains and the shouting." At any rate the description would not be misapplied to Eclipse, the direct descendant of the Darley Arabian. Cumberland, and as a judge of horses he was unsurpassed, must be credited with a knowledge of the value of Arab blood. We have seen that in 1750 he possessed a chestnut Arabian which he exchanged for a brown colt subsequently named Marsk, from which it may be inferred that he was then breeding Arabian horses, or thought sufficiently well of them to include one in his stable. Indeed to the end of his life he appears to have kept at least one Arabian in his stud.* However that may be, in breeding from Marsk and Spiletta he combined three Eastern strains and showed his confidence in the value of that blood. The great-grandsire of Marsk was the Darley Arabian through Squirt and Bartlett's Childers, while Spiletta held the blood of the Godolphin Arabian (a barb) and the Lister Turk.†

The performances of Eclipse are too well known to require restatement. Moreover they lie altogether outside the years covered by Cumberland's career. It may suffice to say that he was a horse of an incomparable mettle, and of so abominable a temper that it was thought improbable that he could be raised as a stallion. As a colt, however, he was entrusted to a rough-rider at Epsom, who is said to have combined poaching with rough-riding, and to have worked Eclipse without respite, using him at night for the less legitimate branch of his craft. During his racing career he was ridden by Fitzpatrick and Oakley, who used neither whip nor spur, but would sit quiet in the saddle without any attempt to dictate to their mount. He won his first race at Epsom in 1769. At Newmarket on October 3, 1770, he won the " 150 guineas and upwards," starting at 70 to 1 on; the following day he walked over for the King's Plate. In the same year he walked over the course at Nottingham, Lincoln, and Guildford, and at York he won 319 guineas against

* See Heber, *Historical Account of Matches Run*, p. 91.

† The blood of Eastern sires in Eclipse is given in *The Horse-breeder's Handbook*, 5th ed., p. xliii, as including that of the D'Arcy White Turk, the D'Arcy Yellow Turk, the Lister Turk, the Leaders Arabian, Huttons Bay Barb, the Akaster Turk, the Darley Arabian, and the Godolphin.

Mr. Wentworth's Tortoise and Sir Charles Bunbury's Bellairs. That was the end of his brief racing career. He won in all 2,149 guineas.* Eclipse was never beaten, but not running till 1768 he never carried the purple jacket of the Duke. On the Duke's death he was bought by Mr. Wildman, a Smithfield salesman, for 75 guineas, subsequently passing into the hands of Dennis O'Kelly. But in breeding King Herod and Eclipse, in founding the Jockey Club, in reviving Ascot, and in kindling a general interest in racing and the improvement of racehorses, Cumberland probably did more for the Turf than any man either before or since his day.

* See a contemporary advertisement of Eclipse at the stud quoted T. A. Cook, *Eclipse and O'Kelly,* p. 289.

CHAPTER XXI

THE Newcastle-Fox Administration was soon in heavy weather. On the one hand was Fox fretting for an authority he could not obtain, on the other Newcastle possessed of an authority he was determined not to delegate. It was a lamentable conjunction. It was distracted by jealousy. Squabbles between Newcastle and Fox were an almost daily incident. Even the ill success of British arms failed to produce any unity in the Cabinet. There was as much acrimony and division as in the Royal House itself. The affair of Minorca had brought on the heads of Ministers a storm of accusation and odium. It was all very well to try to appease popular clamour by promising to execute Byng, but it now looked as if the public were determined to hold Ministers themselves responsible as well. Fox made no attempt to conceal that the task of defending Newcastle and his colleagues in the House of Commons in the coming session (November 1756) was not only distasteful but in the highest degree difficult.

> You will be surprised to hear [he wrote to Hanbury Williams] that I am more alarmed than either the D. of Newcastle or Ld. Chancellor. They have indeed much more courage than I have; and as yet show no other sign of fear than making up to me with the strongest professions of sincere and cordial union. But if they see things truly, they would see that I can neither leave nor save them. And therefore, for all our sakes I will make them look out for other and more help.*

Such a frame of mind in the pilot charged with the duty of navigating the ship through the storm which was waiting to burst, was little calculated to reassure the anxiety of those whose fortunes were committed to the vessel. Personal

* H. Fox to Sir C. Hanbury Williams, Aug. 7, 1756 (Phillips MSS.); cited Lord Ilchester, *Henry Fox,* I, p. 341.

motives were entering into the counsels of those in authority to a degree not reconcileable with the business of carrying on the government in one of the most critical periods of English history. There was the inherent defect in the Administration, that the Minister who could command the strong battalions, and without whom a Parliamentary majority could not be relied on, was among those least capable of dealing with a crisis such as now confronted him.

Newcastle saw too many sides of too many problems at one and the same moment. He was for ever halting before the emergence of new difficulties. A thousand apprehensions would cross and confuse any given line of action to which he inclined. It was little use, therefore, that his general view was correct. He was prolific in suggestions for re-establishing the position. He proposed a variety of plans, such as regaining Minorca in the spring of 1757 if possible, or taking Corsica or Belleisle, or launching expeditions against the coast of France or Martinico or St. Domingo, or again concentrating on Louisbourg in Canada, or " such offensive measures as may employ and divert the naval Force of France in such manner as may give His Majesty's fleet more liberty to act against them." * Each of these measures was sound if taken as part of a general scheme, but in the crude form in which they were suggested by Newcastle they were little more than acts of retaliation, bearing little or no relation to the main objects of the war. And now power was slipping from his hands. Minorca was followed by the loss of Calcutta (June 1756); Calcutta by the loss of Fort Oswego, which in August fell to Montcalm, with the command of Lake Ontario and the headwaters of the Ohio. At home Murray, the Ministry's most powerful supporter in the House of Commons, was insisting, in the face of every art of persuasion, on his right to the post of Chief Justice vacant by the death of Chief Justice Sir Dudley Ryder. Fox was only waiting for the most favourable moment to resign. Public opinion was alarmed and exasperated. It was apparent to everyone that, unless the Ministry acquired a notable accession of strength, its life could not be prolonged.

* Cabinet Memoranda, Aug. 6, 1756, Add. MS. 32997, f. 18, and Aug. 15, f. 30.

Once more and in a humbler spirit negotiations were opened with Pitt. It was now that he exclaimed to the Duke of Devonshire, "My Lord, I am sure I can save this country, and nobody else can." But he made it clear that if the country was to be saved by him the process was to take place without the assistance of Newcastle. On this he was inflexible. He visited Lady Yarmouth. The favourite was ready to support his cause, and to act as intermediary with the King. George II —and in this he did not differ from his fellow-men—detested to have it thought that feminine influence could deflect his will. He was petulant and resentful at the manner in which it was sought to persuade him; that, however, did not prevent his being persuaded. Newcastle and Fox resigned on November 11. The Duke of Devonshire became the nominal head of the Government. Pitt became Secretary of the Southern Department.

Cumberland's influence in these negotiations is a matter of conjecture. We know that he favoured co-operation between Pitt and Fox. We may assume that he would deprecate power passing into the hands of Pitt at the expense of Fox. Walpole considered that Fox, by his threatened resignation, "hoped to terrify and to obtain an increase of sway." * If this were the case he would certainly have had the support of Cumberland. Both the Captain General and Fox desired nothing better than to see Newcastle unseated, nor did they very much care how badly he might be hurt in his fall. Fox, however, was under an eclipse in the esteem of the King. A crisis had arisen at Leicester House, and with this Fox had become associated. In June the Prince of Wales, the future George III, had come of age. It was necessary to appoint for him a household. The Princess, his mother, who had allowed her widowhood to be tempered by the assiduity and attention of Lord Bute, desired that Bute should be appointed Groom of the Stole. This was violently opposed by the King. The King was never more palpably sincere than when he hated. The King hated Lord Bute, and he hated the Princess of Wales, and he was quite prepared to hate those who did not act as if they in their turn hated both Bute and the Princess. Fox in

* *Memoirs of George* II, p. 252 (ed. 1846).

this case thought it politic that the Princess should be humoured. The King thought otherwise. Bute with his gift for private theatricals, with the symmetry of his leg of which he was so conscious, with his polished and rather disdainful manner and his slightly histrionic gestures, was not the personality calculated to appeal to George II. Besides that, had not whispers drifted down the backstairs of Carlton House and Kew, and out upon the world, to stir up speculation and suggest that the observances of propriety in those residences were less conventual than they seemed? But the King had to give in. On October 18 Fox had one of his final audiences at Kensington Palace. The King was in ill humour. " You have made me," he said, " make that puppy Bute Groom of the Stole "; but when he went on to suggest that Fox was trimming his sails to catch the favours of Leicester House, Fox answered : " Sir, what I am so happy in, my attachment to your son [Cumberland], might have assured you against that." Cumberland in the background was no doubt on the fringe of the storm, but he cannot have escaped a share of the responsibility for the conduct of Fox. Their association was too close and well known. The King must have looked with small favour on Cumberland's part in the affair.*

If the ventures on sea and land of the Government now about to retire had not been attended with success, they had at least made some advance in the strengthening of the country's armaments—not, it is true, such as Cumberland had constantly urged, but still much to the good as far as they went. As we have seen, they had added in January 1756 ten new regiments

* Fox's own account of what occurred is contained in a letter to Hanbury Williams : " The short epitome of politics is the D. of N. would not let me go on with him and then found he could not go on without either Pitt or me : try'd Pitt and resigned : Pitt would not join with me : I could not take the whole : Pitt is single, imperious, proud, enthusiastick, has engaged the Torys, who instead of strength are weakness : has Lord Bute and Leicester House absolutely. Upon these and the belief that the D. of N. and I shall not join against him and above all in the confidence he has in his own superiority over all mankind, he comes, or, having gout, sends Legge and Grenville to talk miserably to a majority set against them and who only forbear dividing out of regard to public tranquillity " (Stowe Papers, 263, Fox to Hanbury Williams, Dec. 26, 1756).

to the Army.* They had brought over the Hessians and Hanoverians, and obtained the necessary powers to raise four battalions in America. In the dockyards the activity had been such that in August 1756 there were 125 ships of the line, 79 frigates, and 126 other armed vessels at the disposal of the Admiralty—a force greatly superior to the naval power of France. And since the pressgang had been in active operation, the personnel of the Navy under Lord Anson had risen to 50,000 men. But far more was needed.

The situation was grave in the extreme. England had been worsted in every theatre of war. Frederick, it is true, had made himself master of Saxony and had defeated an Austrian army in Bohemia; but he was now shortening his long lines of communication and withdrawing into winter quarters, and as he surveyed the scene of Europe he had every reason for that uneasiness of mind which he now began freely expressing to the British Government. Fronting him were the armies of Austria, against whom no final decision had been obtained; on his right, when he should again advance into the Empress's dominions, was the threat of France; on his left was Russia, who might at any moment move her forces against East Prussia; while in rear there was the menace of Sweden. Of the Princes of the Empire few could be counted as allies, several needed only a failure on the part of Frederick to turn openly against him. Later he likened himself to the quarry in a stag hunt organised by the Kings and Princes of Europe, who had issued invitations to their friends to be present at the kill. † For the moment his anxiety was to see England exerting herself in the common cause, with the right means at the most advantageous time and place, instead of which she seemed to be entirely taken up with her Ministerial crisis, while Hanover was actually contemplating a neutrality. Had he backed the wrong horse? Had he made an alliance with a country already in its decline? Was this new combination into which he had

* The total forces, including the Plantations, Gibraltar, Jersey, Guernsey, and Minorca, on the Establishment in 1756 were 63,637, exclusive of the Hanoverians and Hessians (Abstract of the Forces for 1756, Holland House MS.).

† *Political Correspondence*, XIV, p. 254, Frederick to the Margrave de Baireuth, Feb. 7, 1757.

entered going to betray him? That such doubts were in his mind is made abundantly clear by his correspondence. * He was determined at any rate that England should realise her danger. He began therefore, and continued at every opportunity, to put before George II and his English Ministers suggestions for their guidance. He warned them of what the enemy intended. He outlined, and filled in with no little detail, the general scheme by which those intentions might be defeated. This was early in November.

It was during those days that Ministerial resignations and readjustments were occupying the energies and distracting the minds of those responsible for the Government. It was during those days that, to Frederick at any rate, England appeared to be without a directing hand, without a plan, without even the necessary capacity for developing her resources. Frederick proceeded to formulate his conception of the strategy to be employed.

Bearing in mind what the genius of Pitt accomplished in the years that followed, it is worth while to examine, with more attention than the subject has usually attracted, the possible origin of the ideas which it was his fame to execute.

On November 9, 1756, Frederick wrote † from his headquarters at Sedlitz in Saxony to inform the English Government that the French plan was to move an army of 50,000 men under Marshal d'Estrées against Hanover early in March 1757. On November 20, from Dresden, to which he had withdrawn on the approach of winter, Frederick wrote a more reasoned aperçu of the situation. He pointed out that France had gained important advantages both in Europe and America: she had taken Minorca, she was about to transfer troops to Corsica, she was in fact establishing a dominant strategical position in the Mediterranean. In America she had taken Fort Oswego, which gave her a marked superiority for conducting a campaign on that continent. It was now her intention to send strong reinforcements to Canada, to despatch a fleet and troops to Pondicherry and drive the Eng-

---

* *Political Correspondence*, XIV, letters of Jan. 27, 1757, p. 229; Feb. 7, pp. 252-4; Feb. 17, pp. 276-7; March 11, p. 358.

Political Correspondence, XIV, pp. 27, 28, 31

lish from Madras, and at the same time to continue her threats of invasion, and thereby contain the English fleet in the Channel and keep the country on the defensive. He went on to point out that England had made two cardinal mistakes: first in not sending succours to Minorca, secondly in adopting the defensive as an answer to the French coastal preparations. There followed a brief dissertation on the advantage of offensive operations, much in the vein of the head of a staff college communicating instruction to his pupils. What therefore was to be done?

He recommended further attempts to form alliances, with Holland, with Denmark, and with any Princes of the Empire who might be willing to furnish troops in return for subsidies; he begged that every effort should be made to keep Russia from moving, that preparations should be pushed forward at top speed and a march thereby stolen on the French, above all that some offensive operation should be devised and put into execution. As to the protection of Hanover against the army to be formed under Marshal d'Estrées, he pointed out that by returning the Hessians and Hanoverians from England, and drawing on the Dukes of Brunswick and Gotha, together with the succours that Frederick himself would be able to add, it would be possible to have an army of 54,000 men ready by the spring, and for this army he drew up in the same memorial a complete plan of campaign.

On December 9,* the very day on which he learnt that the Czarina had determined to move an army of 70,000 men to the assistance of Austria, he wrote a more precise and extended memorial. This is what he urged. England should

(1) Make a diversion by threatening the coasts of Normandy or Brittany;

(2) Take Corsica as a set off to Minorca;

(3) Move an army (composed as in his first memorial) towards the Rhine early in the spring;

(4) Stir up the Turks to make a diversion against Russia or Austria.

As to what could be done in Africa, America, or Asia, his

* *Political Correspondence*, XIV, p. 119.

knowledge of the position did not enable him to suggest; the English themselves must decide as to this.

Such then were the proposals of Frederick. Not all were adopted. But, and it is this that should be noted, the measures put into force, though they may not have been inspired by Frederick, were in accordance with the plan which he outlined for the benefit of the British Ministry. The basis of Pitt's schemes can be seen in these Memorials prepared by a consummate master of the art of war. And it was armed with these ideas that Pitt stretched forth his hand in a gesture of conquest, and raised England from the humiliations she had suffered to the highest point of her renown.

Meanwhile the new Government had entered into power. Lord Holdernesse continued as Secretary of State, the Lord Chancellorship was put in commission, Lord Chief Justice Willes, Judge Wilmot, and Baron Smyth being appointed " Commissioners of the Great Seal," Legge again became Chancellor of the Exchequer, Lord Temple head of the Admiralty in place of Lord Anson, while places were found for other Grenvilles, the relatives of Pitt. It was a Ministry forced on the King—forced on him, not by the House of Commons but by the nation, by a tide of popular feeling which Newcastle, although commanding a majority in Parliament, was unable to contend with, deprived as he was of Fox and Murray. The change denoted a new standard of political measurement. The opinion of the country had penetrated into the House of Commons with an unaccustomed insistence. It had disregarded Newcastle's artificial majority. Without an election the voice of the people had prevailed, just as without an election and with still greater force it was to prevail again before a year had passed. Without acquiescence, the King had been obliged to accept a Ministry of which he disapproved. To those capable of interpreting events the situation had a novel significance. Newcastle himself recognised that a new factor was at work, and that a majority in Parliament was not enough by itself. " Misfortunes," he wrote to Yorke, Minister at the Hague, " incidental to all wars, and more particularly to be expected from this, have, though unjustly, created a Flame, which though it did not extend to the members of

Parliament made it necessary to have the assistance of Mr. Pitt and Mr. Fox, or at least one of them." *

In the King's Speech prepared by Pitt, this new temper found immediate expression. It was no longer a document of formal affirmation between King and Parliament; it was an appeal by the King to the nation—"relying," he was made to say, "with pleasure on the spirit and zeal of my people in defence of my person and realm." Now too defence of the Protestant interest in Europe appears for the first time as a call to the people. George II complained bitterly of the length of the speech, and said that as much of it as he was able to read seemed "stuff and nonsense." He returned it to be shortened. George II was no master of English, but he had an adequate vocabulary for expressing disapproval. He was blunt in his language. He was impulsive in denunciation. The speech was shortened. But the "stuff and nonsense" were not in the speech, but in the intrigues which had made the speech necessary. †

In the speech no reference was made to the formation of an army on the Continent. The succour and preservation of America figured in the forefront; the formation of a national militia was indicated as the remedy for home defence, and the nation was assured that the Hanoverian troops should be immediately restored to their country.

Now the return of the Hanoverian troops, and an incident which followed, have to be borne in mind when considering later Cumberland's campaign in Germany. Pitt's hostility to Hanoverian measures was notorious. It had been one of the not too numerous threads which had run with any consistency through his political career. There was a clause in the Address of Thanks from the House of Lords thanking the King for the service of the Electoral troops in England. This clause formed the subject of a violent attack by Lord Temple, now

---

* Add. MS. 32869, f. 29, Newcastle to Yorke, Nov. 12, 1756.

† One Robert King was arraigned before the House of Commons for printing and publishing a spurious Speech from the Throne. George II expressed the hope that King would be leniently dealt with, as for his own part he thought the spurious speech the better of the two.

16

head of the Admiralty, who denounced it as tantamount to applauding a policy which from first to last was to be deprecated. The clause, however, was retained. In the Address from the Commons a similar clause was suggested. Pitt refused to accept it. He made its omission a condition of his taking the seals.* The clause was omitted. The King, when pressed to accept Pitt as Secretary of State, had said, " But I don't like Pitt; he won't do my business." In his own mind the King's business was Hanover, and here at the very dawn of the new Ministry's existence, they were confirming his fears. It was evident that they were as hostile to Hanover as ever. How could such a Ministry give any sincere support to measures designed to assist that unfortunate Electorate? That question was to recur. That question, and the answer which in their own minds the King and Cumberland gave to it, were to exert a powerful influence on events in 1757.

The winter of 1756–7 settled upon Europe with bitter severity. Snow blocked the mountain passes and lay heavy in the plains. War was suspended, but the cantonments outspread in every quarter of the Continent spoke of a Europe under arms. On every anvil were being hammered the means of war. Russia, Sweden, Austria, France, Prussia, and the Princes of the Empire—all were either armed or arming. Under the dark skies of winter the minds of men were turned in those months with misgiving to the coming struggle. No man could foretell its limits or conjecture its consequences. Frederick, far seeing and unshaken in resolve, saw, but saw without faltering, the hosts that were gathering against him. All that genius could accomplish by way of preparation had been done. Under his command was assembled the finest army in Europe. His magazines were full, his supplies abundant, his armament all sufficient. His troops were disposed so as to conform with the most advantage to such plan of campaign as he might determine for the coming spring. He had provided for every eventuality, for every mischance. Exact orders were given to his Minister of State as to what

* Add. MS. 32869, f. 253, Hardwicke to Newcastle, Dec. 6, 1756.

was to be done, in case of defeat, with the Royal Family, and the treasure and garrison of Berlin; if Frederick himself were killed, things were to go on exactly as if he were there; if he had the misfortune to be taken prisoner, no regard was to be had to his person, no attention was to be paid to anything he might write from his captivity. " Si pareil malheur m'arrivait, je veux me sacrifier pour l'État." * Mindful always of that possibility, he carried on his person in " a small glass tube " the means wherewith to complete the sacrifice. Meanwhile he had two things to wait for. He had to wait till the grip of ice and snow had relaxed, and he had to wait till the dispositions of his adversary should determine him where to strike. All through that winter he was writing to urge the English Ministry to hurry their preparations, to mobilise their army of observation in Hanover, to second his efforts by making some offensive threat to France, and protect his coasts from Russia by despatching a fleet to the Baltic. He was met by assurances. The policy of Pitt was to support him by every means. It was the intention of the British Ministry to form an army in Hanover. Were not the Hessians and Hanoverians being evacuated from England for that pur- pose? But they had their own coasts to defend, their distant possessions to provide for, and above all operations to carry on in America, the true theatre of war in which to obtain a decision against France. They would do what they could; but a fleet for the Baltic!—if they had the ships, well and good, it should be done, but for the moment the scope of their strategical plans did not allow of it.

George II was still casting eyes of regret on the "old system," † now fast disappearing bag and baggage over the horizon. Holdernesse, who remained as Secretary of State and communicated all Cabinet information to Newcastle as though he were still of the Government, retaining as he did his lodgings in the Cockpit, comments on the reluctance of the King "to go in roundly with the King of Prussia," and observes even "a remaining delicacy towards the House of

* *Political Correspondence*, XIV, p. 198, Frédéric au Ministre d'État, Jan. 10, 1757.

† Add. MS. 32869, f. 422, Holdernesse to Newcastle, Dec. 29, 1756.

Austria." * George II was apt at this time to be more aware than usual of his dual capacity. One day he would speak as the King, another as the Elector. Whatever he might write to Frederick, he had in his mind a way out for Hanover. And the more precarious Frederick's situation became, so did the reservations in George's mind pile up, and so did his determination not irrevocably to commit himself grow. Visions of Hanover overrun and devastated by the French haunted his imagination. Indeed both Newcastle and Hardwicke agreed that the King of Prussia, in his desire to frighten the King, had been too successful. He was making pictures. England seemed to do nothing for his Electorate. And here was Pitt now his principal Minister—Pitt, who had openly advocated the policy of leaving Hanover to its fate and who would not even thank him for the presence of the Hanoverian troops in England. He was losing faith in the professions of his English Ministers. What made the thing worse was that Pitt was so ill that he could not attend the House, and could only come to interview the King on the very rare occasions when his gout permitted.† All this was creating an atmosphere and producing in the King a certain definite mentality which has to be taken into account when considering Cumberland's conduct of affairs in 1757, not necessarily by way of excuse, but certainly by way of explanation.

On February 17, 1757, Pitt presented to the Commons a message from the King in reference to the formation of " An Army of Observation for the just and necessary defence and preservation " of his Majesty's Electoral dominions, and those of his good ally the King of Prussia. A sum of £200,000 was voted for the support of the Army. Frederick had been importuning George II to give the command of his Army to Cumberland. He was profoundly distrustful of the Hanoverians; whether with or without the connivance of the King of England, he was convinced that they intended to make the best terms they could for their own preservation. He considered that if the command were given to General Zastrow,

---

* Add. MS. 32869, f. 121, Holdernesse to Newcastle, Nov. 22, 1756.

† *Bedford Correspondence*, II, p. 230, Mr. Rigby to the Duke of Bedford, Feb. 3, 1757.

the Hanoverian, as was proposed, it would be disastrous to the common cause. Writing on March 21, he said that the only chance of imposing the necessary authority on such a heterogeneous force as the Army of Observation was to be found in the appointment of Cumberland to the command. Cumberland, he said, has commanded armies in the field, he is familiar with the methods of the French, and both by his birth and character will be able to exercise a degree of authority over a mixed command not seen since the days of Marlborough.*

Cumberland himself was reluctant to undertake the task. He had been ill. The wound in his leg had been once more causing its constantly recurring trouble. He saw a Ministry in power avowedly unfavourable to Hanover interests. He knew from the first that with a totally inadequate force drawn from mixed sources he would be called on to oppose a vastly superior and united army of France. The country in which he would have to operate was ill adapted to the defensive warfare which it would be his mission to carry on. Moreover by the very title given to the force, " An Army of Observation," it was clear that his movements would be restricted and his liberty of action closely circumscribed. He hesitated. The task had nothing to commend it. It meant separation from the Army which it was the passion of his life to command, and an exchange to the captaincy of half-hearted Hanoverians and subsidised mercenaries to be pitted against the finest troops of France arrayed in a crushing superiority. George II insisted. Frederick of Prussia declared it to be essential. Cumberland chose the arduous course. He yielded. He accepted the command, and in so doing identified himself with one of the disastrous episodes of the Seven Years' War.† It has been said, and it has been habitually repeated, that Cumberland made it a condition of his acceptance that Pitt should be driven

* *Political Correspondence,* XIV, p. 397, Frederick to George II, March 21, 1757.

† In many quarters it was recognised as being in the nature of a forlorn hope. Fawkener wrote: " Your R.H.'s appointment to a command which with your sentiments could not be refused though you saw there were not such dispositions made to support you as cou'd give you any reasonable hopes of success " (Cumberland MS., July 12, 1757).

from office. So stated the suggestion is misleading. From the first, George II had shown a steady determination to get rid of Pitt and his associates. Pitt he found intolerable—" with his long speeches which were possibly very fine but for the most part beyond his [the King's] comprehension, and his letters which were affected, formal and pedantic." While as to Lord Temple, " he was so disagreeable a fellow, there was no bearing him; that when he attempted to argue he was pert and sometimes insolent; that when he meant to be civil, he was exceedingly troublesome, and that in the business of his office he was totally ignorant." * In February the King began negotiating through Lord Waldegrave with the Duke of Newcastle. " I know he is apt to be afraid," he said to Waldegrave; " therefore go and encourage him: tell him I do not look on myself as King, while I am in the hands of these scoundrels; that I am determined to get rid of them at any rate."

Newcastle was too wary to take office at such a juncture. Supply had still to be voted; the enquiry into the responsibility of Newcastle's late Ministry for the Minorca disaster had still to be held. Obviously it was no moment for him to embark on a new Administration. Every conceivable combination was tried. The King even suggested Lord Waldegrave himself as First Minister. Cumberland and Fox declared their willingness to support Newcastle if only he would try to form a Ministry. Finally Fox received orders from the King to draw up a plan. The key to the plan was Newcastle. He and Hardwicke were to be lured by the nomination to high office of their friends. But no bait could blind Newcastle to the inexpediency of taking office at the moment. Time was on his side. He had only to wait. When he was cleared, as he felt confident he would be, on all charges of neglect in connection with Minorca, it would be time to negotiate in earnest.

The Devonshire Ministry meanwhile was being sorely embarrassed by the fate of Byng. The trial at Portsmouth had concluded late on January 27. At dawn on the 28th an express had reached Kensington Palace, and there had been handed to the King the long-awaited verdict of the court-

* James Earl Waldegrave, *Memoirs*, p. 95.

martial. Munchhausen, the Hanoverian Minister in attendance on the King, was directed at once to write to Newcastle to ascertain his views, but to state that the King had already made up his mind to confirm the sentence.* Before nine in the morning Newcastle's reply was in the hands of the King.† He respectfully urged His Majesty to summon a Cabinet, over which the King himself should preside, and take the opinion of each individual member before deciding what should be done. Had the advice been followed Byng's life would have been spared. Pitt, Temple, and Cumberland, it is known, were for mercy. The advice was disregarded. There followed the unseemly discussions in Parliament and the succession of events (too well known to be referred to here) which culminated in the execution of Byng on March 14. But Newcastle's letter, which hitherto seems to have been overlooked, acquits him of that vindictive determination against Byng with which tradition, assisted by Horace Walpole, has saddled his already overburdened reputation.

Cumberland had every reason to suppose that if, in taking up his command, he left on the one hand a Ministry unfavourably disposed towards Hanoverian measures and resolved to cut down all Continental commitments to their lowest point, and on the other hand a King determined to rid himself of that Ministry, both his command and the interests of Hanover would suffer. Some settlement before he set out was imperative. But to say that he was responsible for the dismissal of Temple and Pitt, which took effect in the early days of April, is entirely to misrepresent the situation. That dismissal was the work of the King, in accordance with his fixed resolve. Cumberland may well have urged—did in fact urge—that some decision should be come to before he left, but that is the utmost that can be attributed to his influence on the occasion. Indeed Hardwicke went no further than to believe that Cumberland had concurred in the action of the King.‡ In a letter to Henry Fox Cumberland in fact expressly averred that what he most

---

* Add. MS. 32870, f. 125, Munchhausen to Newcastle, Jan. 28, 1757.
† *Ibid.*, f. 127, Newcastle to Munchhausen, Jan. 28, 1757.
‡ *Ibid.*, f. 396, Hardwicke to Newcastle, April 9, 1757.

desired to see was "a junction of Ministry between the D. of Newcastle and Pitt with you Paymaster." * "If the King can bear it," he added, "which is my first view and desire, it would be the thing I most wish, for then they might undertake the whole, and our ambition would no longer be the tedious topick of Jacobites and Lyars." The allegation automatically repeated that Cumberland was hostile to Pitt, and made his dismissal a condition of accepting the command of the Army of Observation, is thus disposed of.

It was in this manner then that Pitt's first term of high office was brought to a close. † He had failed to secure the support of the King, and he had found that without the assistance of Newcastle and his Parliamentary majority government could not be carried on. He had miscalculated his strength. Popular opinion might force the hand of the King, might even insist that Pitt should be at the head of affairs, but without the good-will of the King and Newcastle not even Pitt could remain there. Before he again took office he had secured a fusion of these two sources of strength. The King had come to recognise him as an inevitable evil, the Whig oligarchy had realised that a compromise was essential. Pitt had added a third constituent, the nation.

The Devonshire Ministry had not succeeded in bringing about any conspicuous change in the military situation of the country. They had passed a Militia Bill through Parliament. They had obtained the assent of Parliament to the raising of two battalions of Highlanders for service in America. ‡ Pitt had

* Holland House MS., H.R.H. to Mr. Fox, May 23, 1757. This letter has been printed by Lord Ilchester in *Letters to Henry Fox Lord Holland* (the Roxburgh Club, 1915).

† Walpole's account of this transaction is highly fanciful and gives a very misleading rendering of what occurred. See *Memoirs,* II, p. 377. On the other hand, in the Holland House MS. there is a detailed account of the transactions drawn up by Fox, without any reference therein to Cumberland.

‡ The information as to the much debated authorship of the idea of enlisting Highlanders for this purpose is too conflicting to be of much value. There is evidence to show that it was originally a proposal of Cumberland; on the other hand Newcastle in one of his letters declares that both the King and Cumberland had opposed the suggestion.

also given a slightly new turn to the relations between the American colonies and the mother country.   He had endeavoured to enlist their co-operation rather than make them the subject of requisitions.   Eight thousand infantry and a powerful squadron under Admiral Holbourne had been despatched * to North America, and these it was hoped, as the result of Pitt's policy, would be assisted with rather more cordiality than had hitherto been manifest.   Two other squadrons had also been detailed for the protection of trade routes and the convoy of merchantmen.

* Owing to various delays it was not till April 7 that the expedition set sail from Cork.

CHAPTER XXII

On the Continent the military situation in the early months of the year was as follows. Frederick, whose army now numbered some 150,000 men with a reserve of 40,000, was in March still at Lockwitz in Saxony, maturing his final preparations for the invasion of Bohemia. Sweden was known to be threatening a descent on Pomerania with a force of 17,000. Russia was pushing slowly forward, and while waiting on events might at any moment cross into East Prussia from Courland and Livonia with an army not less than 100,000 strong. France had formed and had already set in motion an army of more than 100,000 men under Marshal d'Estrées to operate against Cumberland and threaten Hanover. This army, known as the army of Westphalia, advancing in five columns from Longwy, Sedan, Lille, Valenciennes, Maubeuge, had in the early days of April occupied by an advance guard the fortress of Wesel at the junction of the Rhine and Lippe. That fortress had been garrisoned by six Prussian battalions. The fortress was strong. It was reputed in its powers of resistance to be comparable to Luxembourg. But Frederick, when he learnt in the first days of March that the French were directing their advance on the fortress, ordered the garrison to demolish the fortifications, withdraw with their guns, and join the army to be commanded by Cumberland. By April 27 d'Estrées had established his headquarters at Wesel. There he received pressing orders from Versailles to advance against the army covering Hanover.

It was the project of the French Ministry to obtain an immediate and decisive result in Hanover. That result they believed would have political consequences likely to affect the course of the war. Their political judgment was at fault. Hanover was no more than a counter in the struggle with

England. The issue at stake was one not to be measured by the fate of a German Principality, even though the ruler of the Principality was the English King. But Versailles thought otherwise, and they were impatient for a decision. The Hanoverian army which d'Estrées was being urged to bring to action was at the end of March on a line parallel to and behind the Weser, extending from Werden in the north to Hameln in the south; while the Prussian contingent withdrawn from Wesel, under Prince Frederick of Hesse, was holding Lippstadt on the west side of the river.

On April 1 a further treaty between France and Austria was signed. The treaty allocated the prospective spoils of victory. It provided that Silesia, Glatz, and Crossen should be restored to Austria; Magdeburg and Halberstadt should be surrendered to Saxony; Pomerania to Sweden; while Ostend, Nieuport, Furnes, Ypres, Mons, Chimay, and Beaumont should pass into the hands of France. Such an arrangement set the seal on the ambitions of France, and betokened in unmistakeable terms the danger to British interests in the North Sea.

Such was the situation when Cumberland left St. James's Palace at 6 a.m. on April 9 in his travelling coach for Harwich. It was the last time he was to leave the shores of England. He was wearing his scarlet coat and buff waistcoat, his three-cornered hat with the familiar cockade, and the high jack-boots of the period; and as he passed out of London and his coach swung on to the road which he had traversed so often on the way to war, his mind must have travelled back over the strange vicissitudes he had known, to his campaigns in the Low Countries, to Dettingen and Laffelt and the slopes of Fontenoy, to the armies he had commanded, to the Dutch who had failed him so often and made victory so hard to come by, to the Austrians who were now ranged against the interests of Britain, then to the triumph of Culloden and his blaze of popularity which had suffered eclipse like a flaming torch flung upon the waters, and then to the sharp revival of his public fame, and lastly to the Army where his heart was set and which he was now leaving for an untried and precarious field with little to encourage and much to daunt. What could he hope? What could he look for in this new mission to protect his father's dominions? What likelihood was there of achievement or success? and what of his Orders handed to him by his father on March 30? These Orders, which have hitherto lain unexplored among the Cumberland Papers at Windsor Castle, throw a new and illuminating light on the campaign which followed. They are definite and explicit. They admit of no two interpretations. They lay down in precise terms the plan to be followed. No man saw them but their author, George II, and the commander to whom he confided them.

In the first place Cumberland is to have under his command an army composed as follows:

> 27,045 Hanoverians
> 6,241 Brunswick troops
>   800 Saxe-Gotha troops
>   800 Schaumberg-Lippe troops
> 12,000 Hessians

to be strengthened by the six Prussian battalions drawn from the fortress of Wesel. The Orders go on to say:

> When the French draw near Wesel it will be time for our Army to advance towards the Lippe. Should the enemy proceed from Cleves, further into Westphalia towards our German dominion, the first thing to be done, will be to detach the whole, or part of the Cavalry, to carry off all the Provision and Forrage on the Road to our German Dominions and bring it to our Army, or quite into our own Country, and to destroy what cannot be brought off . . . that by this proceeding the Subsistence may be cut off to the enemy on their march to our German Dominions, and perpetually to harass them, but yet not to come to an Engagement with them, without necessity and advantage, but maintaining such a Position, that the detached Corps are not cut off, but may always retire to the Main Body of the Army.
>
> As to the Position to be given to Our Army, and the Operations to be undertaken with it, the first and fixed Object is, not to wait for the Enemy on Our Borders, but if what is mention'd in the foregoing Paragraph should happen, that the enemy has thoughts of penetrating into Westphalia, Our Army is to advance, and to post itself in a convenient and safe Place, on foreign Territories.

The Position and Operations of Our Army must however be directed to Our Chief Aim. This is: not to act offensively, neither against the Empress Queen, nor any other Power, but merely protect Our own Dominions, those of the King of Prussia in Westphalia, and those of the Landgrave of Hesse, from hostile Invasions of Foreign Troops, and repulse Force by Force.

If therefore it is observed the Crown of France has no Views of penetrating into Westphalia, but that the said Crown's sole intent is, to send an Assistance of Troops into Bohemia, it is not in such a case Our intention, that Our Army marches against them, and oppose them.

But if the Crown of France will penetrate into Westphalia, and so thro' Our Dominions, and those of Our Allies, then is the time for acting, and opposing the Enemy.

We have mention'd in the foregoing 5th Paragraph, that when the Crown of France, advances to Wesel, it will then be time for Our Army, if not sooner, to advance to the Lippe, at all events. And when this happens, according as necessity, or the motions of the Enemy may require it, move forward, to the right or left, or retire back. It will chiefly depend on this, whether the Enemy's Army marching against Ours, be much superior to it, or not. In the first case We depend on the presence of Our Son, and on the Bravery of the Troops, that all that is humanly possible, will be done.

Foresight however will be required, that in the position taken, or the Alterations to be made in it, that the Protection of Our own Dominions, be the chief Aim, and to keep a retreat towards Stade open and free, that in case of the utmost extremity, which the Allmighty in His Mercies avert, Our Army may retire to, keep and maintain itself there; to wait the issue of what the Times may bring forth.

On the other hand if Our Army is equal to that of the Enemy's, We think it unnecessary to point out to Our Son, how such an advantage is to be improved, and not only prevent the Enemy from approaching the Borders of Our Dominions, and those of Our Allies, but to drive them back with Loss out of Westphalia.

Such then were the instructions which Cumberland carried with him, when he left England on April 9, 1757. They are not instructions to an English Commander, going to command an English army, destined to take part in a campaign on behalf of English interests; nor indeed did he receive any instructions whatsoever from the Government at home. They are instructions to a general who is being sent out to take over the captaincy of a Hanoverian army, for the most part in Hanoverian pay, with a defined and strictly limited object. That object does not emerge as the encounter and defeat of the enemy forces; on the contrary, it is a purely defensive object limited to Hanoverian interests. Indeed it is only in certain eventualities that the enemies of England are to be regarded as the enemies of Hanover.

If Hanover is threatened by a march into Westphalia—then and then only is Force to be met by Force. If then it can be protected, well and good. But if the attacking power is much superior in numbers, care is to be taken to keep open a retreat to Stade, " that in case of the utmost extremity our army may retire to, keep and maintain itself there." This document therefore sets at rest once and for all the question which has occurred to every military authority who has turned his attention to the matter, why when the time came Cumberland retreated to Stade? Between the day of his appointment and the day of his setting out, these instructions must have formed the subject of many discussions in secret between George II and his son— between on the one hand an autocrat with a political scheme of his own and a definite military conception of how that scheme should be carried out, and on the other hand his confidential servant appointed to put into execution the military plan, and inspired by tradition, by habit, and by training, to obey to the letter the authority of the autocrat from whom his orders were received. George II had no more doubt about his right since Dettingen to be considered a master of the art of war, than he had about his claim to be regarded as a Lothario. And here, he was drawing up a plan of campaign in a country he knew, without even reference to any authority who might know as much and probably more. It was a plan that Cumberland might be counted on to follow in every detail. But Cumberland left England with more in his mind than the actual instructions: he carried with him the purely Hanoverian atmosphere in which the instructions were given, and the Hanoverian point of view by which they were dominated. George II was never tired of insisting that Hanover would not have been attacked "on account of American quarrels," and that it was only "en haine de l'alliance avec le roi de Prusse" that France directed her forces against the Electorate.* It is essential that these considerations should be borne in mind in judging the events that followed.

When later blame was blowing up from every quarter and lying heavy on the head of Cumberland, Hardwicke, maintaining his customary judicial equilibrium of mind, wrote to Newcastle: "I wish your Grace would see the Duke's original instructions. It is to me extremely material, if an eventual retreat to Stade was there originally pointed out." † Now owing to the Cumberland Papers we are in a position to show, not merely that the retreat to Stade was "pointed out," but that it was definitely ordered.

It was at first intended that Cumberland should proceed to the Hague and post thence to Hanover, a distance of some 300 miles. Cumberland was exercised about the conveyance in which he was to travel, and wrote to Yorke to beg him to secure a coach or a chariot. "I must trouble you," he wrote, "to procure me a good travelling carriage rather for four, but if that is not too easily had, for two. The reason I give you this commission is the King's carriages are all open and I love a coach or a chariot." ‡ In the end neither coach nor chariot was used; the French were pushing forward, and it was considered risky to venture on the road from the Hague to Hanover. The capture of Cumberland might be a political counter second only in importance to the occupation of Hanover. In fact, in view of the possibility of Cumberland taking the road from the Hague to Hanover, posts were pushed out as far as Ippenburen in the hope of capturing him. § Cumberland accordingly abandoned the Hague as his port of landing and sailed for Stade, where he landed on April 14, and where by the irony of fate and the orders of his father he was eventually to find himself again at the end of his campaign.

---

* Cumberland MS., H.R.H. to Mitchell, April 23, 1757.

† Hardwicke Papers, No. 190, f. 143, Hardwicke to Newcastle, Oct. 16, 1757.

‡ Cumberland MS., H.R.H. to Yorke, April 1, 1757.

§ Leeds MS., Cumberland to Holdernesse, April 22, 1757.

From Stade he posted to Hanover. There he was met by the representative of the King of Prussia, Lieutenant-General Schmettau, who assured Cumberland that he might count on "strong and effectual succours" * from the King his Master, but Cumberland learnt at the same time with apprehension that the command of the Prussian contingent had been given to Prince Frederick of Hesse. †

In May 1739 Prince Frederick had married Princess Mary, the daughter of George II. On that occasion Cumberland had acted as proxy for the Prince, and to the objections to such a proceeding raised by the Church and the Law, George II had said to Sir Robert Walpole: "I will have no more of your Church nonsense, nor of your Law nonsense. I will have my daughter married and will have the marriage complete." The King's determination had condemned Princess Mary to an irksome destiny. Prince Frederick had treated her with consistent unkindness. He was tall and handsome, but reputed to be brutal in his disposition. Recently (1754) he had given offence to his father-in-law by being received into the Roman Catholic Church. "One is so unused," wrote Walpole, "in this age to conversions above the rank of a housemaid turned Methodist, that it occasions as much surprise as if one had heard that he had been initiated in the Eleusinian Mysteries." ‡ It had made no slight stir among the Protestant Princes of the Empire, and had been the subject of diplomatic representations and protests. Now it was to some extent marring the outward unity of the Protestant Powers. It was a blemish on the sincerity of the appeal being made on behalf of "the liberties of Europe and the Protestant cause." George II was for having him at once removed from the command. More than once Prince Frederick had been a visitor at the Court of St. James's, and in 1746 had entered the lists as a disconcerting rival to Cumberland for the affections of the beautiful Lady Rochford. If he was bad as a husband he was worse as a commander. He was a dealer in troops rather than a soldier himself. At almost any time and for almost

---

* Leeds MS., Cumberland to Holdernesse, April 19, 1757.
† He became Landgrave in 1760.
‡ Walpole to Richard Bentley, Nov. 30, 1754.

any cause he would arrange for the hire of the army of Hesse-Cassel in return for adequate remuneration. Occasionally he would seize the opportunity himself to obtain the position of commander in the field, as when in 1746 the Hessians were hired for service in Scotland.* Now he was in command of the Prussian battalions withdrawn from Wesel and holding the important positions of Lippstadt and Rietberg. He was given the command, as Schmettau explained to Cumberland, because the Prussian King did not know where else to put him." † Cumberland's apprehensions were soon to be confirmed. On April 26 Prince Frederick withdrew from and abandoned Lippstadt and Rietberg, just as he had proposed to withdraw from and abandon Perth in 1746 on the capture of some outposts by the Highlanders. News of the loss of these important posts reached Cumberland simultaneously with the information that the French, 8000 strong, had occupied Münster.‡

Cumberland remained at Hanover till May 2. He found a very sketchy organisation for carrying on the war—and had, as he wrote to Ligonier, himself to act not only as Commander-in-Chief but as " General, Quarter Master, and Commissary." § To Henry Fox he wrote:

The King is surprisingly good to me here, for he approves implicittely all I do; and yet I am forced to change and alter most things, for they were in a thorough state of confusion and as much hatred and party as amongst us in England. But a little resolution, and one may knock their heads together for the service of their master. . . . This is the most difficult and not the most brilliant campaign that ever man was engaged in; as yet I am satisfied with what I have hitherto done. I hope I shall continue to be so, for I know myself to be a severe judge.‖

Ever yours,

William.

But he did not despond. No man could be more tranquil

* See *William Augustus Duke of Cumberland*, p. 257.
† Leeds MS., Cumberland to Holdernesse, April 22, 1757.
‡ *Ibid.*, Cumberland to Holdernesse, April 26, 1757.
§ Cumberland MS., H.R.H. to Ligonier, April 26, 1757.
‖ Holland House MS., H.R.H. to Fox, May 31, 1757.

17

and composed in a difficulty than Cumberland. He had given orders to cross the Weser. He was even congratulating himself on the possession of Lippstadt, " a Post of the utmost importance to this country, the Landgrave's, and to cover Paderborn." At the very moment that he was writing the words at Hanover, Prince Frederick of Hesse, in defiance of the most direct orders to the contrary, was filing off with his Prussian battalions on the supposed advance of the French. It was not without reason that Ligonier wrote to Cumberland, " I wish your Royall [*sic*] Highness the success which I was going to say from your situation I hardly dare to hope." *

On May 2 Cumberland left Hanover to take up his headquarters at Bielefeldt, where he had concentrated 25 battalions and 20 squadrons. Bielefeldt was in a central position about six German miles† distant from Münster and Lippstadt, and rather more from the nearest point of the River Weser. His purpose in crossing the Weser was not in order to take the offensive, but " to stop the incursions of the enemy's advanced Bodies." ‡ The French were ravaging the country wherever their troops penetrated. For the moment it was a fight for subsistence. The French were wasting, and it was Cumberland's policy to accelerate the process.

Lippstadt in the hands of the French was now a serious hindrance to any advance that Cumberland might desire to make. Lippstadt lay to the extreme left of his line. It was the pivot on which his army would naturally manœuvre. It threatened his access between the Weser and Lippe to a part of the country where he would have found supplies for his troops, and it gave protection to the right flank of the French. To protect his left flank Cumberland therefore occupied Paderborn with 12 battalions and 10 squadrons.

The French were devouring the country like a plague of locusts : they were seizing cattle and horses and means of transport; they were requisitioning offhand whatever they required. The peasants were being driven to take up arms, and francstireurs began to harass the invaders. Trumpets passed between

* Cumberland MS., Ligonier to H.R.H., May 15, 1757.
† About 30 English miles.
‡ Cumberland MS., H.R.H. to Mitchell, May 6, 1757.

From an Engraving in the Royal Library at Windsor.

d'Estrées and Cumberland relative to this feature of the war. They wrote in the grand manner; they observed the courtesies of intercourse between friendly Princes. Cumberland signed himself " votre ami affectionné," and deplored the action of the peasantry, just as with civility he deplored the provocative excesses of the French—had not the officer bearing the letter of d'Estrées shot a woman dead on his way to Cumberland's camp? * These were the things responsible for the existence of francs-tireurs.

Trumpets, on the other hand, were being sent into the Hanoverian camp with suspicious frequency. Trifling occurrences were made the occasion, with an elaboration of punctilio and benevolent profession, for the despatch by d'Estrées or the Prince de Soubise of an officer bearing a message. These officers in the course of their mission appeared to be exercising uncalled for powers of observation. Cumberland thought it time to protest. "Enfin nous faisons la guerre poliment, si ce n'est pas commodément." †

In the early days of June Cumberland was still at Bielefeldt, with an army of 22,000 men encamped between that place and Rietberg, with a detachment of 10,000 men in the neighbourhood of Paderborn.

The French were facing him on a line from Münster to Lippstadt with a force at the moment of 86 battalions and 84 squadrons, approximately 70,000 men. ‡ Battalions in the French Army at this epoch numbered 685 effectives, and were divided into 17 companies, 1 of grenadiers and 16 of fusiliers. Each battalion carried with it a gun of light calibre drawn by 3 horses and provided with 55 rounds of ammunition. Officers and sergeants alike carried a musket: the officers in addition were armed with a species of lance seven feet in length and carrying at the end a blade some eight inches long. The cavalry unit was the regiment, consisting of two squadrons, each squadron having 4 companies of 41 effectives per com-

* Leeds MS., Cumberland to d'Estreés, May 6, 1757.

† Cumberland MS., H.R.H. to Ligonier, May 23, 1757.

‡ The total command of d'Estrées appears to have been 110 battalions and 127 squadrons. These were not all assembled in this area. See *La Guerre de Sept Ans*, I, p. 391. Pajol gives different figures.

pany, a total of 328. A large preponderance of young soldiers filled the ranks, deficient both in training and discipline, but the march from their places of assembly on the frontier, under conditions of weather calculated to try the most stedfast, had been endured with surprising spirit. The experience had done much to consolidate the army and prepare them for the campaign. Half the Princes and nobility of France either had commands or were attached to the headquarters staff. The Duke of Orleans, the Prince of Condé, and the Comte de la Marche, princes of the Blood Royal, were present to embarrass d'Estrées with their feuds, jealousies, and intrigues. Hundreds of horses were required to transport the aristocracy of the headquarters staff; coaches and chariots of Princes and Dukes blocked and impeded the lines of march; secretaries, aides de camp, and retainers by the score had to be provided for by the commissariat. The fashionable world of Paris had indeed set out on the campaign, and the contrast between the lot of the common soldier and the lot of those in high place provided one of those sources of discontent, the recognition of which was so rapidly finding a place in the consciousness of the people of France. Moreover the scheme of subsistence had been based on a delay of two months for the siege of Wesel. Now Wesel had surrendered, and the 300,000 rations which were to have been at Münster according to programme, were now no more than 22,000.

Hitherto the French had been able to draw their supplies from the Rhine, but as they advanced from their base their difficulties multiplied in a ratio wholly disproportionate to the mileage traversed. They were operating with 100,000 men in a country in which the great Turenne had found it difficult to subsist an army of 25,000.* Cumberland moreover had swept up all the forage and subsistence in the area between Münster and the Weser. The embarrassments of the French would daily be accentuated, and Cumberland rightly reckoned that he had no reason to fear a rapid advance.

But continual pressure was being exercised from Versailles, urging d'Estrées to force a decision, and Cumberland was necessarily in doubt. He had no light cavalry, and it was

* Pajol, *Les Guerres sous Louis XV*, IV, p. 64.

" only by paltry spies that he could get information whether the enemy was at six German miles or two." * He wrote in vain to the King of Prussia to ask for a handful of Hussars.† Frederick had not a man to spare. His promises of substantial succours were melting into vacancy. Cumberland thereupon formed a corps of Hunters, ‡ recruited from the gamekeepers of the landed proprietors in Hanover. They were famous marksmen, and " could shoot a single ball to a but no bigger than the crown of a man's hat at 200 yards distance." § In their green uniforms and with their adequate if rather melodramatic equipment of " a rifled-barrel gun, a broadsword, a dagger, and four pistols," they soon made themselves feared by the French. They were formed in two companies of horse and two of foot, and were greatly approved by the King ‖ No help was to be looked for from England. In England the " Army of Observation " was regarded as little more than a distraction for the French and a sop to Frederick. Ministers could not be expected to look on it with either the sympathy or the interest due to a purely English commitment.

By June 9 d'Estrées had moved to Warndon with 57 squadrons. Soubise was at Lippstadt with 20 battalions and 20 squadrons. D'Estrées now began to press the Hanoverian forces. His movements suggested an attempt to work round Cumberland's left and cut him off from the Weser. He was operating on both flanks of Cumberland's line: with one force he was threatening Hameln and Minden, where the Duke's magazines were established; with the other force he was making demonstrations towards East Friesland. Cumberland decided to withdraw. In face of the preponderating superiority of his adversary Cumberland's movements were sound, indeed hardly admitted of an alternative. Leaving a rearguard at Hervort, he began his march on June 14 towards the Weser, which he successfully crossed on June 16 by two bridges which he had thrown across the river at Vlotho and Rehme. The attempts

* Cumberland MS., H.R.H. to Mitchell, June 7, 1757.
† *Ibid.*
‡ Cumberland MS.
§ *Gentleman's Magazine,* XXVII (1757), p. 374.
‖ Cumberland MS., H.M. George II to H.R.H., April 26, 1757.

of d'Estrées to harass this movement were repelled with the loss to the French of some 200 men. On June 20 d'Estrées moved to Bielefeldt.

The position on that date was as follows: Cumberland, now on the east or right bank of the Weser, with his main body was guarding the two bridgeheads; the Prince of Hesse with the Prussians was holding Minden, while on the left Hameln was occupied by a force of Hanoverians.

D'Estrées with his great superiority in numbers was in a position easily to effect the passage of the river. On July 5 he began his operations. His army was divided into three corps. His plan was to make a demonstration in force on the lower Weser and occupy the attention of Cumberland's right; at the same time, by means of another corps provided with pontoons as though to effect the passage of the river at some point opposite Bielefeldt and in the vicinity of Vlotho, to cause a concentration of Cumberland's forces at that point, while with his third corps he effected the real purpose of the movement by covering the construction of two bridges at Holtzhausen and Corvey, some 25 miles up the river above Hameln.

On July 11 Cumberland, convinced that the enemy's real design was to force a passage of the river at or above Hameln, moved his army to that locality. His situation was further complicated at this date by the surrender of the town of Emden, at the mouth of the Elbe, hitherto held by a Prussian garrison, to a small party of French, thereby cutting his communication with England through that port and by a per-emptory order from the King of Prussia to detach the six Prussian battalions from the army and send them to garrison Magdeburg.

While these operations had been in progress, news had been received of the heavy reverse which Frederick had sustained at Kolin (June 18) at the hands of Marshal Daun, and the consequent raising of the siege of Prague. The scene was now one of unrelieved gloom. The Russians were on the march. Sweden might be expected at any moment to join. The forces of Prussia had suffered a severe defeat. Princes of the Empire were stirring uneasily towards the rising sun

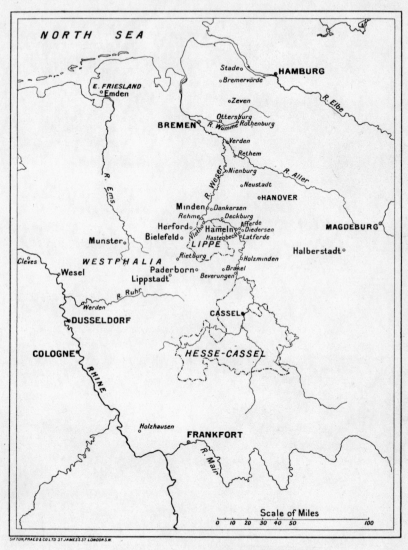

HANOVER AND THE CAMPAIGN OF 1757.

of Austria. On the other hand, in England the Ministry, after ten weeks of intrigue, bargaining, and the display of ignoble dexterities, had finally been formed. The seething activities, the scuttlings hither and thither, the clandestine conferences, the trepidations and the outwittings had ceased. Pitt, though Newcastle was nominally conjoined with him, was supreme. The great Administration of the Seven Years' War had begun.

On July 16 Marshal d'Estrées with his whole army crossed the Weser and encamped at Holzminden. On the 18th he issued orders for a general advance down the right bank of the Weser, timed to take place on the 20th. Hitherto Cumberland had outgeneralled the French commander. His dispositions had kept a superior force inactive, and at the last moment he had, with the utmost secrecy and with complete success, withdrawn his army and crossed the river in his rear.

So well had he screened his purpose, that it was only by the accident of one of d'Estrées' lackeys mounting a church tower, to spend the leisure of a summer afternoon in surveying Cumberland's camp at Hervord through a spy-glass, that information reached the Marshal that Cumberland's whole force had abandoned their camp and were already some leagues on their way.* Cumberland's operations had in fact extorted the admiration of the French, and even of that candid and critical soldier Ligonier. In Paris the army of d'Estrées was known as "l'armée de l'admiration," as they were so far reputed to have done nothing but express admiration for Cumberland's skill.†

---

* Jean Lemoine, Correspondance Amoureuse et Militaire d'un Officier pendant la Guerre de Sept Ans (1905), p. 53. Letters of great interest which give a clear account of the French movements.

† *Ibid.*, p. 65, Madame de XXX à M. de Mopinot, July 28, 1757.

CHAPTER XXIII

THE French commander, Louis-César Lettelier, Count and Marshal d'Estrées (1695-1771), between whom and Cumberland a decisive action was now pending, had, like other officers holding high station in the French Army, begun his career under Marshal Berwick in Spain. There he had served with distinction. In 1718 he had been given a regiment of cavalry, which was sent to Alsace as a guard of honour for Stanislas Leczinski when that monarch, forced to leave Poland, sought the protection of France. D'Estrées quickly became a favourite in the family of Stanislas. His youth and station, his distinction as a soldier, and his ingratiating presence quickly found favour in the eyes of Marie, then sixteen years of age, the eldest daughter of the King. An engagement followed, to which Stanislas gave his consent, provided that d'Estrées could procure a dukedom for himself. The Regent was unwilling to concede the required attribute. The engagement was broken off. Marie Leczinska was reserved for a more exalted if less fortunate destiny. On September 5, 1725, she was married to Louis XV at Fontainebleau.

D'Estrées next saw military service in the War of the Austrian Succession, first in Bohemia, and later under Marshal Saxe in Flanders. As a cavalry leader he had been opposed to Cumberland at Fontenoy, at Raucoux, and at Laffelt. At Fontenoy he had twice charged the British infantry at the head of the famous Maison du Roi, and played a conspicuous part in the victory over the Allies. Flanders had therefore made him familiar with the tactics of the Commander who was now facing him on the banks of the Weser.

D'Estrées had the reputation of being obstinate and cautious. Every factor of the problem to be solved had to be clear, ponderable, and exactly known, before he would proceed.

His plan had to be matured in every detail and every element of uncertainty eliminated before he would act. Attending himself to the minutiæ of every branch of his command, he was continuously at work. For a week before the battle he had been in the saddle twelve to fifteen hours a day, and for only three hours in the twenty-four had he rested. He was reserved—he would admit none to his confidence; he would allow none to interfere. Gifted with a singleness of purpose and an exacting sense of duty, he held aloof from intrigue and ignored the jealousies and cabals with which his entourage were clouding the conduct of the campaign. He had powerful enemies. Madame de Pompadour in Paris was working for his downfall. Duverney, the Commissaire Général, whose arrangements he had criticised, was using his immense authority for his undoing.

At the seat of war he was singularly unfortunate in having as Chief of the Staff Maillebois,* who employed his leisure in writing to Paris derogatory criticisms of his Chief. Day after day couriers would leave the army bearing letters from Maillebois, each more damaging than its predecessor. They alleged that d'Estrées was timid and without a plan, that he exaggerated the strength of his opponents, saw difficulties where none existed, and took upon himself every duty connected with the management of an army except that of leading it, that he was deaf to advice, and that he inspired mistrust among the officers and indiscipline among the men;† in short, if the campaign was to show any results, the sooner d'Estrées was superseded the better for France. But d'Estrées went his own pace, preparing step by step the means for success. His methods were patient and laborious, if uninspired. In the end, as the result of intrigue, he was to be superseded; but the blow was only to fall when the victory was already his.

Cumberland, in conformity with the motions of the enemy,

* Maillebois was later confined in a fortress on account of a pamphlet he wrote criticising d'Estrées.

† See especially Maillebois to Paulny, Bielefeldt, June 29, 1757 (Archives de la Guerre); cited Richard Waddington, *La Guerre de Sept Ans,* I, p. 417.

had moved his headquarters from Dankerren, first to Deckborg and then to Affrede near Hameln, whence he had written on July 15 * to inform Holdernesse that the French had laid two bridges across the river at Corvey and Holtzhausen, and were passing small bodies of troops to the right bank and levying contributions in the Electorate; at the same time intimating his intention to deal with this phase of the campaign. On the following day the main French army effected without opposition the passage of the river. Why had Cumberland not opposed? That was a question freely asked at the time. But the answer is not far to seek. Cumberland could not have contested the passage of the river without dispersing his forces. D'Estrées, as we have seen, had made feints at stated points on the long line of river which Cumberland had to watch. It was quite uncertain at which point he meant to cross. Cumberland's numerical inferiority did not allow him to divide his army. His tactical obligation was to keep it together and to maintain such a position on the right bank as would render it necessary for d'Estrées to attack him before advancing on Hanover. This Cumberland did, by establishing himself in the neighbourhood of Hameln, above which (though at what point was a matter of doubt) d'Estrées was bound to cross the river. It has to be remembered that Cumberland's plan of campaign was imposed on him. His instructions, as we have shown, were clear. He was to act on the defensive. It was the essence of that plan to delay a decision.† He had been told to count on Frederick. Through all these weeks, his eyes had been turned anxiously to the east for the promised reinforcements. Only a few days before his defeat in Bohemia, Frederick had written to George II to say that, when his heavy artillery arrived, Prague would fall, and that he would then be able to detach a considerable force to assist Cumberland.‡ Kolin had followed. The siege of Prague had been raised. Frederick then had need of every man he could

* Leeds MS., Cumberland to Holdernesse, Affrede, July 15, 1757.

† On April 12, 1757, Frederick had asked that Cumberland should hold up the French for six weeks (*Political Correspondence*, XIV, p. 493).

‡ Add. MS. 32871, f. 325, Apostille du Roi à Son Altesse Royale Monsgr. le Duc, June 17, 1757.

procure. Reinforcing Cumberland was out of the question, and it was now Frederick who was appealing to England to send troops to Cumberland, and urging that 6000 foot and 3000 cavalry * should be despatched at once to Stade.

But Pitt in the meanwhile had evolved a plan of his own. To appreciate how this had come about it is necessary to bring into view the other aspects of the military situation. From beyond the Atlantic Loudoun, in command of the land forces, had in March informed the Government at home of his intended attack on Canada. There is good reason to suppose that the plan was initiated by Cumberland. Through the Cumberland Papers † we are at any rate able to establish that the Captain General had, as far back as December 1756, sent to Loudoun a plan of operations (the execution or abandonment of which he left entirely to Loudoun's judgment), having as its object an attack on Louisbourg and subsequently Quebec. If therefore the design was not actually inspired by Cumberland, it was certainly in accordance with his scheme of operations. In March Loudoun sent home the scheme he intended to carry out. That scheme had as its primary purpose the capture of Louisbourg, with a view to an attack on Quebec by the highway of the St. Lawrence. By the end of April Loudoun had concentrated his force at New York. There he awaited news of the arrival of Holbourne, who, with seventeen of the line, five frigates, and a number of cruisers, accompanying the transports with the seven battalions on board, had left Cork in April bound for Halifax. Loudoun waited. May passed, and June came with no news of Holbourne. French fleets were known to be concentrating according to plan at Louisbourg. Bauffremont with five of the line from Brest, du Revest also with five of the line from Toulon, and finally la Motte with the main squadron from Brest, had arrived or were drawing near to Louisbourg. Still there

* Add. MS. 32872, f. 325, Mitchell to Holdernesse, July 9, 1757.

† Cumberland MS., H.R.H. to Lord Loudoun, Dec. 23, 1756: "Prepare your own plans for an army up the St. Lawrence Rv. and for the other to keep the enemy in check where yr. army now is. I will send you my thoughts more fully with a Plan of mine for your operations which you shall be at liberty either to adopt in part or not at all as you shall find it proper from your better information."

was no news of Holbourne. Further delay would be fatal
to the scheme. On June 20 Loudoun with a weak convoy
sailed from New York. It was a bold move, depending for
its success on the possibility of evading the French ships. But
it succeeded. The expedition reached Halifax unmolested.
On July 9 Holbourne arrived. But the strength of the French
fleet, the advanced season of the year, the insufficient chance
of possible success, the disproportionate disaster of possible
failure, led to the abandonment of the attempt on Louisburg.
Loudoun returned to New York. Such was the position at
this time on the American continent.

At home the constitution of the new Ministry, of the great
Administration of the Seven Years' War, had been finally
settled on Saturday June 18 at Kensington Palace. At 5.30,
after a final day of negotiation, Lord Dupplin was able to
write to Newcastle that the King's assent had been given to
the suggested distribution of offices.* As that same day drew
to a close and darkness fell on the field of Kolin, in Bohemia,
Frederick, after a last effort to rally his cavalry, had begun his
retreat to Nimberg and the Elbe. It was the end of the
campaign he had planned and the hopes he had entertained
of a decisive victory. The news of this disaster reached
London on June 24. Elsewhere, the Russians had entered
East Prussia and were advancing on Memel. Sweden had
declared against Frederick, and was moving 17,000 men into
Pomerania. Kolin had necessitated the evacuation of Bohemia.
Hesse had been overrun by a portion of the army of d'Estrées.†
With the surrender of Emden the command of Friesland had
gone.

> O temps! O mœurs! [wrote Frederick to his sister] Il
> vaut, en vérité, autant vivre avec les tigres, les léopards, les
> loups-cerviers que de se trouver, dans un siècle qui passe
> pour poli, parmi ces assassins, ces brigands et ces perfides
> hommes qui gouvernent ce pauvre monde. Heureux, ma
> chère sœur, l'homme ignoré dont le bon sens a renoncé dès
> sa jeunesse à toute sorte de gloire, qui n'est ni envieux par-
> cequ'il est obscur, et dont la fortune n'excite pas la cupidité

* Add. MS. 32871, f. 335, Dupplin to Newcastle, June 18, 1757.
† 20,000 men under the Duc d'Orléans.

des scélérats. . . . J'ai cru qu'étant roi, il me convenait de penser en souverain, et j'ai pris pour principe que la réputation d'un prince devait lui être plus chère que sa vie.* Frederick had reached the lowest depth of his despair, that despair from which he was such a past master in extricating himself and his fortunes.

By July 7 Pitt had determined to make one of those diversions against the French coast which had, under totally different circumstances, been suggested by Frederick in his letter of November 20, 1756.† Rochefort was to be the objective. It was while this expedition was being formed that Frederick wrote urging that assistance should be sent to Cumberland from England. Newcastle, Hardwicke, and the King were for sending the troops.

> We had last night [wrote Newcastle to Ashburnham] some little difference of opinion whether we should send 9000 men to reinforce the Duke upon a demand from the King of Prussia for that purpose. My Lord Hardwicke and I were strongly for it. Pitt was against it but in the most decent and friendly manner possible. . . . I rather think we shall send the troops. ‡

By July 30 the friendliness and decency of manner had undergone a change, and Pitt had made it clear that he would not allow a man to be diverted from the purpose to which he had now set his mind.§ But Newcastle had sound reason on his side when he wrote on July 25:

> I found the Closet as much for sending the troops [i.e. to Cumberland] as it has ever been against it (the Measure I always thought right) . . . such a reinforcement might certainly enable the Duke to do more than I am afraid we should do by any attempt on the French coasts. It would give spirit to the Protestant cause—to the Princes of the Empire and to the Dutch and it would show we were in earnest and not altogether deserving the Reproaches the

* *Political Correspondence*, XV, p. 243, Frédéric à la Margrave de Baireuth, July 13, 1757.

† See ante, p. 238.

‡ Add. MS. 32872, f. 358, Newcastle to Ashburnham, July 27, 1757.

§ *Ibid.*, f. 397, Newcastle to Ashburnham, July 30, 1757.

King of Prussia makes us from abroad and I daily hear at home. On the other hand I see the difficulties and I make no secret of them in the Closet—sending troops abroad, disclaimed by everybody not only Mr. Pitt, but by Mr. Fox by the Duke's order as I told the King—The obvious answer was *Circumstances are altered.**

The expedition against Rochefort, hastily conceived, planned on insufficient information, and in the end executed with all the faultiness that hesitation on the part of the commander and ill-adjusted concord between the Army and the Navy could bring about, was the first of Pitt's strategic conceptions. As late as July 25 not only the military authorities but the Admirals themselves considered the scheme was incapable of being carried out.† But Pitt was inflexible. On August 2, after a Cabinet meeting, when a French pilot gave his views on navigation and a Captain Clarke stated what he knew of the fortifications at Rochefort which he had examined three years previously,‡ opinion veered, and both soldiers and sailors became convinced of the practicability of the undertaking.§ It was on such a basis that Pitt's determination rested. It was on such a hazard that he withheld 10,000 men from Cumberland and sent them on what was to prove an abortive attack on Rochefort. "His Majesty was very severe," wrote Newcastle after an interview on July 25, "upon Mr. Pitt both with regard to his abilities and intentions."‖

This expedition or raid has been held up as an enlightening illustration of a minor offensive conducted within the sphere of a general defensive.¶ Its primary object was to create a diversion in favour of Frederick and Cumberland. It was believed that an expeditionary force mobilised for the purpose of operating against an unrevealed objective would embarrass the French military dispositions and draw away troops from the main armies for coastal defence. Incidentally it would

---

* Add. MS. 32872, f. 320, Newcastle to Hardwicke, July 25, 1757.

† *Ibid.*, f. 320, Newcastle to Hardwicke, July 25, 1757.

‡ See *Gentleman's Magazine*, XXVII, p. 441.

§ Add. MS. 32872, f. 413, Holdernesse to Newcastle, Aug. 2, 1757.

‖ *Ibid.*, f. 320, Newcastle to Hardwicke, July 25, 1757.

¶ See J. Corbett, *England and the Seven Years' War*, I, Chap. IX.

also have the result of affecting French credit and imposing on the French a redistribution of their naval strength. It was the less direct alternative to reinforcing Cumberland with troops from England. What did it actually achieve? Sir Julian Corbett has extolled it as a measure " absolutely correct and bearing with it all the elements of success." * He has pointed out that, as a consequence of the assembling of troops at Chatham and the concentration of ships, every French general on the coast believed himself to be threatened, and that certain battalions on the march to the Army of Westphalia were diverted to garrison Ostend and Nieuport.† But in spite of this, the salient, the actual, and the dominating fear of the French was that the destination of the expeditionary force was to be Stade. Stade would have meant timely and for-- midable succour for Cumberland, it would have meant the co-operation of a British force based on the sea, with unin-terrupted sea communications in rear. It would have altered substantially, instead of only slightly affecting as did the Rochefort raid, the whole strategical situation. The French commander who succeeded d'Estrées in the Army of West-phalia made no disguise of his apprehensions:

> Mais si les Anglais embarqués à Chatham viennent à Stade, et que le roi de Prusse y joint quelques Prussiens, ce qui n'est pas impossible, cela deviendra sérieux [he wrote on Aug. 12], car tout ce que nous avons ici, se perdrait aussi vite qu'il a été pris, si nous éprouvons quelque malheur : je ferai bien en sorte qu'il n'arrive pas. ‡

If therefore the desirable military operation was that opera-tion which would have caused the maximum embarrassment and in its execution the most serious menace to France, ought not the destination of the expedition to have been Stade rather

* *Ibid.*, I, p. 209.

† Add. MS. 32872, f. 259, Vice-Consul Irvine to James Wallace, July 15, 1757. The occupation of Ostend and Nieuport by the French might in any case have necessitated the diversion of troops, quite apart from any threat to the coast.

‡ Richelieu to Duverney, Aug. 12, 1757 (Waddington, *La Guerre de Sept Ans*, I, p. 462).

than Rochefort? Cumberland's own view was expressed to Henry Fox when he wrote:

> I hear you send two thousand men more to North America, what for, God knows. Here I am sure you'll send none, tho' perhaps they would be more necessary than anywhere England can imploy them. I am labouring on, but to what purpose I yet can [not] tell. We shall [do] our utmost, but it is not the most favourable prospect that it carries with it.

The best way of helping Frederick was to keep the Army of Observation as " a force in being " by sending help to Cumberland, as Frederick himself urged. †

This could only be done by strengthening Cumberland's command. The landing of troops at Stade would, it is true, have involved an operation eccentric to the general defensive, but a similar course of action was adopted in the following year, adopted moreover by Pitt, and it is difficult to believe that it was not political rather than military considerations which at this time determined Pitt in his selection of an objective. Hanover in fact was once more tainting the motives of action. Cumberland was to be left to himself. The Ministry did, however, several weeks later, on September 5, go so far as to resolve that a squadron of ships should cruise at the mouths of the Elbe and Weser. ‡ Pitt's failure at this juncture has been lost sight of under the blaze of light that envelopes his subsequent triumphs. Moreover it was deprived of its most dangerous consequences by the victories of Frederick which immediately followed. But judged in its relation to the general position in July 1757, it is open to more adverse comment than it has hitherto received. In fact the heresy here put forward, that Pitt either blundered, or sacrificed military to political considerations, finds at least as much support as the orthodox view.

Frederick, in writing to Cumberland, had no reserve:

> Il serait à souhaiter [he had written on July 8] que l'on

* Holland House MS., H.R.H. to Fox, Affrede, July 1757.

† See *Political Correspondence*, XV, p. 230, Mitchell to Holdernesse, July 9, 1757.

‡ Add. MS. 32997, f. 252, Cabinet Memoranda, Sept. 5, 1757.

pensât en Angleterre à renforcer l'Armée de Votre Altesse Royale par des Troupes Anglaises. Si jamais les libertés de l'Europe: la Religion; et la Ballance des Pouvoirs ont couru Risque c'est à présent, et je m'étonne qu'une Nation qui a tant dépensé d'Argent, et tant versé de sang pour le soutien de ce système, voie à présent avec des yeux indifférents les grands hazards que court l'Europe d'être subjuguée par la Force prépondérante de ce Monstre Politique. . . . En vérité on regrettera, mais trop tard, l'indifférence avec laquelle on regarde en Angleterre la guerre de terre ferme.*

Cumberland in his reply was discreet and guarded. He lamented the absence of reinforcements, assured Frederick of the loyalty of George II, and intimated that he had been too long away from England to have knowledge of the political considerations which were responsible for the policy.† To Henry Fox, on the other hand, he wrote: "I trouble none of my friends in England with our affairs, for you neither heed them nor understand them."‡ It will be seen therefore to what extent Pitt's first intervention in the Seven Years' War had jeopardised the interests of the new alliance, and how conspicuously it failed to bring any relief to the military situation.

* Add. MS. 32872, f. 327, Frederick to Cumberland, July 8, 1757.
† *Ibid.*, f. 329, Cumberland to Frederick, July 15, 1757.
‡ Holland House MS., Cumberland to Fox, May 2, 1757.

18

CHAPTER XXIV

WE must return now to the Weser and the encounter that was preparing on the banks of that river, where Cumberland with a force of between 30,000 and 40,000 men was endeavouring to defend Hanover against d'Estrées, who had at his disposal no fewer than 65,000 and probably more than 70,000 troops.* In what followed, it must be borne in mind that Cumberland was not a free agent. He had his father's orders to keep open a retreat to Stade. He was not at liberty to base himself on Magdeburg, as Frederick was later so urgent he should do.† He was not even free to retire in a direction which would keep open communications with Prussia. He was definitely restricted to a plan of campaign which, when the moment to retreat came, and come it must as everyone recognised, would find him with the road to Stade and the sea open to his army. Whatever the strategical advantages of a move in an easterly direction might be, these were therefore denied him.

Clearly d'Estrées could have no knowledge of these secret conditions, any more than the English Ministry. The military task of d'Estrées was to occupy Hanover. French strategy was directed by the political assumption that, if Hanover was in French hands, it would be possible to exercise effective pressure on England. By crossing the Weser at the point he

* The exact figures cannot be given. Every writer differs. We know that on May 6 Cumberland had 44 battalions and 44 squadrons (Add. MS. 6835, Mitchell Papers, May 6). These included six Prussian battalions withdrawn before the battle. The French forces were estimated by Cumberland to be 80,000 effectives (Add. MS. 6835, Mitchell Papers, Cumberland to Mitchell, Aug. 1, 1757). Moreover Cardinal Bernis, writing to Richelieu on Sept. 12, credits him with 100,000 men (*Correspondance des Généraux Français*), Allemagne, 1757, Vol. 595, French Foreign Office Papers).

† Cumberland MS., Holdernesse to H.R.H., Sept. 16, 1757; Add. MS. 32873, f. 290, Frederick to Michel, Aug. 27, 1757.

had chosen, d'Estrées had interposed himself between Cumberland and any chance of assistance from Prussia. Now, if he could bring Cumberland to action and defeat him, the road to Hanover would be open. At the same time d'Estrées had secured his flanks by occupying Cassel on the right and Emden on the left.

Skirmishes between the advanced posts of the two armies were now of daily occurrence. On July 14 Cumberland moved his headquarters from Deckberg to Afferde. He had thrown forward the Grenadiers of the army into the " Pays de Gottingen " to withstand the depredations of the French. The Grenadiers were attacked by a force of great superiority, and Cumberland had found it necessary to " make a movement with the second line of the army " to disengage the Grenadiers.* On July 20 the operation was successfully carried out without loss. Cumberland had formed the impression that it was the intention of d'Estrées to get round his left flank. At any rate the Duc de Randan, with two brigades and 18 squadrons, had pushed out as far as Einbeck, and was menacing Cumberland's communications with Hanover.† This was the force with which the Grenadiers had become involved.

The position on July 24, two days before the battle, was as follows: Cumberland's headquarters were at Afferde. The army was posted on the low ground that separates the hills on the east from the Weser. On Cumberland's right Major-General Fürstenberg, in command of the outposts, was in occupation of the village of Latford. On the left, the defiles of Bessinghausen and Volkershausen were held by Major-General Hardenberg with the Grenadiers who had retired from the Pays de Gottingen. The main body of the army was disposed on the low ground in rear of the wood of Lafferde.

Upon the advance of the French on July 24 Cumberland abandoned the village of Latford, and withdrew General Fürstenberg to the wood of Lafferde. Here Fürstenberg sustained and successfully resisted an attack by the enemy. Simultaneously an attempt by the French under M. Chevert to force the defiles held by Major-General Hardenberg was repelled.

* Leeds MS., Cumberland to Holdernesse, July 22, 1757.
† Waddington, *La Guerre de Sept Ans*, p. 424.

The French encamped on the afternoon of July 24 in front of the allies. During the night of July 24 Cumberland withdrew unobserved, and took up the position which he had prepared and where he had resolved to give battle to the French. Here his extreme flank was protected by the river Weser, which at this time, though of no great width, ran swift and clear as far as the fortress of Hameln, at which point it began to widen out. Immediately in front of his right wing lay a morass passable only by certain ill-defined causeways, and traversed by the small Hameln river. In front of his centre lay the village of Hastenbeck, from which ran a covered way to a point on the edge of the wood where Cumberland had stationed a battery of twelve-pounders and howitzers. The position was strong and well chosen. Immediately to the left of Hastenbeck the ground rises sharply, and where it breaks from the plain is diversified by ravines, which, rocky and steep as they are, present a natural obstacle. It was on a spur with a ravine in front that the battery was placed. Above this the land slopes with rapidity to a height of some 700 feet, the sides of the hills being thickly clothed with oak, with beech, and with pine up to the crest, beyond which the land falls again into a broad ravine.

D'Estrées, viewing the situation from the Buckeburg, an eminence close to the Weser and surmounted by a clump of willows which tradition still associates with the occasion, realised that Cumberland's right was unassailable, and that the centre with Hastenbeck and a redoubt which had been constructed in the defile between the village and the wood was too strong to be forced by direct assault. The attack therefore, if it was to succeed, must be by an enveloping movement along the crest of the range and through the woods which protected Cumberland's left wing. His plan was made accordingly. To M. Chevert, one of the most capable commanders in the French Army, was allotted the difficult task of forcing his way through the wood on Cumberland's left, with four brigades of infantry—Picardie, Navarre, Eu, and La Marine—some light troops and 16 pieces of cannon. Armentières at the head of a division of the same strength was to advance along the edge of the wood, capture the battery situated on the spur, and so flank the principal attack against the redoubt and the village of Hastenbeck. The rest of the army was disposed on the parallel principle and extended towards the river, with the Duc de Broglie, who had crossed the Weser the previous day, on the extreme left, while the cavalry was drawn up in rear.

Throughout the day of July 25 the cannon on both sides were active, but the superiority of the French artillery was painfully apparent, and by the evening it had dominated that of the allies. Both sides held their ground, and when night fell no alteration had occurred in the tactical situation. When, before dawn of the 26th, Cumberland after his third night in the open mounted his horse to reconnoitre the position, a thick mist, which had been forming through a night of intense stillness and heat, lay over the theatre of battle. As the dawn widened the mists thinned out, and by 5.30 Cumberland could see the forces of France drawn up in the same situation as the day before. Chevert, however, since midnight had been advancing with his division through the wood and climbing towards the crest of the hill, arduously dragging with him his 16 pieces of cannon. When day broke he was drawing near to his position on the extreme left of the Hanoverian army. Later, as the sunlight drifted through the mist, the flag of Picardie could be seen planted on the highest crest of the Schekenberg. Between 7 and 8 o'clock, the sound of musketry fire proceeding from Chevert's attack was the signal for a cannonade along the whole line and a movement in advance by the entire French army. Cumberland had stationed in the wood above and to the left of the battery three battalions of Grenadiers and some Chasseurs, with some six pieces of twelve-pounders under Count Schulenburg. During the night or the late evening of July 25, Cumberland had reinforced Schulenburg with four more battalions of Grenadiers under Major-General Hardenberg. Behind the village of Hastenbeck were drawn up the Hessians, with a strong battery of twelve- and six-pounders, to form which it had been necessary to make a draft on the guns of the fortress of Hameln. It was against these that the enemy's artillery was principally directed. As the musketry firing in the wood increased in volume, Cumberland ordered Major-General Behr with three battalions of Brunswick troops to support General Hardenberg "if necessary."

It was in this quarter that the key to the battle lay. No matter what might happen in the centre, it was clear that, unless Cumberland could beat off the attack of Chevert, his line of retreat would be threatened and his whole army in jeopardy. By 11.30 the French attack appeared to be succeeding at every point; Schulenburg, attacked by Chevert on his left flank and by the Grenadiers of Armentières, who had ascended the slopes of the Ohnsburg on his immediate front, had been driven back, drawing off his cannon. Hardenberg was being overwhelmed by force of numbers. The battery at the point of the wood had fallen into the hands of Armentières and was being used against the Hessians, who were defending the village of Hastenbeck with great steadiness. It was then that the Duke of Brunswick, placing himself at the head of a battalion of Wolfenbüttel guards and one of Hanoverians, advanced up the ravine and with fixed bayonets drove off the enemy and recaptured the battery. But it was too late; Chevert on the higher slopes had passed on, and was now in a position not only to enfilade the entire Hanoverian line, but to take Brunswick and the recaptured battery in rear. Brunswick was consequently forced to retire. At the same moment d'Estrées ordered a general advance. Four columns on the left, under MM. de Broglie, de Guerchy, de Leyde, and de Souvre, moved forward against Hastenbeck and the Hessians. Armentières pressed his attack. Chevert began to close in on the left flank and in rear of the Hanoverian position. It was midday, the battle seemed over. Cumberland, seeing that he had been outflanked, that "the enemy were in possession of a height which commanded and flanked both his lines of infantry," and that his line of retreat was in jeopardy, gave the order for a general withdrawal towards Hameln. It was at this moment that a circumstance occurred which was within an ace of altering the whole fortunes of the day. When early in the day Cumberland saw that the Grenadiers of Hardenberg were being pressed back and forced to retire nearer to the left of his army, he gave orders to Colonels Dachenhausen and Briedenbach, with three battalions of Hanoverians and six squadrons, to march by Afferde on Diedersen, and so in rear of the westerly slopes of the Schekenberg, down which Chevert was forcing the grenadiers of Hardenberg. It was about 12.30. Cumberland had given the order to retreat. D'Estrées with his staff, viewing the situation from the captured redoubt, was counting the victory as won, when suddenly there was heard the sound of firing from the crest on the extreme right and from the slopes which lay beyond and below that crest—in rear and to the left, that is to say, of Chevert, who was by this time descending the hill towards Hastenbeck. Almost at the same moment word reached d'Estrées that Hanoverian troops had appeared on the extreme right and in rear of the French army, that a new phase of the battle had opened, and that assistance was urgently required. This was followed in rapid succession by officers bearing the news that the brigade of La Marine had been obliged to retreat, that ten cannon had been lost, and that the Austrian troops were in difficulties.

D'Estrées saw himself confronted with three alternatives— to alter his position, to retreat, or to dispose his forces so as to attack the Hanoverians if they were pressing a serious attack on his right wing. He did in fact give orders for the infantry and artillery to retire across the ravine of Hastenbeck; he did at the same time send instructions to Chevert to fall back on the main body of the army.

What had happened to bring about this dramatic moment in the battle? It will be remembered that Cumberland, in order to relieve the situation on the Schekenberg, had despatched Briedenbach with three Hanoverian battalions and Dachenhausen with six squadrons to march round the wood and ascend the ravine to Diedersen. Arrived at Diedersen and finding no sign of the enemy, Briedenbach, leaving Dachenhausen to continue his march up the valley, turned to the right and climbed the hill, on the other side of which heavy firing could be heard. The ascent was arduous. His progress was slow. By the time the summit had been reached Cumberland had given the order to retreat. On the summit were still stationed the regiments of Eu and Enghien. These troops resting in the heat, aware from their commanding position of the progress of the battle, and totally unapprehensive of any possibility of attack from the quarter from which the Hanoverians were approaching, were taken by surprise. A panic ensued. The regiment of Eu abandoned their post and their cannon, and pursuing their way down the slope in great disorder found before them the Swiss regiment of Reding. Mistaking these for Hanoverians, they opened a fire which was at once returned, and had Briedenbach at this moment followed up his attack there is no doubt the whole French army would have been forced, momentarily at any rate, to retire. But Briedenbach when he reached the summit with his battalions had a commanding view of the plain below; there he could see the French army still in position between himself and the glistening course of the Weser; at the same time, as he looked north towards Hameln, the clouds of dust which were hanging grey over the landscape told him that the Hanoverian army was in full retreat towards that fortress. Briedenbach therefore, dragging off nine cannon with him and spiking the remainder, descended again to the valley to begin his march in order to rejoin Cumberland. At Diedersen he was joined by Dachenhausen with his cavalry.

Thus had come about the strange situation in which, at the very moment when Cumberland was drawing off his forces, d'Estrées had thought it necessary himself to take measures to retreat. Had Cumberland been able to keep in touch with Briedenbach the result might have been different; as it was, it is not too much to say that the army of the allies was saved by Briedenbach. Had his action not produced its panic on the slopes of the Schekenberg, had it not raised such anxiety in the minds of the French General Staff, d'Estrées, in spite of the heat and it spite of the fatigue of his troops, who had lain for three consecutive nights on their arms, would have been able to pursue the Hanoverian army and turn an orderly and unmolested retreat into a disastrous rout.

On both sides the losses were small. The total casualties on the Hanoverian side were 1500, including "missing," while the French on their side suffered a total loss of some 2300.

Cumberland had shown judgment in the choice of his position, and he had manœuvred skilfully so as to bring about a battle on the actual theatre of his choice. He has, however, been criticised for not strengthening his left. It has been said that he should have placed not 8000, but 25,000, infantry in the woods,* and that he should have relied on the morass to protect his right. His total available force, however, including cavalry, was nearer 30,000 than 40,000 men. His total frontage was rather more than 18,000 paces. If we omit the morass, which, while it was an effective protection, was not altogether impassable, he had a front to defend of about 9000 paces, that is to say about 9000 paces was the width of the defile which extended from the edge of the morass to the slopes of the Ohnsburg. Had he transferred 25,000 men to the wooded slopes, he would have left his centre dangerously weak. It cannot be claimed for Cumberland that he had military genius—that was a gift possessed by one commander alone in Europe—but it would be unfair to criticise him from any platform but that of the standards of the day. Did he conform to these? were his dispositions sound, having regard to the military theories of his time? To these questions the answer must certainly be in the affirmative. It must be remembered that it was a battle of position, a set piece, and that once his troops were advantageously placed, the result rested with the fighting capacity of the men, their relative numbers, and the handling of the artillery. Mobility, that factor in war which the genius of Frederick was introducing, with such brilliant results, on the field of battle, had not found its way into current military conceptions. Otherwise it might well be that Cumberland, holding his cavalry in rear of his line instead of stationing them on the extreme right, might have used them in support of Briedenbach and Dachenhausen with decisive effect. As it was he was pinned down by the rigidity of his plan; the correctness of his scheme was in fact its weakness.

Napoleon, in one of his most illuminating military criticisms, containing as it does a statement of the qualities which the ideal general should possess, attributes the failure of d'Estrées to obtain a decisive victory to the incompetence of the French General Staff in those days. He blames d'Estrées for not employing cavalry to follow up Chevert's attack, and for seeing

* Lloyd and Tempelhoff, *The History of the Seven Years' War in Germany*, I, p. 228.

in the attack of Brunswick and the movement of Briedenbach a co-ordinated plan justifying his order to withdraw.*

The subsequent movements of Cumberland and his army are of no interest, either military or political. He withdrew on the line laid down by his father, keeping always some two days' march distant from the French.

* Montholon, *Mémoires de Napoléon*, VII, pp. 207–8.

REFERENCE TO PLAN OF BATTLE OF HASTENBECK

A.   Position of the Duc de Broglie on the 24th July.

B.B.B. Positions of the Division of Chevert after he had forced the defiles near Bessinghausen and Volkershausen.

C.C.   Out-posts of the Allies under General Fürstenberg after they had retreated from Lafferde.

D.D.   Rear-guard of Grenadiers under Major-General Hardenberg before they quitted the heights above Bessinghausen.

E.   Corps of the Duc de Broglie.

F.   Four battalions of Palatine troops.

G.G.   French Cavalry.

H.H.   Attacks under the Duc de Broglie.

I.I.   Columns of the Grenadiers of France and the Brigades of Orléans, Vaubecourt, Lionnois, and Mailly, under the Marquis de Contades.

K.   Division of General d'Armentières in position before the attack and march by the right upon the flank of the Allies.

L.   Four regiments of dismounted dragoons.

M.   General d'Anlezy with the Brigades of Champagne and the Swiss of Reding.

N.   The Austrian Brigade, and the French of Belsunce, La Couronne, and Alsace.

O.P.   March and attack of General Chevert with the Brigades of Picardie, Navarre, La Marine, and Eu.

Q.Q.   Hanoverian Grenadiers under General Hardenberg.

R.   Grenadiers, light troops, and riflemen, commanded by General Schulenburg.

S.   Brunswick Infantry, under General Behr.

T.   Battery of twelve-pounders.

U.   Hessian Infantry and Cavalry.

W.   Hanoverian Cavalry.

X.X.   Attacks under Colonels Briedenbach and Dachenhausen.

Y.   March and attack of the Prince of Brunswick.

Z.   Retreat of the Allies.

CHAPTER XXV

CUMBERLAND—and here he was in agreement with everyone who had given a thought to the matter—had never entertained any hope of defeating the French. Writing on August 22 to Henry Fox he said:

> I wont tire you with a three days' battle, you'll neither care nor understand it, but we had as brave a handfull of men as ever fought but we had a most numerous enemy that might have overpour'd us when they pleased, but had not hearts equall to half their number.*

Cumberland's task, in accordance with his father's orders, had been to preserve his army from falling into the hands of the enemy: this he had done, and with the limitations imposed on him this was about all he could do. He made no reproaches. He recognised that here and in this campaign he was acting for the Elector of Hanover and not for the King of England. England was not prepared to help. Cumberland was not even in a position to ask for help. The struggle was unequal and could have but one result—a result which when the time came would, as Cumberland knew, be subject to the political aims of Hanover. He may have thought with his aide-de-camp, Lord Albemarle, who wrote: " 20,000 men at Hastenbeck would have been more good than your new expedition " † (i.e. to Rochefort). But he kept his counsel to himself.

News of the defeat reached England on August 2. " The fate of Hanover is now decided," wrote Newcastle to Hardwicke. " The Duke's army was beat on the 26th of last month, and H.R.H. is retired to Meyenburgh which leads to Bremen and Stade." The King's determination was quickly formed.

* Holland House MS., H.R.H. to Henry Fox, Aug. 22, 1757.
† Holland House MS., Lord Albemarle to Henry Fox, Aug. 22, 1757.

Hanover must be saved.   On August 3 Newcastle was admitted to an interview.

> His Majesty [he wrote] was calm,* he said he must do the best he could.   He had stood it as long as he could and he must get out of it as well as he could—that he had taken his part, which I found was to make his Peace.

Hardwicke took the view that the King could not be prevented from making his own Peace, and thought that the King of Prussia would do the same.† On August 9 a despatch was written by Munchhausen,‡ the King's Minister in London, to Steinberg at Hanover.   In view of what subsequently occurred this document is of the highest importance.   It shows conclusively what George II as Elector was prepared to do.   Steinberg was directed to order his son, the Hanoverian Minister at Vienna, to inform the Court of Vienna that George, in order to secure peace for Hanover, was prepared to break up the Army of Observation, to send back all the auxiliary and subsidised troops to their respective countries, to return the Hanoverian troops to their ordinary quarters, and to guarantee as Elector that, so long as the war in Germany lasted, he would neither directly nor indirectly take any further part, " Sa Majesté en qualité d'Électeur ne donnera de secours à qui que ce soit, ni par ses Troupes ni d'aucune manière, ni directement ni indirectement." §   It was by such means that he hoped at this time to save his army and relieve his Electorate.   These terms were submitted to Cumberland.   Every means was to be taken to get them accepted.   President Munchhausen, brother of the Minister in London, was himself to negotiate directly with d'Estrées. ‖   Bernstorff, the Danish Minister at Copenhagen, was to enlist the good offices of the King of Denmark.   Steinberg was to bring pressure on the Court of Vienna.   Peace rumours were in the air.   It was even rumoured that Frederick himself was negotiating for separate

---

* Add. MS. 32872, f. 426, Newcastle to Hardwicke, Aug. 3, 1757.
† *Ibid.*, f. 441, Newcastle to Hardwicke, Aug. 4, 1757.
‡ *Ibid.*, f. 490, Munchhausen to Steinberg, Aug. 9, 1757.
§ *Ibid.*
‖ *Ibid.*, f. 405, Newcastle to Hardwicke, Aug. 6, 1757.   President Munchhausen was the brother of the veteran Minister who resided in London with George II.

terms at Paris. He did in fact on September 5 write to Richelieu a pacific proposal. * Pitt expressed his own anxiety to Newcastle, and said that as a condition of carrying on the war Spain must be bought by the cession of Gibraltar, and if that failed then England must make the best peace it could.† At the same time Mitchell was writing to Holdernesse that Frederick's situation was hopeless.‡

Frederick had good reason to write:

> Les Anglais ne voullent soutenir ni leurs affaires de Mer ni la guerre de Terre ferme; je me trouve comme le dernier Champion de la Ligue prêt à combattre, s'il le falloit même sur les Ruines de ma Patrie. Je suis dans le cas de dire la Fortune est pour César mais Caton suit Pompée. §

The expedition to Rochefort was still detained by contrary winds. So far as Frederick was concerned, not a thing had been done by England to assist the alliance. ‖ The British Government had refused his repeated requests for a few ships to be sent to the Baltic. They had in fact done none of the things he asked.

Nothing indeed is more extraordinary in connection with the Army of Observation than the complete inaction of Newcastle and Pitt. They had been in office since early in June. It was during Pitt's previous Government that the Army of Observation had been proposed, organised, and formed. Hastenbeck had been fought on July 26. Thereafter they had known that Cumberland and his forces were in deadly peril. Early in August they knew that the King was negotiating a separate peace, from which they apprehended the gravest and most fatal consequences. It was plain to every man that unless something was done and done at once the Army of Observation would be lost, the French in possession of the whole Electorate, the alliance with Prussia in jeopardy, and the ability

* *Political Correspondence*, XV, p. 336.

† Add. MS. 32872, f. 492, Newcastle to Hardwicke, Aug. 10, 1757. This at least was Newcastle's version of his interview with Pitt.

‡ Add. MS. 32873, f. 21, Mitchell to Holdernesse, Aug. 11, 1757.

§ Add. MS. 32874, f. 34, Frederick to Mitchell, Sept. 11, 1757. This was six days after he had written his peace proposal to Richelieu.

‖ See *Political Correspondence*, XV, p. 228.

of England to carry on war with France seriously compromised. Yet nothing was done. The question of the Army of Observation seems rarely to have been discussed; it hardly appears at all in the correspondence of Ministers; and even in Newcastle's Cabinet Minutes it is only found as a question for occasional consideration, and never till September 5 as the subject of a practical Resolution. Yet on August 16 Newcastle's Memoranda * for the Cabinet contain the following entry: " To consider the State of the Army in the Dutchy of Bremen, the means of providing for their Retreat by a sufficient number of vessels in the Elbe and a proper convoy. Nothing is so material as to keep that Army on Foot in some way or other." Again nothing was done. At last, and as we know too late, on September 5 a Cabinet Resolution was passed: " That a squadron of ships should be kept cruising to guard the mouths of the Elbe and Weser as long as the season will permit. Ordnance Stores and Provisions to be sent." †

What was the explanation? None, so far as we are aware, has been offered, because here again the later triumphs of Pitt have blotted out all recollection of his failure at this juncture. It has been perhaps regarded as an episode of no further significance than to show how near it is possible to approach disaster in a war without reaping the consequences that seem destined to follow. Everyone saw the importance of maintaining the army as a fighting force, yet no one did anything. Hardwicke, Newcastle, Granville, and the King were all in favour of sending assistance, but Pitt stood across their path, and such already was the force and sway of his personality that he could extort obedience from his colleagues, apparent submission to his view from the King, and impose on soldiers and sailors an operation of war in which none of them had believed, and against which each in turn appears at first to have protested.‡ Pitt indeed was as absolute in authority at this time as at any moment of his career. He was virtual dictator; §

* Add. MS. 32997, f. 245, Memoranda for Cabinet, Aug. 16, 1757.
† *Ibid.*, f. 252, Sept. 5, 1757.
‡ See ante, p. 269.
§ It is only through the Newcastle and Hardwicke Papers that any idea can be formed of how completely Pitt dominated his colleagues and every department of the executive at this time.

and if Newcastle could boast, as he did, that except for " occasional vivacities " his relations with Pitt were harmonious, it was only because those relations spelt dictation on one side and submission on the other.

It was therefore Pitt's own policy that was followed, and it was here that his will to keep clear of Hanover entanglements determined him to adopt any method of assisting Frederick except the obvious means of sustaining the Army of Observation. This, we must in fact conclude, is what made him ignore Frederick's suggestion and engross himself in the diversion against Rochefort. That was why the naval and military expedition which sailed from Portsmouth in the early days of September appeared before the French port and not off the mouth of the Elbe, and that is why no attempt was made to avert the doom which was very surely advancing upon Cumberland and his army.

Cumberland had written to the King that in view of the great superiority of the French he would eventually have to retreat to Stade, " where," as he warned the King, " it would be impossible for the troops to winter," * while the absence of rain and the dryness of the country would enable the French to follow him. In such an hour of gloom, Pitt came forward with a proposal to pay the Landgrave of Hesse £20,000 † by way of compensation for the losses he had sustained, and £100,000 for the support of the Electorate. This had pleased the King, but had left the military situation precisely as it was. It was scarcely as much as applying a watering-can to quench a conflagration. But in his alarm at the effect which the King's seeking after peace might have on Frederick, Pitt was ready to depart from his settled policy. He was prepared to agree to a substantial subsidy to Prussia.‡ The war could hardly have opened in a less auspicious manner.

* Add. MS. 32874, f. 16, Newcastle to Duke of Devonshire, Aug. 11, 1757.

† *Ibid.*; also Grenville Papers, I, p. 206, Pitt to Grenville, Aug. 11, 1757.

‡ See *Political Correspondence*, XV, p. 193. As far back as June Frederick had given an urgent hint to Mitchell that this was one of the things he desired.

And now George II, wrung " by the cries and tears " of his people, had definitely committed himself to the negotiation of a separate peace. The divorce of his dual interests was to receive a final sanction. Hitherto, inconsistent as those interests had often appeared, they had never failed to be reconcileable. Now for the first time they were to be set specifically in opposition to one another. Hanover was to fall out of the alliance. If England was unable to help Hanover, then neither could Hanover help England or her allies. On August 11 George II despatched to Cumberland a series of notes which mark the crucial stage in the events which led up to Klosterzeven.

The first note * sets forth the desperate straits in which the King is placed: his most fertile territories overrun; the impossibility of sending reinforcements from England or obtaining recruits in Hanover; the inability of the King of Prussia to send succours; and finally the likelihood of the Landgrave of Hesse and the Duke of Brunswick recalling their troops from the Army of Observation. In the face of this situation he asks Cumberland to consider the desirability of a separate Peace or Convention.

The second note emphasises the necessity for treating without delay: he urges Cumberland to summon such Ministers of Hanover as are accessible and consult with them as to the terms to be proposed; and then to lay the terms before the French General without waiting for ratification from him (the King); if the terms are unacceptable, then to save his army by the best terms he can get.

The third note insists on the necessity for " une paix particulière ou une neutralité, ou même un accommodement préliminaire, aussitôt et aussi bien que possible, afin que tous ces pays soient soulagés et les troupes conservées." Moreover the fact that the French commander may not be invested with full powers to treat is not to stand in the way of the conclusion of a treaty, articles, or convention.

Finally, there is added to these notes or apostilles a commission to Cumberland conferring on him full powers to enter

* Cumberland MS., George II to Cumberland, Aug. 11, 1757; also to be found in Add. MS. 32873, f. 1.

into and conclude negotiations with the French Commander.

The Commission could hardly have been expressed in wider terms, and as it has never yet been printed in any English account of these transactions, it is here given in full, as it appears in the Cumberland Papers.

PLEINS POUVOIRS DE SA MAJESTÉ ÀS.A.R. MGR LE DUC DE CUMBERLAND POUR TRAITER ETC AVEC LE GÉNÉRAL DE L'ARMÉE DE FRANCE. KENSINGTON, LE II D'AOÛT 1757.

IIme *Août.* 1757.

George Second par la Grâce de Dieu Roi de la Grande Bretagne, de France et d'Irlande, Défenseur de la Foi, Duc de Bronsvic et Lunebourg, Archi-Trésorier et Électeur du St. Empire Romain, à tous ceux qui ces présentes Lettres verront, Salut. Comme Nous avons fort à cœur, de contribuer autant qu'il est en Nous à mettre fin aux maux de la Guerre dans Nos États d'Allemagne, y compris la Comté de Bentheim, laquelle Nous possédons à present, en vertu du contract conclu avec le Comte de ce nom, et dans les États de Nos chers Cousins les Ducs de Bronsvic-Wolfenbüttel, de Saxe-Gotha, et le Landgrave de Hesse-Cassel, comme aussi dans la Comté de Lippe-Schaumburg, Nous confiant entièrement en la Capacité, Expérience et Zèle de Notre très cher Fils, Guillaume Auguste, Duc de Cumberland, Duc de Bronsvic-Lunebourg, Notre Capitaine Général. Pour ces Causes Nous avons commis, et par ces Présentes, signées de Notre main, commettons le dit Notre très-cher Fils, et Lui avons donné et donnons Plein-pouvoir, Commission et Mandement spécial, pour, de Notre Part, en qualité d'Électeur convenir avec le Général en Chef de l'Armée de Sa Majesté Très chrétienne, arrêter, conclure et signer, Lui-même, ou par telle ou telle personne qu'il y autorisera, tel Traité, Articles ou Convention que ledit Notre très cher Fils Avisera bon être; Promettant en qualité d'Électeur, d'avoir agréable, tenir ferme et stable à toujours, accomplir et exécuter ponctuellement, tout ce que le dit Notre très cher Fils aura stipulé, promis et signé en vertu du présent Pouvoir, sans jamais y contrevenir, ni permettre qu'il y soit contrevenu, pour quelque cause, ou pour quelque Prétexte, que ce puisse être. Comme aussi d'en faire expédier Nos Lettres de Ratification, en bonne forme, pour être échangées dons le Tems dont il sera convenu. En Témoin de quoi Nous avons fait mettre Notre Seel(sic) à ces Presentes. Donné à Notre Palais de Kensington le 11ᵐᵉ d'Août, l'An de Grâce Mille Sept Cent Cinquante Sept, et de Notre Règne le Trente-unième.

GEORGE R.

[Seal here.]

The position therefore in the middle of August was as follows: George II had determined on behalf of his Electorate to make peace, and had given full powers to Cumberland for that purpose. He held the view, and had impressed it on Cumberland, that Hanover had no lot or part in the storm now raging. If it had not been for England's alliance with Prussia, France would never have invaded the Electorate. In order to bring relief to his territories and to preserve his army, he was prepared to go the lengths which he had indicated in his notes to his son and in Munchhausen's letter to Steinberg. Moreover he had imposed on Cumberland a retreat towards Stade—a military operation the political object of which, it can hardly be doubted, was to keep clear of Prussia and the complications connoted by a junction with Frederick. George II was in fact playing a double game. With advancing years motives not infrequently become complex and diffuse. It was so with George II. His singleness of mind had faltered. His purpose was becoming confused. He was holding communications with Cumberland that were not consistent with his professions to his Ministry in London or to Frederick, the ally of England. It is here that we must seek an explanation of the ungovernable fury with which he later received the news of Cumberland's action at Klosterzeven, and his unbalanced efforts to direct against and focus on his son the outcry to which that action gave rise. As will be seen, he had by that time partially repented of the course he had adopted. But things were *in extremis*. The recantation was too late. He was to suffer all the mortification of a private repentance without any of the reward of public merit.

Cumberland, in accordance with his instructions, wrote from his headquarters at Verden on August 21, 1757, to the commander of the French Army to propose a suspension of arms, preparatory, as he said, not to a peace, " car je ne connois point de Guerre déclarée entre la France et l'Électorat d'Hanovre, mais d'un Accord." * The commander whom Cumberland had to deal with was no longer d'Estrées. On August 6 Richelieu, in accordance with a commission dated as far back as July 16, had taken over the captaincy of the French forces. It was therefore with a very different personality and a much more highly trained negotiator that Cumberland had now to contend.

Louis-François-Armand de Vignerol du Plessis, Duc de Richelieu, great-nephew of the Cardinal, was born in 1696 From his first introduction to Court life, in the atmosphere of which his rank, his beauty, his high spirits, and his adventurous temperament ensured him a rapid succession of favours, he had dedicated his energies to those pleasures to which the licence of the age and his own natural advantages could be counted on to secure him access. In 1711, at the age of fifteen, he was married to Mademoiselle de Noailles. In the same year the scandal caused by his relations with the Duchesse de Bourgogne led to his temporary seclusion in the Bastille.† That fortress he was fated twice to revisit as a prisoner—once in 1716 as the sequel to a duel, and again in 1719 on account of a supposed plot against the Regent. His amorous adventures, to which there was an infatuated willingness to contribute on the part of one after another of the beauties of the time,‡ soon became a bye-word in Paris, openly canvassed in the streets and publicly brandished in songs, quatrains, and couplets. But neither the likelihood of publicity nor the certainty of being forsaken seems to have affected the trustfulness of those to whom his advances were made. At the time of his third imprisonment in the Bastille two princesses, Mademoiselle de Charolais and Mademoiselle de Valois, putting aside for the occasion their jealous rivalry, were found co-operating in a common endeavour to secure his release. His infidelities,

* Cumberland MS., H.R.H. to Duc de Richelieu, Aug. 21, 1757.
† Richelieu, however, denies this in his *Mémoires*, published in 1918.
‡ "Il a été le dompteur de toutes les femmes, au point que l'on a remarqué celles qui lui avaient résisté."—*Mémoires du Président Hénault* (édition Rousseau, 1911), p. 124; cited Paul d'Estrée, *Le Maréchal de Richelieu*, p. 107.

for the time being, were obliterated by his peril, and when during one hour of the day he was allowed to take exercise on one of the towers of the prison, the street of St. Antoine from which he could be seen would be regularly frequented by those who had been the sundry victims of his fascination but could still lament over his predicament. An author has recently * traced in fiction the characters which probably owe some of their features to the inspiration of Richelieu. Among these are to be numbered the Selim of *Les Bijoux Indiscrets* of Diderot, the Lovelace of *Clarissa Harlowe,* the Valmont of *Les Liaisons Dangereuses,* and the hero of *Le Lovelace Français,* a play which appeared in Paris in 1796.

In spite of the claims of his intrigues, Richelieu had found leisure for more permanent achievements. In 1721 he was elected to the Académie Française, three years later he left Paris as Ambassador to the Court of Vienna. There he was successful in combating the influence of Spain at the Court of Charles IV. On his return in 1729 he directed his attention seriously to soldiering, and in 1733 joined the Army of Marshal Berwick on the Rhine as colonel of a regiment of infantry. Accompanied by his usual pomp and ostentation, he arrived at the theatre of war with 30 horses, 72 mules for the transport of his baggage, and tents no less luxurious than those of the King himself. Luxury, however, did not hinder him from acting on every occasion with conspicuous valour. His facile successes in the fashionable world of Paris in fact found their counterpart in the military sphere of the Rhine campaign, and in 1738 he was rewarded with the Governorship of Languedoc. During the intervals of campaigning, he had married in 1734 Mademoiselle de Guise, Princess of Lorraine.† Voltaire, his friend, admirer, and eulogist, celebrated the occasion by his well-known *Epître à la Duchesse de Guise.* The marriage was founded on affection. It signalised what was probably the most genuine devotion of his career, and it surpassed expectation in suspending for some six months the usual course of his intrigues. At the outbreak of the War of the Austrian Succession he stood high in the

* Paul d'Estrée, *Le Maréchal de Richelieu.*
† His first wife died six months before his second marriage.

favour of Louis XV. That position he had attained, not only by his finesse in all the arts of a courtier and his distinguished services, first as a soldier and then as Governor of Languedoc, but as well by the tact and skill with which he was able to cater for the less reputable pleasures of the King. The war added fresh lustre to his name. At Dettingen where he fought with the greatest gallantry at the head of his regiment of horse and was the last to cross the bridge over the Main, at Fontenoy where he persuaded Louis XV to remain on the field of battle and changed the fortunes of the day by his cavalry charge, and again at Laffelt where he fought side by side with d'Estrées, he strengthened his claim to high command. In July 1748 he was appointed to succeed the Maréchal de Boufflers in command of the Army operating against the Austrians in Italy. In October he was made Marshal of France. It was in this year that the discovery by M. de la Pouplinière of an ingenious and secret entrance through a fireplace between a house which Richelieu had hired for the purpose and the room of Madame de la Pouplinière in the Rue Richelieu, caused a scandal which, while it would seem to have left the Marshal's reputation unscathed, was the topic of the salons and overflowed into the streets, where verses commemorating the episode and toys which represented the scene that had been enacted were openly sold by hawkers. At the beginning of 1757 Richelieu suggested the attack on Minorca. He was entrusted with the command of the expedition. His success here was rewarded by an order from the King not to return to Paris but to remain in Provence.* The Marshal replied that Provence was no longer in danger, and that the air of the country was "too dry" for his health. He set out for Paris. On his arrival in the capital his popular triumph was discounted by the King, who at the prompting of Madame de Pompadour received him coldly, and is said to have addressed him with some callous enquiry as to the quality of the figs in Minorca.

Hitherto Richelieu had been one of the few courtiers able to retain their popularity with Louis XV in spite of the hostility of Madame de Pompadour. The Marshal and the Mistress

* *Mémoires de Richelieu*, p. 132.

habitually intrigued against each other with all the subtlety and authority which they respectively commanded; and it was certainly not the least of the achievements of Richelieu that he should have been able to carry on a scarcely veiled hostility to the favourite without entirely forfeiting the confidence of the King. His advancement had been in spite of her. Madame de Pompadour was now at the height of her power. Ambassadors, Secretaries of State, and Commanders of armies alike felt their tenure dependent on her favour. Even Frederick the Great, as a way out of his difficulties in October 1757, sought her favour as the opening move, and proposed that she should be offered the Principality of Neuchâtel and Valangin.* The direction of foreign policy was largely in her hands. Recently she had secured the dismissal of d'Argenson, the Secretary of State, and Machault, the Minister of Marine. The Cardinal Bernis, who was now to be given the Ministry of Foreign Affairs, was one of her protégés and had risen entirely through her favour. The Cardinal was gifted with a talent for occasional verse and ornamental prose. Madame de Pompadour had not disdained his assistance in the odes she composed and the letters she addressed to the King after Fontenoy, Laffelt, and the French victories in the Low Countries.† Now in order to displace d'Estrées, who had been given the command of the Army of Westphalia in preference to her favourite Prince de Soubise, she had in August 1757 entered on a course of intrigue, one move of which had necessitated a *rapprochement* with Richelieu. That temporary reconciliation was followed by the dismissal of d'Estrées at the moment of victory, and the substitution of Richelieu as Commander in Hanover. This change it was believed would in the end benefit Soubise. It was in such a way that the whims of the favourite determined matters of State and affected the course of military operations.

Richelieu has been held up as representative of many of the characteristics of the France of the eighteenth century. As a

---

* *Political Correspondence*, XV, p. 391. After Kolin he had suggested that she should be offered 500,000 crowns for peace (*id. ib.* p. 218).

† *Mémoires de Richelieu*, p. 132. See also Goncourt, *Madame de Pompadour* (ed. 1831), p. 204.

PIGALLE—LE DUC DE RICHELIEU MARÉCHAL DE FRANCE (LOUVRE).

duellist and a cavalry leader he certainly typified that particular form of indifference to danger and self-respecting courage which may arise as much from caste or sense of manners as from temperament or sense of duty. His easy self-possession was never at fault, whether on the battlefield or in a duel, whether dealing with his Parliament in Languedoc or disentangling himself from an intrigue in Paris. An inflexible will, a refined irony of mind, a scepticism which induced in him a tolerance of every form of creed, a taste for the arts and graces of life, for letters and the enlargement of knowledge, were his in the highest degree. He knew no scruples. He affected no standards. From the moment when he first appeared as a boy at the Court and was described by Madame de Maintenon as " la plus aimable poupée qu'on puisse voir," to the day when at the age of ninety in a spirit of bravado he climbed the high tower of the Bastille where in his youth he had been a prisoner, he was governed by an undiluted worldliness of outlook. That which contributed to his pleasure or advancement was good, that which stood in the way of either was bad. Egoism could go no further. His conduct, which at first seemed a caricature of contemporary morals, in the end became a pattern which claimed many disciples, and impressed itself on a society already sufficiently averse to inhibitions. In cynicism he had no rival. The cynicism which attributed to a husband who had surprised his wife with her lover the remark, " Quelle imprudence, Madame, si c'était un autre que moi," * has been pointed to as peculiar to the France of the eighteenth century; it was certainly the vein of cynicism which found in Richelieu its most notable exponent.

By what qualities did he attain his great position? He did not triumph by force of intellect or of moral qualities; he was impelled by no principle; he was fired by no cause. On the other hand he was a consummate courtier, knowing when " to crook the pregnant hinges of the knee," bearing a great name, endowed with personal qualities of distinction and unrivalled charm, with a keen and ironical wit, flawless tact, and a devouring ambition. He could win the affection alike of women and men. He knew from whom to take counsel, and

* Goncourt, *La Femme au dix-huitième siècle,* p. 234.

when his judgment was determined he could act with celerity and strength. On the field of battle his courage inspired those he commanded, and on occasion he could seize an opportunity, as at Fontenoy, and exploit an opening; but as a general he had no outstanding qualities. At the siege of Port Mahon, and it is on the capture of Minorca that his military fame rests, he carried the position by the superiority of his numbers, and now when facing Cumberland he could look to an even greater superiority to ensure him victory.

In stature he was below the middle height. His features were regular, and his eyes of a notable brilliance. The expression of his countenance was frank and engaging. Slimness gave distinction to his figure. But as the years advanced and his excesses wrote their mark on his features, he wore an appearance older than his age. He was one of the persons whom Horace Walpole was most curious to see in 1765 on his visit to Paris. Richelieu was then sixty-nine years of age. At the age of eighty-four he married the widow of an Irishman, Michael Rothe, who had joined the French service and been naturalised in 1736. The widow was thirty-five years of age and of attractive appearance.* Walpole is not flattering to the Duke in his comments. "I saw the Duc de Richelieu," he wrote, "in waiting, who is pale, except his nose which is red, much wrinkled, and exactly a remnant of that age which produced General Churchill, Wilks the player, the Duke of Argyll, etc." † Later he wrote: "The Duc de Richelieu is a lean old resemblance of old General Churchill, and like him affects still to have his Boothbies." ‡ Richelieu, however, did much more than merely "affect." Later Walpole wrote an even less favourable account. Richelieu "is an old piece of tawdry, worn out, but endeavouring to brush itself up; and put me in mind of Lord Chesterfield, for they laugh before they know what he has said—and are in the right, for I think they would not laugh afterwards." § But Richelieu

* "La Reine demanda un jour au maréchal si sa femme était grosse: il répondit qu'il ne le pensait pas—à moins, ajouta-t-il, qu'elle ne le soit d'hier ou de ce matin."

† Walpole, *Letters*, VI, p. 311.

‡ *Ibid.*, p. 327.

§ *Ibid.*, p. 372.

was far from done with, and it was not till 1788 that his strenuous activity ended in death.

Cumberland's first move towards peace had no success. On August 22 Richelieu replied, declining to entertain any proposal for a suspension of arms. " Le Duc de Cumberland se moque de moi avec son armistice," he said to Hardenberg, the Hanoverian Minister entrusted with the negotiation, and his language plainly showed that, at the head of 100,000 men, he had no other idea but to harry the country and squeeze every possible penny out of the Electorate.* None the less Richelieu had difficulties of his own. He did not know, as Cumberland did, that the fortress of Stade was " without Bombs, Cannon Ball or Grenades ";† he saw before him an autumn and winter spent in a formal siege, in a marshy and unhealthy country, far from his base, with subsistence difficult and transport precarious, and with the incalculable Prussians in rear of his operations. He too was therefore revolving in his mind some favourable way out of the situation which had been created by the retreat towards Stade. On August 23 he addressed a letter to President Ogier, the French Minister at Copenhagen, in which, after frankly exposing the military position, he suggested that Denmark should intervene and put forward, with a view to an accommodation, a proposal that he should halt in his pursuit; otherwise, as he pointed out, there would be no alternative but to follow Cumberland to the fortress of Stade, and there bring him to action and destroy his army—that army which must presently find itself hemmed in, with its back to the sea and with no fleet present to further its escape. From the French point of view, moreover, it was highly desirable that an end should be put to these hostilities, which were an embarrassment, and that the army should be free to undertake the siege of Magdeburg.‡ This missive reached Ogier on August 27. In the meanwhile Richelieu had been pressing his pursuit, and continually threatening to outflank Cumberland's left. Cumberland had conducted his retreat in three columns, himself com-

---

* Add. MS. 32873, f. 285, Hardenberg to Cumberland, Aug. 26, 1757.

† Cumberland MS., H.R.H. to George II, Sept. 6, 1757.

‡ Richelieu to Ogier, Aug. 23, 1757; cited Waddington, *La Guerre de Sept Ans*, I, p. 467.

manding the centre column composed of Hanoverian troops. On August 28 he had established his headquarters at Rothenburg, the army being encamped on the north side of the Wümmer, on a line which extended to Ottersburg in the west. * Here he received another urgent despatch from Kensington Palace. George was distracted about the fate of his army. He could neither eat nor sleep. That was his habit when worried, though he remained in excellent health. Ministers could do nothing with him. His private peace negotiations seemed to be making no progress. Now he wrote to Cumberland :† it is possible that the French may insist on disarming my troops, or making them prisoners of war, or they may insist "sur d'autres conditions dures et nullement acceptables"; therefore consult with those of my Ministers in whom you have confidence, and my generals, devise some means in order that "mon armée soit délivrée et conservée, pour qu'elle ne tombe d'aucune façon entre les mains des ennemis." Here it appears that his great and present preoccupation was to preserve his troops, and prevent their being made prisoners of war. That at any rate was the construction put upon his orders by Cumberland. When he told Cumberland to consult with the Hanoverian Ministers, he well knew that he was giving hostages to all that was flabby in counsel and timorous in action. He well knew that the Hanoverian Ministers, now with their bags, baggage, and families, their state treasure and household effects, in refuge at Stade, were and always had been in favour of a weak-kneed policy, and a neutrality on almost any terms. It was difficult enough for George to see the mutuality between the policy of England and the policy of Hanover. To the Ministers in Hanover the very idea was not unnaturally repugnant. What therefore could Cumberland see in this, the most recent of George's despatches, except another and an emphatic step in the settled trend of the King's personal policy?

The retreat continued. By September 1 Cumberland was at Selsingen, by September 4 he was at Bremervorde. Here he was visited by Count Lynar, on behalf of the King of Denmark, and here, after consultation with the Ministers of Han-

* Cumberland MS., H.R.H. to Holdernesse, Aug. 28, 1757.
† Add. MS. 32873, f. 111, George II to Cumberland, Aug. 16, 1757.

over and the generals, he consented to the opening of negotiations through the intermediary of Count Lynar. To what extent Cumberland regarded himself as strictly the servant of his father in his capacity of Elector of Hanover, is shown by the fact that, when writing to Holdernesse on September 6,* he refrains from mentioning that negotiations had begun. The conditions first proposed by Richelieu were considered unacceptable. Count Lynar visited both headquarters. Finally, on September 10, 1757, after taking counsel with the Hanoverian authorities, Cumberland affixed his signature to what is known in history as the Convention of Klosterzeven.

Before considering the terms of the Convention it would be well to glance at the circumstances present to the mind of Cumberland at this date. He and his army were hemmed in between the sea and the Elbe, in a locality not of his own choosing but forced on him as the result of a military operation dictated by his father. At his back was the sea, destitute of shipping which could facilitate his escape, and across which he knew no succour could be expected from England. Before him was a victorious army of some 100,000 men. All chance of help from Prussia was at an end. On August 31 Mitchell had written to him from Frederick's headquarters saying that the Prussian King's situation was desperate and that nothing could save him. Moreover, though Cumberland had no certain knowledge of the fact, Frederick had on September 5 actually written his peace proposal to Richelieu. The last news of the Russians was that they had defeated the Prussians at Jagersdorff on August 30. From America had come the melancholy tidings that Lord Loudoun and Admiral Holbourne had abandoned the attack on Louisbourg. Despatch after despatch had reached him from his father urging him to effect an accommodation, save the army, and prevent it from being disarmed or falling as prisoners of war into the hands of France. He himself did not consider that it was possible to winter his army in the country about Stade, but before any such question could arise he, with between 30,000 and 40,000 men, would have to fight and defeat Richelieu with his 100,000. He had been told to seek the advice of George's Hanoverian Ministers. He

* Cumberland MS., H.R.H. to Holdernesse, Sept. 6, 1757.

had sought it. The Ministers had advised acceptance of the terms offered by Richelieu.

Again it must be remembered that in this transaction Cumberland was acting not for the King of England but for the Elector of Hanover. He was at the head of an army which had been put in the field to assist Frederick, but on the understanding that Frederick would be able to reinforce it. Frederick had not reinforced it; on the contrary, he had withdrawn the six battalions which had at the opening of the campaign formed part of the Army of Observation. Cumberland, on the other hand, from April to September had contained the whole power of France. That large force, first under the command of d'Estrées and then of Richelieu, had been prevented from falling on Frederick at the most critical period of his campaigns. If terms could not be arranged with Richelieu, then a battle must follow; to that battle there could only be one result—either Cumberland's army would be driven across the Elbe if the passage of the river could be effected, or it would have to lay down its arms as prisoners of war. Such then were the main considerations present to the mind of Cumberland when, on September 10, 1757, he put his hand to the Convention. In doing so he had every reason to believe that he was carrying out his father's intentions; he was certainly giving effect to the views of his father's Ministers, whom he had been told to consult. It was not a mathematical problem capable of an exact solution that he was called on to deal with, but a tangled issue of military and political considerations. He was not a free agent; he was tied both as a soldier and a negotiator by a strict interpretation of his father's orders. King George's grievance, as will appear, was that Cumberland obtained no relief of any value for the Electorate itself. How could he? it may well be asked. The French were in possession. Only force could expel them. Cumberland had no such force at hand. The issue could be stated in this form. " The French are there and will remain; is it better that the army should be preserved by negotiation or be destroyed as the result of a battle? " Reticent as Cumberland was, it is not difficult to infer from his laconic letters that politically he felt he had been forced into an equivocal situation. Although he corresponded with Lord Holdernesse, he could not consult with him. Although he was Captain General of the British Army, he was fighting as a foreigner, taking his orders from the Elector of Hanover, well knowing that the Elector and the King of England were distinct entities for the immediate objects of the Army of Observation. "I trouble none of my friends in England with our affairs, for you neither heed them nor understand them," * he had written to Henry Fox in May 1757, and as the weeks went by the justice of the statement became more and more apparent. Again, in the last days of June, he had written to the same correspondent:

I own I am pleased at the spirited manner with which the King insisted upon your being Paymaster, as it does H.M. honour, and is a further proof of his goodness to me. I am sure you know my heart too well to think that clamour can alter my oppinion or Love and esteem for a friend I have not only known but tried so long: beside I have a personal reason, you know too well, not to allow much weight to clamour. Indeed, Fox, you need not regret your not being in a more active situation on my account, for I hope not to be very much longer the object of hatred and malice; for I am quite tired with running my head against the wall for to do good, and in that respect I wish Ld George had been Secretary at Warr, that I might have had still more reason for retiring from the bustle. Dont repeat to any one what I write, not from the bitterness of heart but from serious reflection as what would sute [*sic*] my private satisfaction and ease of mind more than anything, for you know how much I despise the dirty means necessary amongst us even to serve the publick, and how happy a private man I can be either in town or at Windsor.†

* Holland House MS., Cumberland to Fox, May 2, 1757.
† *Ibid.*, June 30, 1757.

CHAPTER XXVI

THE terms of the Convention were briefly as follows:

Art. I.   Hostilities to cease within 24 hours.

Art. II.   The auxiliary troops Hesse, Brunswick, Saxe-Gotha, and Buckeburg to be sent to their respective countries.

Art. III.   Those Hanoverian troops not capable of being accomodated in Stade, to pass the Elbe with H.R.H. the Duke and take quarters in the country beyond that river.

Art. IV.   The whole Hanoverian army to retire under Stade within 48 hours.   The French army to retain the posts and countries of which it is in possession.

Art. V.   The aforesaid articles to be performed under the faith of his Majesty the King of Denmark's guaranty.

It would be tedious to trace in detail the correspondence which, following on the despatches of August 11 already referred to, George II carried on with his son.   It is easy to surmise from his letters that the King was alarmed at the effect produced by his negotiations for a separate peace.   The indignation of Frederick of Prussia, the disapproval of his own English Ministers, and the representations made to him by Lady Yarmouth that a separate peace would be "contrary to his Honor and would taint his memory hereafter," * had combined to throw him into a state of feverish bewilderment.   In answer to the charge of deserting his allies he could only repeat, "It was over with the King of Prussia."   Nevertheless, in his letters to Cumberland, his tone had changed, his requirements had sensibly hardened, and on September 13, taking his courage in both hands, he wrote a definite instruction to Cumberland that nothing was to be concluded till "Steinberg's Despatches [from Vienna] shall have come to my hands, and that after having weighed the contents, you shall have received my answer

* Add. MS. 32873, f. 545, Newcastle to Hardwicke, Sept. 10, 1757.

and resolution about it. My affection towards you is perfect and unalterable." *

Again on September 16 † he wrote to Cumberland of the "heavy complaints" which were being made by the King of Prussia in respect of the applications to the Courts of Versailles and Vienna for a separate peace. He deplored his inability to break off these negotiations, and the necessity of agreeing a peace if those Courts accepted his terms: at the same time they might refuse; and if that happened, then everything was to be left open until he had been given an opportunity of seeing what was proposed. Now too for the first time he calls on Cumberland to consider how the King of Prussia's proposal that Cumberland should "march along the Elbe to the neighbourhood of Magdeburg" can be carried out. Long before these letters reached Cumberland, the Convention had been signed.

They were the last letters in which Cumberland was to receive assurance of a perfect and unalterable affection. On September 20 he received the following from Lord Holdernesse:

Sir, WHITEHALL, *September* 20, 1757.

I obey, with Grief and Reluctance, The positive Orders, I have received from The King, which are, To acquaint Your Royal Highness with His Majesty's Disapprobation of the Convention Your Royal Highness has signed; And The King's Surprise That Your Royal Highness should have carried It into Execution without waiting for His Majesty's Ratification.

Your Royal Highness will have seen, by my Dispatch of last Friday, and by the Declaration made to The King of Prussia, That this Negotiation was begun, and has been carried on, without the Participation of The King's English Servants, and His Majesty has thought proper to order Baron Munchhausen to lay before Them the Whole of This Transaction; And The King has required Their Advice, in what Manner His Majesty may, yet, extricate Himself out of the present Difficulties. I have received The King's Commands, upon this Occasion, to require The Attendance

* Cumberland MS., George II to Cumberland, Kensington, Sept. 13, 1757.

† *Ibid.*, Sept. 16, 1757.

of all Those Persons who are usually consulted upon His Majesty's most Secret Affairs.

I have the honour to be with the greatest deference and respect

Sir,
Your Royal Highnesses most dutifull
and obedient Servant,
HOLDERNESSE.*

The news of the Convention could hardly have reached King George at a worse moment. A comparison with what Frederick was doing seemed to add a fresh and intolerable ignominy to King George's responsibility for the Convention. Frederick was by a series of rapid marches advancing to attack the army of Soubise, now (September) in the neighbourhood of Erfurt.

> Pour moi, menacé du naufrage,
> Je dois, en affrontant l'orage,
> Penser, vivre et mourir en roi.

It was thus that Frederick, breaking into verse, as was his wont in moments of stress, addressed himself to Voltaire. It was by the resolution and expedition of his movements that he was making his desertion by Hanover appear such a shameful action.

Why had George II ordered the retreat to Stade? why had he postponed till too late communicating Frederick's suggestion that Cumberland's army should move on Magdeburg? why had he given those full powers and those renegade orders to his son?—these were the questions now assailing the King and driving him into an exhibition of frenzy.

The King was pleased to say that His Honor and his Interest were sacrificed by it [wrote Newcastle after the news of the Convention had reached London]. That His Majesty had by it been given up tied hand and foot to France—that he did not know how to look anybody in the face—that he had lost his Honor and was absolutely undone. That he thought the Duke's head was turned or he had lost his courage. That he could not tell what to make of it, but that he would not have it lay upon him. If anyone but his

* Leeds MS., Holdernesse to H.R.H., Sept. 20, 1757.

son had done this he would have said he had been bought
by the French. I own I was so moved by what I saw,
that I was not able to bear it, as I ought to have done.*

Hardwicke thought a word of caution was necessary, and
wrote to remind Newcastle that the King had said things
hardly consistent with his present indignation, such as " I will
order him to make " or " a convention may be made at the
head of the two armies." † Everyone, from the King down-
wards, was for extricating the Electorate from its obligations
under the Convention. Pitt was strongly for losing no time
in sending orders to Cumberland's successor to fall upon the
French immediately. ‡ Hardwicke and Lord Mansfield, more
sensitive to the sanctity of a written agreement, hesitated to find
a special plea for its repudiation. George himself wrote to his
Hanoverian Ministers to take advantage of any technical breach
and reopen hostilities—suggested in fact on October 3 that such
a breach could be found in the outrageous exactions of the
French. § Kensington Palace remained during those days in a
state of turmoil. Munchhausen, as though he were paraphrasing
the famous speech of Jaques, depicted the King as now " sans
Pais, sans armée, sans sujets et sans argent." ‖

Meanwhile Cumberland, unconscious of the storm he had
aroused, was engaged in carrying out the terms of the Convention. On September 23, hearing that Richelieu was proposing to disarm the Hessians who had begun their march to
their own country, he at once ordered them to halt, and
despatched Count Lynar to the French Commander to declare
his " most positive resolution never to submit to so unjustifiable
and disgracing a Pretension and encroachment of Marshal
Richelieu's, *let the consequences be what they will.*" ¶ Here
he was putting his foot down on behalf of one of the conditions
for which his father had stipulated. For this he was prepared
to perish in the last ditch, though George was now trying to

---

* Add. MS. 32874, f. 148, Newcastle to Hardwicke, Sept. 18, 1757.
† *Ibid.*, f. 147, Hardwicke to Newcastle, Sept. 20, 1757.
‡ *Ibid.*, f. 412, Newcastle to Hardwicke, Oct. 3, 1757.
§ *Ibid.*, f. 448, George II to Ministry in Hanover, Oct. 5, 1757.
‖ *Ibid.*, f. 173, President Munchhausen to Newcastle, Sept. 20, 1757.
¶ Leeds M.S., Cumberland to Holdernesse, Sept. 29, 1757.

20

make out to all the world that that was the situation in which he had all along desired to see his son. On September 29 Cumberland was congratulating himself that this last difficulty had been satisfactorily disposed of. Richelieu had agreed not to pursue his intention of disarming the Hessians. The Hanoverian Ministers were in high spirits * at the success of the negotiation. All indeed seemed for the best when, on the evening of that day or on the morning of the 30th, there arrived a King's Messenger in the camp with Holdernesse's despatch of September 20 and a long letter from the King expostulating against what Cumberland had done. To the King Cumberland replied in justification:

> Je me console uniquement par l'espérance, que lorsque votre Majesté voudra bien comparer dans leur suite les Ordres gracieux qu'elle m'a donnés, avec ma conduite, elle me fera la justice d'avouer qu'autant que j'ai pu entrer dans ses intentions, je n'ai hasardé dans la moindre chose de m'en départir.†

That in a sentence is the case for Cumberland; nor does a perusal of the lengthy correspondence between George and his son leave the reader with any other impression than that Cumberland had ample and compelling reason for interpreting his father's intentions in the way he did. It is true he acted with precipitation, but Richelieu was within two days' march. It is true that he did not consult his father, but he had been told to act on the responsibility of himself and the Hanoverian Ministers. On the other hand, he had saved the army from falling as prisoners of war into the hands of the French, and that had been the condition above all others that George II had insisted on. The intolerable element, as far as the King was concerned, was the fact that no relief was obtained for Hanover. But neither George nor anyone else had ever suggested how it could be brought about. Even Frederick's plan had been withheld from Cumberland till too late.‡ To

---

* Add. MS. 32834, f. 218, Munchhausen to Newcastle, Sept. 22, 1757.
† *Ibid.*, f. 258, Cumberland to George II, Sept. 30, 1757.
‡ *Ibid.*, f. 258, Cumberland to George II, Sept. 29, 1757.

Holdernesse Cumberland replied as follows:

STADE, *September 30, 1757.*

My Lord Holdernesse, yesterday I received your Dispatch of the 16: by *Pollock* the Messenger, who was immediately forwarded to Mr. *Mitchell.* And, this Day I received yours of the 20: containing the Orders you received from the King to acquaint me with His Majesty's Disapprobation and Surprise, of the *Convention's* being carried into Execution, without waiting for His Majesty's Ratification. Nothing can give me So much concern as that His Majesty thinks I have merited this severe Reproof. I have acted as it appeared to me most agreeable to His Majesty's Orders, and for the Good of that army and country that His Majesty had entrusted to my Care. I was not ignorant that His *Negotiation* was begun without the Participation of His Majesty's English Servants: and, I most sincerely wish that now His Majesty has thought proper to order Baron *Munchhausen,* to lay before them the *whole* of this Transaction, they may be able to give such advice that His Majesty may extricate himself out of the present Difficulties, which, if I might be allowed, tho' immediately concerned, to say, are not encreased by this unfortunate *Convention.*

According to His Majesty's orders, I propose Setting out as soon as ever the captain of the 50: Gun Ship is ready to receive me, that I may the sooner be able to throw myself at the King's Feet; and, if not justify myself, submit, as I ought, to His Will and Pleasure. I remain your very affectionate Friend,

WILLIAM.

The effect produced at Fontainebleau by the Convention was not dissimilar, except in degree, to that produced in London. On September 12 Bernis wrote to Richelieu that he had acted without authority in the negotiations, and that those negotiations must be broken off at once. Peace with Hanover must be conditional on peace with England. The Capitulation was bad in substance because it did not provide for disarmament of the Army of Observation, and bad in form because the signatories had no power to execute the Convention. The terms in themselves were prejudicial to the interests and honour of

France, at a moment when Richelieu at the head of 100,000 men was in a position to impose any terms he pleased.*

> Nous aurons à nous reprocher d'avoir donné dans un piège et d'avoir négocié à la tête de cent mille hommes et d'une façon humiliante pour nous une suspension d'hostilités avec un ennemi fugitif qui n'en a pas trente mille. La négociation trop légèrement hasardée par M. le Président Ogier ne pouvait avoir d'autre objet que de faire gagner du temps à nos ennemis et de nous en faire perdre.

But by this time the matter had gone too far. Louis XV felt himself compelled to acquiesce and state his willingness to ratify so soon as the Convention should be ratified by the Elector.

Napoleon, speaking of this Convention, declared it was incomprehensible: at the moment it was made, he went on to say, the Duke of Cumberland was lost, there was nothing for him to do but to lay down his arms and surrender, any other terms of capitulation were inadmissible.† Indeed in the course of history there can have been few bargains entered into by the representatives of two countries which have been so completely displeasing to both sides. A little more knowledge on either side and the terms might have been different. Had Cumberland known of Richelieu's anxiety to move elsewhere with his army, or had Richelieu known that Stade was ill prepared for a siege, the Convention might have contained terms that would have been more consonant with the wishes of one side or the other. In the Archives of the French Foreign Office is an account of the transaction written by Richelieu in 1772, in which he set forth his motives for entering into the Convention. He there says that he was anxious to withdraw his army to Halberstadt, and put the territory of the King of Prussia under contribution along the line of the Elbe; that by the terms he had arranged, the Army of Observation would have been dispersed, and once in their several countries would

---

* The correspondence between Bernis, Richelieu, and Ogier is to be found under the heading "Hanovre: Mémoires et Documents. Brunswick et Hanovre, 1757-1758. Capitulation de Closterseven," *Archives des Affaires-Étrangères*, Vol. 10 (Paris).

† Montholon, *Mémoires de Napoléon* (ed. 1830), VII, p. 209.

have found themselves among French troops, and their disarmament would then have been a mere matter of procedure. Bernis had ruined this plan by compelling Richelieu specifically to undertake not to disarm the Hessians.* Thus on both sides there was disapproval of the terms which the generals in the field had arranged. But while Richelieu was left in command and was able to continue the exactions by which he enriched himself sufficiently to build the Maison Hanovre in Paris, Cumberland was recalled with every mark of anger and disapproval on the part of his father.

At Kensington Palace the temperature had been visibly rising. Each day seemed to bring a fresh aggravation calculated to make George II's action look more shabby and dishonourable. By September 25 it was known that the Russians after their victory at Jagersdorff had withdrawn to their own territory. "And now," said the King on hearing the news, "if my son had not made this Convention what a good situation we should have been in." † Frederick had advanced to Erfurt: single-handed as he now was, he was driving back the French and holding Europe at bay. Nor had he failed to express his anger at the Convention, which he attributed to neither George II nor Cumberland, but to the Regency in Hanover.‡ Nor if George surveyed affairs at home could he find much ground for satisfaction. Attempts to put the Militia Act into operation had led to the outbreak of riots throughout the country. Chief and petty constables had been assaulted and forced to give up the lists on which the call to arms was to be based. Country houses had been threatened by angry mobs, troops had been requisitioned, and Woburn Abbey had been considered in such danger that a troop of the Blues had been despatched post haste from London for its protection. The general cry of the people was "that they would have no such laws as had been. That the gentlemen just kept poor men alive

* "Allemagne: Mémoires et Documents, 1772 à 1777," *Archives des Affaires-Étrangères*, Vol. 115.

† Holland House MS., Duke of Devonshire to Henry Fox, Sept. 29, 1757.

‡ *Political Correspondence*, XV, p. 357, Frederick to Mitchell, Sept. 20, 1757.

to fight for them. That they would not fight for the pay of
H.M.'s troops. That they were resolved to stand by one
another and not to serve as Militia." * This manifestation
had gained impetus from a breach of faith in the previous
year on the part of the Government, when two regiments
raised for service at home by Lords Ilchester and Digby
had been forcibly shipped at Portsmouth to reinforce the
garrison of Gibraltar. As Anson wrote, "Not one event
from the beginning of the war that has not been unfortunate." †
It was on the top of all this that news came to the effect that
Cumberland had adjusted the question of disarmament with
Richelieu. An opportunity for breaking the Convention had
thus been lost. George was beside himself. "His rascally
son; His Blood was tainted " ‡—these were expressions at which
Newcastle shrugged his shoulders and ventured to suggest that
His Majesty should wait and at least hear what his son had to
say—whereupon the King added: " A scoundrel in England
one day may be thought a good man *another*. In Germany
it is otherwise, I think like a *German*," a proposition that Newcastle made no attempt to deny. Moreover it was now known
that the Rochefort expedition had failed and was on the sea
bound for home. On this Pitt was " outrageous," and imputed
the failure to a prevailing opinion that neither the King nor
Cumberland wished success to this expedition so that a German
war might appear to all the world as the only practical way of
carrying on the contest.§ Between the King and his colleague,
Newcastle was at his wits' end, and to make matters worse
the King desired that Newcastle should wait on Cumberland
on his arrival and inform him of the King's views.

And now the day of Cumberland's arrival, attended with so
much apprehension by those who had access to the King, drew
near. On October 10 he disembarked from a fifty-gun ship
at Harwich. On October 11 " towards evening he pass'd over

* Add. MS. 32874, f. 157, Duke of Ancaster to Newcastle, Sept. 19,
1757.

† Lord Anson to Lord Hardwicke, Oct. 6, 1757; cited Yorke, *Life of
Hardwicke,* III, p. 186.

‡ Add. MS. 32834, f. 471, Newcastle to Hardwicke, Oct. 8, 1757.
Hardwicke, III, p. 186.   § *Ibid.*

London Bridge for Kensington in a very private manner."* At the Palace he found Windham, Napier his military secretary, Sir E. Fawkener his private secretary, and his friend Henry Fox awaiting his arrival. "You see me," he said to Fox, "as well as ever I was in my life both in body and in mind"; † and when Fox in reply said that he had feared to find him distressed in mind, Cumberland added: "You have always mistaken me, Mr. Fox. With respect to the King, I am perfectly easy: I have the King's Orders in writing for what I have done, and I have done better for him than I thought the exigency would have allowed of." While he dressed he discussed the military situation with Napier, then leaving his friends Cumberland went to the cupola room, where after his rigid habit the King at nine o'clock had joined Princess Emily and Lady Yarmouth for a party at cards. It was there that these three were now waiting the arrival of Cumberland, the devoted sister shrinking from the ordeal which awaited her brother, the mistress till the last moment gravely seeking words with which to soften the anger of the King, the King himself, now old and embittered, shaken by the fury of his resentment and distraught by the consciousness of his own inglorious part in the drama. Upon this agitated scene there entered the Captain General in all the appointments of his office—a massive figure clothed in his scarlet coat—calm in the knowledge that he had acted in obedience to his father's orders, and already sure of the role he had determined to play, be the consequences what they might. If any hope had been entertained that the King's frenzy would be assuaged or his rage abated on seeing his son after so long an absence, it was quickly disappointed. The Duke of Devonshire had been right when he wrote to Fox before Cumberland's return: "The first conversation between them [the King and Cumberland] will be terrible, and you will do well to prepare H.R.H. for it and to advise him to keep his temper if possible." ‡

"Here is my son who has ruined me and disgraced himself,"

---

* *Gentleman's Magazine*, XXVII, p. 478.

† *Bedford Correspondence*, II, p. 276, Fox to Bedford, Oct. 12, 1757.

‡ Holland House MS., Duke of Devonshire to Mr. Fox, Sunday morning.

were the words with which Cumberland was greeted. The interview was short. Cumberland defended himself by reference to his Orders; the King only became more angry, more insulting. He told Cumberland that "he had ruined his Country and his Army, had spoiled everything and lost his own Reputation." When the King withdrew:

> Cumberland desired Lady Yarmouth, in the most respectful and most submissive manner, to let the King know that he had it not in his power to serve H.M. any longer, and that he had no favour left to ask, but leave to quit. Lady Yarmouth desired him to take no resolution. He answered that his resolution was not now to take: he had had time to reflect on his own conduct, which was irreproachable, and on the impossibility of his showing due regard to his own honour by any other method than what he now pursued. She asked him if he was determined? He said yes, and that he only spoke to her as the person who could with most ease and least offence let the King know it.*

When he again met Fox, the latter expostulated with Cumberland on the resolution he had taken. Cumberland was not to be deflected; he said, "a point of Honor was in question, on which nobody should ask advice. His submission, his duty, his regard to the King, were without bounds on any other subject: but, dear as the King was to him, his own honor was dearer to him than the King." Fox found him as cheerful and at ease as he had ever seen him to be. The King, in the hope of fixing the blame once and for all on his son, sent Munchhausen to lay the papers relating to the transaction before the Conciliabulum of Ministers. The King for the moment was like a dog biting at flies, snapping at every isolated sentence or phrase which would help his case. Here and there in the voluminous correspondence was a word which would serve his purpose. Here and there a sentence which, divorced from the context, would appear to support his view. He and Munchhausen had been busy piecing together an indictment that might convince the Ministers. The mission failed signally in its purpose. "I must," said Pitt after the documents had been read, "as a man of honour and a gentleman, allow every-

* *Bedford Correspondence*, II, p, 276. Fox to Bedford, Oct. 12, 1757.

where that H.R.H. had full powers to do what he has done."
Such perhaps is an adequate vindication for the part played by
Cumberland in this episode of the Seven Years' War. To this
we can add the testimony of Prince Ferdinand of Brunswick,
who in a review of the operations of the Army of Observation
now among the Cumberland Papers at Windsor Castle makes
reference to Klosterzeven and avers that no other course was
open to Cumberland at the time. Abreu, the Spanish Minister,
in writing to Grimaldi, was not far from the truth when he
wrote :

> I can assure you in confidence that the shamefull Con-
> vention signed with the French by the Duke of Cumberland
> was made by His Britannick Majesty's Orders in clear and
> express terms, but H.R.H. not being able to justify himself
> without discovering the secret and bringing his father into
> question with the King of Prussia . . . it was thought
> proper to give to Europe a publick testimony of His
> Britannick Majesty's disgust at his son.*

Two days after Cumberland's arrival and reception, the
King was uneasy at the situation which he had created. He felt
that he had gone to unseemly lengths in denunciation. He was
anxious for Cumberland to reconsider his decision; he begged
that he would at least retain his Colonelcy of the regiment of
guards, and not sever his connection with the Army, so that in
case of invasion he might again be at the head of the Forces.
The Duke of Devonshire was employed as a negotiator by the
King. The Cabinet Council were sent to make their bows to
Cumberland at St. James's. But Cumberland was firm, he had
made his resolution and would abide by it. "The Duke's
resignation," wrote Wolfe, "may be reckoned an addition to our
misfortunes: he acted a right part but the country will suffer by
it." Later, when there was a rumour of invasion, the Duchess
of Bedford told Cumberland that the general expectation was
that he would be sent for to command. "I do not believe,
Madam," replied the Prince, "that the command will be offered
to me, but when no wise man would accept it, and no honest
man would refuse it." †

* Add. MS. 32875, f. 169, Abreu to Grimaldi, Oct. 18, 1757.
† Walpole, *Memoirs,* III, pp. 233.

Through these days, framed as they were to test the character of the strongest, Cumberland showed to the world a largeness of view and a dignity of spirit that might well have given pause to the King in the vehemence of his denunciation. But the load the King had fashioned for himself was too heavy for his shoulders. He saw himself discredited in Europe, his Electorate ruined; he saw himself a mockery in the eyes of his nephew Frederick, and his reign drawing to an inglorious close. He was determined that the blame should lie elsewhere than at his own door. Not content therefore with the result of his personal encounters with his son, he determined to canvass the generals of the Army of Observation for opinions unfavourable * to Cumberland. The Duke sent for Munchhausen and said:

> Mr. Privy Councillor, I hear the King has sent for opinions of Hanoverian Generals on my conduct: here are the opinions of the Hessian Generals and the Duke of Wolfenbüttel. As the King has ordered the former to be deposited among the Archives of Hanover, I hope he will do me justice to let these be registered with them. Take them and bring them back to me to-morrow.

On the next day Munchhausen returned. The King, he said, had read the papers, was now better informed, and took a more favourable view of Cumberland's conduct. Cumberland was well aware that no one had been more active in denouncing the Convention than Munchhausen, who had even described it to Napier, the Duke's military secretary, as "infâme, indigne et lâche," with other words of invective equally offensive. When therefore the Hanoverian Minister fell prostrate before the Duke to kiss the lappet of his coat, the Duke with anger and dignity checked him and said:

> Mr. Privy Councillor, confine yourself to that office; and

---

* General Zastrow's replies are in the Newcastle Papers. (1) He thought only one opportunity of attacking the French had occurred, namely on July 1; but the infantry were so slow in coming up that Cumberland had been obliged to desist. (2) He thought the position at Bremervorde very strong and that it was improbable the French would have attacked. (3) He thought Cumberland could have maintained himself at Stade had subsistence been provided for (Add. MS. 35417, f. 101, Oct. 7, 1757).

take care what you say, even though the words you repeat should be my father's: I have all possible deference for him, but I know how to punish anybody else who presumes to speak improperly of me.

On November 5 all doubt as to the expediency of repudiating the Convention was removed by the victory of Rossbach and the defeat by Frederick of the army of Soubise. Thereafter threats to devastate Hanover could be answered by a threat to ravage Saxony, of which Frederick was now the master. The Army of Observation, which had only partially been dispersed, was once more set in movement under the command of Prince Ferdinand of Brunswick, to operate in conjunction with Frederick successfully against the French. The office of Captain General was never again held in this country. Ligonier became Commander-in-Chief.

Meanwhile on October 15 Cumberland could have been seen in a post-chaise on the Windsor road, in his blue coat, the cockade no longer in his hat, his military trappings finally laid aside, a private man with his mind turned towards the ease and relaxation of country pursuits and unofficial life at Cumberland Lodge. It was the end of his share in the Seven Years' War: henceforward he was to be a spectator of events, rejoicing in the great days that were to follow, and applauding without rancour the successes of his contemporaries and the victories that attended everywhere on British arms.

These last days, probably the most difficult to face in his military career, had seen the supreme expression of those qualities of loyalty and self-discipline which had been the distinguishing marks of his whole public life. Had he given to the world the text of his instructions, he would have protected his fame and reputation. Instinctively he chose the more difficult course. He maintained his reserve. He sacrificed himself and his professional name, he surrendered the calling to which his life was devoted, and this on behalf of a father who had sullied their relationship by his insults and forfeited his claim to generous treatment by his duplicity. The gesture may well claim an abatement of the prejudice which, initiated by the Jacobites, has been so carefully maintained by tradition. By the common consent of his time Cumberland was a man to be trusted, and in whose category of values the Throne and the public service ranked far above all other considerations. Those who would find charm and the lighter graces of human intercourse must seek elsewhere. They were not with Cumberland. His virtues were civic rather than social, his qualities fitted more for the service of the State than the adornment of life.

As a Commander it would be unfair to estimate him by his defeats. He fought on every occasion at a disadvantage, always with a mixed and generally with a markedly inferior force. It would be juster to remember that he conducted a long and difficult campaign for years against Marshal Saxe, certainly without victory, but at the same time without decisive disaster, receiving in the end a high tribute of praise from his great opponent * for the generalship he had shown. On the other hand, he restored the tone, the _moral,_ and the discipline of the British Army, and at a time when it had been demoralised by the defeats of Prestonpans and Falkirk he renewed its prestige and led it to an easy victory at Culloden. Nor should the fact be lost sight of that it was under the leadership of Cumberland that the Army of the Seven Years' War was formed, trained, disciplined, and adapted to its victorious ends.

In his last days as a soldier, in his encounters with his father, he had been true to the best that was in him. He had upheld his just renown for courage and devotion to the Throne. He had subordinated himself, his ambitions, and his interests to a cause which seemed in his eyes to require his own immolation. Walpole, who devoted so much of his vivacity to besmirching the Duke, but who in his final judgment declares him to have been one of the five great men he had known, is constrained to write of this episode in words which may well bring this Memoir of the Duke's military career to a close.

A young Prince, warm, greedy of military glory, yet resigning all his passions to the interested dictates of a father's pleasure, and then loaded with the imputation of having acted basely without authority; hurt with unmerited disgrace, yet never breaking out into the least unguarded expression: preserving dignity under oppression, and the utmost tenderness of duty under the utmost delicacy of

* See ante, p. 27.

honour—this an uncommon picture—for the sake of human nature, I hope the conduct of the father is uncommon too! When the Duke could tear himself from his favourite passion, the Army, one may judge how sharply he must have been wounded. When afterwards the King, perfidiously enough, broke that famous convention, mankind were so equitable as to impute it to the same unworthy politics, not to the disapprobation he had pretended to feel on its being made. In a former part of this history, I have said with regard to his eldest, that the King might have been an honest man, if he had never hated his father, or had ever loved his son—what double force has this truth, when it is again applied to him on his treachery to the best son that ever lived.*

* Walpole, *Memoirs,* III, p. 64.

APPENDIX I

Stallions 1762	Mares	Stallions 1763
Scampson Cade	Old Ebony	Blank
Crab	St. Quinter	Crab
Regulus	Miss Western	Blank
Regulus	Blaze Mare	Regulus
Crab	Godolphin Mare	Crab
Merlin	Blind Mare	Scampson Cade
Careless	Miss Thighs	Bajazet
Careless	Jenny Mare	Careless
Merlin	Spilletta Mare	Maske *
Regulus	Grey Ball Mare	Scampson Cade
Scampson Cade	Silvia	Crab
Scampson Cade	Grey Barb	Scampson Cade
Scampson Cade	Snip Mare	Careless
Maske	Paulina	Morro
Scampson Cade	Salome	Scampson Cade
Crab	Blank Mare	Maske
Regulus	Starkling Mare	Regulus
Cato	Red Rose	Scampson Cade

List of His Royal Highnesse's Horses for 1st May 1764

Sultan	age not given.
King Herod	6 years old.
Gift	6 years old.
Favourite	4 years old.
Bajazet	4 years old—out of Miss Western.
Selim	4 years old.
Bajazet	4 years old—out of Miss Thighs.
Dunce	4 years old.

* See post, p. 321.

Young Cade	.	4 years old—out of the Blaze Mare.
Milk-sop	.	4 years old—out of the Godolphin Filly— Ascot 65.
Habakkuk	.	3 years old.
Regulus	.	3 years old—dark grey colt.
Claudius	.	3 years old.
Regulus	.	3 years old—brown colt.
Crab	.	3 years old—brown colt.
Crab	.	3 years old—bay colt.
Drone	.	3 years old.
Young Cade	.	3 years old.
Achmet	.	3 years old.
Bajazet	.	3 years old.
Keeper	.	3 years old (now four).
Maske	.	3 years old—Ascot 65.
Doctor	.	2 years old.
Moro	.	2 years old.
Maske	.	2 years old—brown—Ascot 66.
Marcelles	.	2 years old.
Maske	.	2 years old—a bay colt.
Blade	.	2 years old.
Snipe	.	2 years old.
Snap	.	2 years old—a bay, no white.
Nelly	.	2 years old.
Young Cade	.	2 years old.
Lion	.	2 years old.
Fear-not	.	2 years old—Ascot 66.
Bully	.	2 years old.
Blank	.	2 years old—out of a daughter of Regulus.
Regulus	.	yearling—out of a daughter of old Traveller.
Regulus	.	yearling—out of Grey Ball.
Bajazet	.	yearling—out of daughter of old Crab.
Cato	.	yearling—out of Red Rose.
Careless	.	yearling—out of Jenny.
Scampson Cade	.	yearling—out of the Barb Mare.
Scampson Cade (A Filly)	.	yearling—out of Salome.
Crab	.	Sucker—out of the St. Quinton Mare.
Regulus	.	Sucker—out of the Blaze Mare.
Moro	.	Sucker—out of Paulina.
Careless	.	ditto—out of the Snip Mare.
Scampson Cade	.	Sucker—out of Salome.

* Maske   .   .   ditto—out of Spilletta.
Maske   .   .   ditto—out of the Blank Mare.
Scampson Cade .   ditto—out of the Blind Mare.
Note in pencil on back of book:
Keeper   .   .   out of a daughter of Regulus.

* These entries finally remove any doubt as to the origin of Eclipse.

APPENDIX II

TRANSLATION OF HIS MAJESTY'S INSTRUCTIONS TO HIS ROYAL HIGHNESS THE DUKE

LONDON *the 30th of March* 1757.

WE George the second by the Grace of God, King of Great Britain, France and Ireland, Defender of the Faith, Duke of Brunswick and Luneburg, Arch Treasurer of the holy Roman Empire &c &c &c.

INSTRUCTIONS

For Our beloved Son, William Augustus Duke of Cumberland, relative to His Command over Our Army to be assembled in Germany.

I

As the hostile Views of the Crown of France, and the dubious disposition of the Court of Vienna, force Us to assemble an Army, therewith under the Blessing of the Allmighty, to guard Our German Dominions, and those of the German Princes in Our neighbourhood in Alliance with Us, from any hostile Invasion, Devastation and Compulsion; It is therefore a great comfort and no small Alleviation, that We have a Body of Troops of Our own, on whose good Will We can depend, and a Son in the Duke of Cumberland's person, to whom We can intrust the Command over the said Troops, as also over the Auxiliaries to be added to them, with the grounded Confidence, that He will exert Himself to His utmost in this Command, to Our Satisfaction, to the increase of His Reputation, and to the safety of Our German Dominions.

2

Our Son is acquainted that this Army including the Train of Artillery consists of

27045 Men of Our own Troops
6241 do Brunswick Troops

322

800   do   Saxe Gotha do

800   do   Schaumburg Lippe Troops

12000 do   of Hessians

which last will be separately supplied by Col. Amherst, from hence with Forrage, Bread & Pay; that Our own Troops are ready for marching, and now cantoon'd along the Weser, and those of Brunswick, Saxe Gotha and Schaumburg Lippe have been required to keep themselves in readyness for marching. There is a Treaty on foot with the Count of Neuwied for a Batt^n of 800 Men, with the Count of Schaumburg Lippe for a small Corps of 100 Hussars, and with the LandGrave of Hesse, that in pursuance of His Treaty of 1755 for a Body of Cavalry, that He may deduct 100 of those, and supply the same number in Hussars. The King of Prussia is sollicited to have a Body of Troops in the neighbourhood of Magdebourg & Halberstadt, which, if the Crown of France invades Westphalia with a superior force, may strengthen our Army, or if the said Crown orders two Armies to advance, and with the One proceed to Our German Dominions, and with the other to the Wetterau, or the Dominions of Hesse Cassell that they may act on the side of Hesse and oppose the Enemy. It is yet uncertain if, and what number of Troops the King of Prussia may have ready to march for this twofold purpose; but the 6 Batt^{ns} that have lain in Garrison at Wesel, may be depended on, after that the Works of that Fortress shall have been blown up, and that they shall have retired to His Dominions in Westphalia the nearest at hand to Ours.

As to the rest, the Subsistance of the Troops has been provided for in such a manner, that there are Magazines of Corn and Forrage along the Weser, sufficient to supply them 'till next October.

We have order'd likewise that Corn & Forrage be brought up in all Places where it can be come at.

The Warlike Ammunition is provided, and the Train of Artillery and Hospital properly settled.

3

Our Son's Command extends itself over all the said Troops, as well home as foreign, as also over Our Militia, and the Corps that may be formed from the Invalids, as the Plan by which they are to be put in Garrisons will be laid before Him at Hannover.

And as Our Son is to repair to Hannover, to take upon Him this Command, He will there find the Orders given to Our Master of the Horse, to hold in readyness out of Our Stables, the necessary Saddle Horses, Bas Horses and Mules, with proper Attendants; to Our Master of the Household, to provide for His Table in the Field, or otherwise. We also write to our Privy Councellors, to lay before Our Son, the Plans and Dispositions hitherto made, and to inform Him fully of every thing that may conduce to the successful managing of the Command, and to assist Him as Ourselves.

Our War Office has the like Orders for what relates to their Department, and besides to furnish Him with the Moneys He shall want as Commander in Chief, on His written Order and Receipt. And to Our General Officers, We send the Orders, to obey Our Son as their Commander in Chief, and to pay Him the obedience due to Us.

We have reason to persuade Ourselves, that all will be punctually obey'd as set forth, and that every one in particular will endeavour to comply with Our Will & Intention.

4

How soon Our Army is to be form'd, and to take the Field, where, and how it shall be posted, will depend on the Motions and Undertakings of the Enemy, on their Strength, and the Situation of Ours.

Our Privy Councillors will not fail to impart without loss of time, the intelligence they receive from our Embassador Walmoden, as also the Correspondence of those sent out for intelligence; and We impower Our Son, to stand at no Price, for the procuring timely and certain information, of the Enemy's Undertakings, of what passes in their Army, and what preparations they may be making to subsist their Army. We leave to Our Son's Disposition the drawing of Our Army in the Field, and the Place of their Encampment.

5

We will not however conceal from Our Son, where Our present Views tend, and what is to be chiefly consider'd in the various occurences that may come to pass.

According to all probability the Crown of France intends to begin its hostile Operations, with the taking the City and Fortress of Wesel; And that this cannot be prevented, the King of Prussia is sensible of, and has, as mention'd above, order'd the Fortifications of Wesel to be demolish'd, and the Garrison to retire.

When the French draw near Wesel, it will then be time, if not sooner, for Our Army to take the Field, and advance towards the Lippe, or where it may otherwise be of most advantage; to assemble at the appointed Place, and possess themselves of an advantagious Camp.

Shou'd the Enemy proceed from Cleves, further into Westphalia towards Our German Dominions, the first thing to be done, will be to detach the whole, or part of the Cavalry, to carry off the Provision and Forrage on the Road to Our German Dominions, and bring it to Our Army, or quite into Our own Country, and to destroy what cannot be brought off, but yet, as much as possible, and as much as the Laws of War will admit of, to spare the Bishoprick of Osnabrug; that by this proceeding the Subsistance, in all manner of ways, may be cut off to the Enemy, on their March to Our German Dominions, and perpetually to harrass them but yet not to come to an Engagement with them, without necessity and advantage, but maintain such a Position, that the detached Corps are not cut off, but may always retire to the Main Body of the Army.

6

As to the Position to be given to Our Army, and the Operations to be undertaken with it, the first and fixed Object is, not to wait for the Enemy on Our Borders, but if what is mention'd in the foregoing Paragraph shou'd happen, that the Enemy has thoughts of penetrating into Westphalia, Our Army is to advance, and to post itself in a convenient and safe Place, on foreign Territories.

The Position & Operations of Our Army must however be directed to Our chief Aim. This is: not to act offensively, neither against the Empress Queen, nor any other Power, but meerly protect Our own Dominions, those of the King of Prussia in Westphalia, and those of the LandGrave of Hesse, from hostile Invasions of Foreign Troops, and repulse Force by Force.

If therefore it is observed the Crown of France has no Views of penetrating into Westphalia, but that the said Crown's sole intent is, to send an Assistance of Troops into Bohemia, it is not in such a case Our intention, that Our Army marches against them, and oppose them.

But if the Crown of France will penetrate into Westphalia, and so thro' Our Dominions, and those of Our Allies, then is the time for acting, and opposing the Enemy.

We have mention'd in the foregoing 5th Paragraph, that when

the Crown of France, advances to Wesel, it will then be time for Our Army, if not sooner, to advance to the Lippe, at all events. And when this happens, according as necessity, or the motions of the Enemy may require it, move forward, to the right or left, or retire back. It will chiefly depend on this, whether the Enemy's Army marching against Ours, be much superior to it, or not. In the first case We depend on the presence of Our Son, and on the Bravery of the Troops, that all that is humanly possible, will be done.

Foresight however will be required, that in the position taken, or the Alterations to be made in it, that the Protection of Our own Dominions, be the chief Aim, and to keep a retreat towards Stade open and free, that in case of the utmost extremity, which the Allmighty in His Mercies avert, Our Army may retire to keep and maintain itself there; to wait the issue of what the Times may bring forth.

On the other hand if Our Army is equal to that of the Enemy's, We think it unnecessary to point out to Our Son, how such an advantage is to be improved, and not only prevent the Enemy from approaching the Borders of Our Dominions, and those of Our Allies, but to drive them back with Loss out of Westphalia.

7

For the confirmation and elucidation of the foregoing, We repeat Our intentions:

That this is the case in which the French are to be consider'd as Ennemies, against whom all possible Opposition and Damage must be offer'd: When the French cross the Rhine at Wesel, or any other Place, from whence they may, without fetching a great Compass, penetrate into Westphalia, or the neighbouring Countries, and that We consider as neighbouring Countries, the Bishoprick of Osnabrug, the Bishoprick of Munster, the Bishoprick of Paderborn, the Principality of Minden, and the Counties of Bentheim, Tecklenbourg, Lingen, and Ravensberg.

But if on the contrary, the French Troops cross the Rhine, at such Places, from whence an Invasion into Westphalia is not apparent, and take the Route of Bohemia, they are not then in the case of being consider'd as Enemies, unless they bend their March too much to the Left, and by the Wetterau or Hesse, come too close to Our neighbourhood.

8

As We have the greatest confidence that Our Son will exert Himself to His utmost, according to these Instructions, to fullfill Our Views and Expectations, We leave Him intire liberty, and by these Presents expressly authorize Him, to make such Dispositions and Preparations, as He may judge proper and necessary.

9

Lastly We desire to have often, and if possible every Post Day, Advices from Our Son, and We think it the most convenient, that His Letters come to Us, by the Channel of Our privy Councellor Munchhausen. Given at Our Palace at St. James's the 30th of March 1757 in the thirtieth Year of Our Reign.

GEORGE R.

Von Munchhausen.

INDEX

Acadia, 116, and Louisbourg, 116
Aix-la-Chapelle Peace, 3, 8, 9, 13, 115
Albemarle, Lord, 123, 134, 146, 283
Amelia, Princess, 20, 34, 37, 52, 53, 55, 70
America, alarming news from, 89, rival powers in, 115, boundaries unsettled, 117
Anson, Lord, 15, 128, 162, 172, 310
Austria refuses support, 156, treaty with France, 251
Austrian Succession War ended, 8, 12, 157

Barnard, Sir John, 168
Barrier towns restored to Dutch, 8
Barrington, Lord, 184, 208
Bathurst, Lord, 46
Bathyany, Marshal, 23
Bedford, Duchess of, 313
Bedford, Duke of, and Gibraltar, 1, country near bankruptcy, 2, adulation of Cumberland, 13, married Lady Dye Spencer, 35, First Lord of Admiralty, 35, Secretary of State, 36, inflexible honesty, 36, hooted in London, 36, mobbed at Honiton, 36, personal appearance and nicknames, 37, sporting tastes, 37, Woburn fashionable centre, 37, Westminster election, 40, and his tenants, 42, Newcastle opposes, 67, and the King, 69, resigns, 70.
Behr, Major-Gen., 277
Berkeley, George, 49
Bernis, Cardinal, 294, 307
Bland, Sir John, at White's Club, 147
Boscawen, Admiral, 28, 149, 161
Bottle Hoax, 64
Bourgogne, Duchesse de, 291
Braddock, Major-Gen., 129, command in North America, 130-3, 146, 149, 162, forces routed, 167, mortally wounded, 167
Breton, Mr., 46
Briedenbach, Col., 278, 280
Bristol, Lady, 44

British Museum founded, 94
Broglie, Duc de, 277, 278
Brotherhood of Medmenham, 17
Brunswick, Duke of, 278, 315
Buckingham, Duchess of, 60
Bury, Lord, 21
Bussy, Francois de, 153, 169
Bute, Lord, and Princess of Wales, 235
Byng, Admiral, to relieve Minorca, 197, failed to engage French, 198, recalled and arrested, 198, court-martial, 246, sentence confirmed by King, 247, executed, 247.

Cadwallader, Mr., 63
Cape Breton, restored to France, 8, 28
Carleton, Baron, 46
Carlton House, 42, 46
Carpet manufactories, 25
Carteret, 35, 48
Chelsea china factory, 24
Chesterfield, Lord, 1, 23, resigned, 2, 36, 38, and reform of calendar, 82
Chevert, M., 275, 276
Churchill, Charles, and Lord Sandwich, 15
Clark, Baron, 61
Condé, Prince of, 260
Conversion of national debt, 94
Corbett, Sir Julian, 271
Cornwallis, Col., 30
Coventry, Lady, and Cumberland, 109
Cox, undersheriff, 61
Cumberland, Duke of, ability of, 13, directing the peace, 13, Ministerial confidence, 14, on King and Cabinet, 14, friendship with Sandwich, 14, in London, 21, cumbersome proportions, 21, scene at a ball, 21, dignity in the saddle, 22, judge of horses, 22, taste in menageries, 22, presents from Empress of Austria, 22, and Marshal Saxe, 22, animal collection at Windsor, 23, culture of plants and trees, 23, Chelsea china factory,

329

Printed in Great Britain by Hazell, Watson & Viney, Ld.,
London and Aylesbury.